BEYOND LOGISTICS & PLANNING

THE EVENT MARKETING HANDBOOK

ALLISON SAGET

Printed in the United States of America

060708 10 9 8 7 6 5 4 3 2 1

Library of Congress Cataloging-in-Publication Data -
Originally published by Dearborn Trade Publishing
A Kaplan Professional Company © 2006

Saget, Allison.

The event marketing handbook: beyond logistics and planning/ Allison Saget.

p. cm. Includes index. ISBN 13: 978-1-4774-6818-0

1477468188

DEDICATION

For my favorite kids

Spenser and Sam Durrick
Simone and Austin Adler
Matt, Steven, and Travis Hornstein
Matthew and Madison Stein
Kirra and Kyle Sponenberg
Penny, Athena, Justine, and David Karp
Sydney Amster
Jenna, Jamie, and Jake Saiz
Aubrey, Lara, and Jennie Saget
And . . . Michael, Robert, and Christina Giannini

PRAISE FOR *THE EVENT MARKETING HANDBOOK*

The Event Marketing Handbook *is a must-read for all those in the marketing discipline—especially those who own their company's event strategy and results.*
CHRISTOPHER BURNS, IBM, WW CHANNEL STRATEGY AND DEVELOPMENT

This handbook is an event in itself—plan to buy it! At last we have a lively, understandable, clear-cut blueprint of do's and don'ts for successful event creation.
PAUL LEVINSON, PHD, PROFESSOR AND DEPARTMENT CHAIR OF COMMUNICATIONS AND MEDIA STUDIES AT FORDHAM UNIVERSITY

[Speaking] as the manager of an exhibit and events team with multiple brands that we have to promote, this easy-to-read book showcases how to expose the brand through events and maximize lead efforts.
KENT EMESON, EVENTS AND EXHIBITS MANAGER, HARCOURT ACHIEVE INC.

This comprehensive resource is rich in advice drawn from the author's experience and that of other experts in the field. It offers step-by-step coaching on how to orchestrate an event strategically, flawlessly, and with maximum results.
FLORINA GOGARNOIU, PRINCIPAL PRIORITY MANAGEMENT CONSULTING

This book takes an integrated approach from building an event strategy to understanding the audience, as well as position and messaging, advertising, PR, and analyst relations—all leading to measurable results and impacting sales.
STUART R. GOLD. PRESIDENT, STUART R. GOLD INTEGRATED MARKETING

Allison Saget has written the definitive guide to strategic event planning and execution in The Event Marketing Handbook. *I would highly recommend this book as a must-have for every marketer's reference bookshelf.*
RONDA THOMAS FARRELL, CEO, THE EXORDIUM GROUP INC. INTERNATIONAL STRATEGIC SPONSORSHIP CONSULTANCY

Remarkable in its breadth of detail, The Event Marketing Handbook *will serve both as a useful tool for the ambitious novice as well as a refresher course for even the most seasoned professionals.*
LAURENCE WHITING, DIRECTOR—CATERING AND EVENTS, THE GETTY VILLA

As a destination management professional who has been producing spectacular events in Las Vegas for over 25 years, I found The Event Marketing Handbook . . . *just that! A handbook and a guide, not only for our clients but also for our internal team to use as a reference.*
KAREN GORDON, DMCP, PRESIDENT, ACTIVITY PLANNERS, INC.

Contents

LEAD GENERATION

Introduction

Whether you work for a large corporation, a mid-size firm, a small company, or a worldwide enterprise, there are four very dirty little words:

"Let's Do an Event!"

Everyone's eyes perk up, a smirk splatters across their faces, and you can hear the acid reflux stir in the room. It really doesn't matter what department you work in or what your title is or what level you're on. Because when you hear those four little words *"lets do an event,"* you know you're company IS going to do it! So, now the fun part! What's next? Oh, yes someone inevitably throws in that fifth dirty little word:

"Let's Do a Great Event!"

Before we proceed let's set the foundation.

- *First:* Understand what events do. This is the most important, and it is my mantra. I will repeat this over and over throughout this book: Event Marketing is all about facilitating, easing, opening, accelerating, and shortening the sales cycle. That's it! Events open the door. Events do NOT close the deal.
- *Second:* Understand that no matter what marketing is done, whether it's print advertising, television or radio commercials, direct-mail campaigns, research, or online communications, at the end of the day people still do

business with people. *Your company wants SALES, right?? You need to interact with people!*

- *Third:* Understand that everyone in the company plays a role in an event. *"Let's Do a Great Event"* needs the support of everyone at all levels; from the top down, from your colleagues or supervisor. Frankly, getting that support is a rollercoaster ride. But, when you apply fundamentals with creative wizardry, everyone wins and support is no longer an issue...it is a given!
- *Fourth:* Understand that event marketers move beyond logistics and planning. Don't lose sight of the value event marketing brings to your company. Why? Because event marketing provides the forum to continue to build and deepen relationships with customers, prospects, partners, analysts, press, and fellow employees from around the world. This one-on-one forum allows your company to penetrate the market, build consistent brand recognition, solicit input and feedback, demo products, as well as educate and build awareness among your desired target audience.
- *Fifth:* Understand that MONEY plays a huge role. Realize that what you believe you can or will spend will be quite different from the end result.

So whether it's a conference, summit, local forum, trade show, seminar, Webinar, live meeting (external or internal), roundtable, meal function, networking reception, and sports or hospitality function, the creative process, marketing activities, planning, management, and coordination follow a very clear process. This book will not only explain the process but show you how to leverage it, moving you beyond the logistics and planning.

Much of the content focuses on the sales and marketing relationship. This is where I start. It doesn't matter if you produce external or internal events, the same principles still apply.

My approach is as follows:

a. Strategic events must be both integrated into but also integral to the larger marketing program.
b. Strategic events should deliver a "high-touch" market-outreach opportunity to connect with clients and prospects within a comfortable, welcoming. and relevant context.
c. Strategic events must succeed in differentiating the brand, products, and services.
d. Strategic events must always achieve these two objectives: *Extend the brand* and *Shorten the sales cycle.*

In *The Event Marketing Handbook,* you'll learn how my approach to events allows your company to concentrate on the target audience while minimizing the logistics requirements and being creative. From an overview perspective, there are only so many formal types of events. Whether one touches two people or 20,000, there is a process that I have developed to get any company to its end goal.

As an event marketing "brand-a-holic" I have an "own and dominate" approach which is achieved through the positioning framework I created called EventBLT™.

The EventBLT is a model that leverages:

- Brand Recognition
- Lead Generation
- Thought Leadership

In addition, the "bread," or money, packages "putting it all together" with ingredients such as:

- Discovery
- Target Audience
- Sponsor, Exhibit, Attend, or Host

- Meeting Technology Platforms
- Strategic Philanthropy
- "Logistics You Need to Know"

I stand by these principles in order to execute the EventBLT approach. In this book, you will uncover ways to:

- Set goals and expectations in a strategic fashion.
- Create the right experience and a "unique" experience for your company and target audience.
- Develop a personality and an atmosphere in which your company can shine and excel.
- Anticipate client needs and desires.
- Be flexible, passionate, and focused on the client experience.
- Create brand dominance and awareness; in other words, "own and dominate."
- Ensure the right blend of communications programs with the event as the nucleus, but enriched by programs that accentuate that experience before, during, and after the event.
- Fundamentally understand the business and its unique value position and differentiation.
- Think like a salesperson: how to build the customer lifecycle and shorten the sales cycle.
- Win loyalty among customers, and build trust, confidence, and competitive advantage.
- Establish discipline, creativity, and rigor in all negotiations with vendors and partners.
- Win customers for life and build new business opportunities.
- Provide a thorough approach to every touch point opportunity and every detail.
- Budget extension and management.

I've created a series of templates that I use over and over. It's how I set the foundation for producing successful events. You will find these templates layered throughout *The Event Marketing Handbook.* The templates, as well as tips and tricks that are included, reflect input and materials from *experts* in PR and analyst relations, lead capture programs, privacy rights, online event management technology, and presentation and content development. I've taken the "best from the best" and created my own. Information in regards to sponsoring or hosting an event and working with your executive team and/or celebrities is also included.

The templates are designed for you to use as a guide. Feel free to customize them to your specific needs since each industry has their own lingo and their own series of requirements. You can find electronic versions at *http://www.eventblt.com.*

It is important throughout your work life to develop a network of relationships. For me, I refer to this as my "event network." The people in my event network range from executives to technical support gurus to creative agencies. These individuals are experts in their field. I believe creating an event network makes you resource rich and will extend the value that you bring to a program. Many of these experts have contributed to the content in this book. I'm an effective event marketer because of my event network and my ability to engage in a relationship. Take a look at who you know—it's as simple as that! Create your event network today!

The Event Marketing Handbook is a professional guide for anyone who is a recommender, influencer, decision maker, implementer, or participator of an event. With information shared in this book, you can create an aura or an experience that will bring your company to life every place an attendee goes. So you will not have a shortfall anywhere.

So now, when you hear those five dirty little words, "Let's Do a Great Event," you'll know you have a way!

Tip

Creating an Event Network

1. Always follow up after you've met someone. Take a business card and e-mail address and write to them within 72 hours of your first introduction. (A simple "pleasure to meet you" is sufficient. Keep your info on file and provide personal data.)
2. Update your contact database. Keep a backup in electronic and hard copy formats.
3. Be memorable. A personal touch that connects you to someone, so even if you call them five years later, they still remember you.
4. When you're in their town let them know.
5. Call or e-mail them for advice when you are working on a project and need assistance.

Acknowledgments

When I set out to write this book, I realized that the reason was because of the many individuals who had contributed to my professional and personal development. In the course of 20 years, I've been fortunate to have worked with some fantastic people—many whom contributed to sections of this book and must be credited accordingly. You make me shine! I also want to thank my family and friends who enrich my life. I want you to know how much I appreciate your continuing energy and support.

THE EVENT NETWORK

Family and Friends

My fiancée Tony Giannini and the entire Giannini clan.

My parents and siblings, Barbara & Lee Adler, deceased father, Samuel "Stan" Saget, Mallory Saget Durrick, Mark Durrick, Debbie Adler, Marlene and Marc Adler

Cousins: Bob Saget, Adam Saget, and all my aunts and uncles, their kids, and their kids on both parents' sides.

Friends: Judie Koss, Monica Stein, Craig Stein, Fern Amster, Elliot Amster, Laura Gold, Meg Moss, Amy Nislow, Lori Wilson, Barbara Lemis, Jeffrey Axelrod, The Cozen Family, Francine and Geoff Schwartz, Debbie and Vince Rocha, Lisa and Jeff Lem

Valued Colleagues

Suzie Naspo, Brian Vanden Broucke, Jennifer Bader, Stuart Gold, Kent Emeson, Kent Larson, Andrea Michaels, Tom Bercu, Lisa Holland, Michael Christman, Bruce Vanden Broucke, Jeff McCaw, Ray Lane, Alicia Read, Jim Welch, Joe Spuria, Garth Humbert.

Susan Roth, Janice Burg-Levi, Michael Westcott, Skip Cox, Ken Mortara, Greg Spector, Cece Lee, Alister Christopher, Stacie Jones, Debbie Chernoff, Kim Millen, Lara Shackelford, John Pino, Mary Ann McNulty, Betty McNulty, Gwen Aman, Carolyn Rammel, Amy Hyatt, Cammy Lopez, Tim McEwen, Robert Sheridan, Laura Villagram, Steve Bailey, Joel Zucker, Lynn Harris, Karen Gordon, Gordon Stake, Geoff Poli, Dan Belmont, Bob Barretta, Jonathan Vatner, Sarah Woodberry, Jonathan Fader, Derek Gordon, Monica Norton, Wendy Colby, Lynn Hughes, Jackie Kuhl, Steve Zahm, Tooey Courtemanche, Courtney Klinge, Mike Lodato, Pete Goettner, Tim Cook, Kimberly Daniel, Susan McKenna, Sally Jenkins, Betsey Signol, Jack Johnson, Kay Hart, Gail Snider, Tom Victory, Jim Conlon, James Hyde, Derek Fredrickson, Tom Slattery, Rob Foley, Stephanie Lane, Victoria Wells, Jon Bromberg, Michele Belanger-Bove, Jennifer Miller, Jon Leland, Linda Kundell, Elise Bauer, Ronda Thomas, Jed Mandel, Andy Herman, Martin Smith, Evan Moltz, Cindy Spuria, Andy McMillan, Ernie Allen, John Walsh, Marci Anderman, Jennifer Harrell, Jeff Frick, David Murphy, Carol Wolf, Linda Lindamood, Rianna Riego, Jeff Zamensky, Larry Wells, Christy Lamagna, Barry Byrne, Rodney Johnson, Annie Yuzzi, Chris Burns, Leslie Hatch, Don Harris, Brooks Bagley, Florina Gogarniou, Christine Porrini, Elliot Levine, Abbe Braitman, Larry Braitman, Claude Saiz, Karen Saiz, Tom Fell, Lisa Fell, Joe Stirlacci, Nancy Stirlacci, Hal Hershman, Hilary Bayer, Mitchell Bayer, Bruce Benjamin, Jodi Benjamin, Bob Eve, Susan Austin, Melissa Gallus, Jennet Nazzal, Carl Fremont, Monica Vila, Andrea Eng, Jeff Aliber, Jill Archer, Tom Grossman,

Glenn Byrnes, Barbara Pasciolla, Rick Carmel, Maria Waclawski, Ellyn Raftery, Chris Paul, Lori Marshall, Ed Phillips, Kimberly Daniel, Jim Welch, Barbara White, Paul Batchelder, Paul Burrin, Bill Freed, Jeff Gloeb, Bill Goerl, LeAnn Holler, David Griffiths, Russell Reeder, Carol Broadbent, Kathy Ury, Craig Weicker, Erin Isselmann, Debbie Juliani, Lisa Weaver, Mark Lobel, Pat Meier, Alan Bednowitz, Kate Potts, Rosie Madison, Gary Gilliam, Brian Simmons, Kevin Buckholtz, Bill Gaylord, Don Montgomery, Tania, Weidick, Karen Hagman, Darlene Smith, Mitch Ahiers, Andrew M. Goldstein, Lou Bertin, Alison Jenks, Chris Janese, Richard Harper, Greg Hughes, Jim Dristas, Renee Robbins, Deborah Lopez, Arturo Fernandez, Lisa Keating, Chimene Vasick, Jalenda Motley, Dave Rathbun, Philippe Suchet, Mark Ogne, Michael Oiknine, Mark Meyer, Rob Rosen, Michele Goldberg, Doug Alexander, Grante Wright, Kellie Shevlin, Hellena O'Dell, Judy Sims, Colin Higgins, Stephanie Pendergast, Ruth Stevens, Laurence Whiting, Susan Feninger, Ray Reo, Dave Coulier, Jonathan Silverman, John Stamos, Scott Weinger, Marshall Herskovitz, Steve Garvey, Candace Garvey, Ron Masak, Arte Johnson, Tom Arnold, Michael Price, Brad Grey, Jill Grey, Paul Pressler, Mindy Pressler, Lori Loughlin, Fuzzy Zoeller, Johnny Miller, Lee Janzen, ICM—Chyna Chuan, Betsy Osha, Charles Spaulding, Wendy Keller, and Pat O'Brien.

Technical Team: Albert Raymundo and Rio Ryan

. . . and Bruce Lev, Becki Lev, and David Lane, who taught me at the age of 16 the foundation of the marketing mix. Kay Koplovitz, from the start-up days at USA Cable Network. Former teachers: Paul Levinson, from Fairleigh Dickinson University and now Professor and Department Chair of Communication and Media Studies at Fordham University, and especially Miss Susan Sloan, my 5th grade teacher. And, to watching Oprah Winfrey every afternoon and who is right: you can do anything you set out to do! Be careful what you wish for! Thank You!

Chapter

1

EVENTBLT

STRATEGIC EVENT MARKETING

Understanding your company's or your internal/external client's sales initiatives and business objectives are the fundamental key for a successful event. This is not tactical–it's interpersonal.

Before we proceed, let's set the foundation.

- *First:* Talk, listen–and network. It's important to take a step back and look at the big picture. Really look at your company. Understand the organization. The atmosphere, the environment and its challenges, as well as how you are interfacing and communicating with your customers, your prospects, your partners, your distribution channel, and your employees. Pay close attention to the press and analysts. *This process is all about your relationships.* You can learn so much just by asking questions. People love to talk. Engage them. Create your own "event network." You'll find champions in your organization that will further your message, at any level.

> *"I firmly believe that people do NOT buy things, people buy from people."*
>
> Kent Larson, CEO & Founder
> M.A. Apparel
> http://www.maapparel.com
>
> *M.A. Apparel is a Minnesota-based promotional products distributor and embroidery manufacturer.*

- *Second:* Realize that understanding and establishing the business objectives for the company and for your particular event or event plan is accomplished through very concise conversations with the business leaders of the company. Depending on the size–whether a large or small company–your contact points will be different, but you will still need to have a clear understanding of the objectives.
- *Third:* Assess the various functions within your organization. For example, it may be customer support, product marketing, engineering, R&D (research & development), or HR (human resources). Become familiar with these groups and understand how and why they interact and work well with each other, solving their customers' needs.
- *Fourth:* Research your company's Web sites and your competitors' Web sites on a regular basis. Often, great content is overlooked when it comes to an event. It is important to note that with each company's pubic Web site, every positioning statement has been approved, every product announcement has been featured, and every bio on executive management has been written. Because this information is already approved, it saves tremendous time on content development.
- *Fifth:* Make friends with Sales. Yes, Sales! It doesn't matter what industry you represent–it's all about Sales. Metrics and measurements are directly linked to Sales! I refer to it

as Event Accountability. Get it—sales are what's measured! That's it! Obtain their target account list. Know who they want to sell and at what level. Know their prospects. Know their customers.

So, what is our mantra?

Event Marketing is all about facilitating, easing, opening, accelerating, and shortening the sales cycle. That's it!

Plain and simple—events create awareness for a company; they allow that company to show the marketplace what they have to offer in its best light; to show a breadth of products, services and solutions that clients can rely on.

Once you understand your company's sales initiatives and business objectives, the next step is making them come alive in an event. What I've learned over the years is that no matter what these initiatives or objectives are, they will be based on three primary ingredients. So, when you hear the words *"Let's Do a Great Event,"* think of the EventBLT ingredients:

1. Brand Recognition
2. Lead Generation
3. Thought Leadership

Whether it's for your Event Strategy or Event Plan, the EventBLT gives you the framework to position the power of events within your company.

Recognize that every event you accomplish is a communications opportunity. Once you take that perspective, it elevates your program into a new light; from how you display your products, to what clothes you wear to how you wine, dine, deal, and schmooze with your customers, prospects, partners, press, employees, and stockholders.

Once you step out of the "event silo," you can clearly identify how an Event Strategy and the individual Event Plan support the company's marketing mix.

- PR initiatives
- Direct, field, or channel-marketing
- Print and broadcast advertising
- Web/Online initiatives

Integrating these efforts into events is a critical component of your marketing communications since there are only a handful of tools (advertising, public relations, direct marketing, sponsorships, online, and events) to get the word out about your company.

Since events are an integral part of the marketing mix, it's important to realize the bigger picture—that information is exchanged through a variety of media. For example, the Web is equally, or as some believe, more important today than traditional media such as newspapers, magazines and television. Look for fresh ways that your Event Strategy can complement these efforts. It's all about experiential marketing and that's what events are all about! Attendees are no longer passive recipients of information and passive advertising doesn't work. It's all about active flow of information and integration.

For integrated event marketing, it is important to understand the Customer Journey as published in the Building Brand Advocates whitepaper from The George P. Johnson Company, and shown in Figure 1.1.

Regardless of what you want to accomplish—whether it's *brand recognition, lead generation, or thought leadership*—by *leveraging each other* you *give and get more impact.* Your ad messages are stronger! Your PR efforts accelerated! Your message is consistent! Everyone is hearing the same thing, and that just blends for a

FIGURE 1.1 *The Customer Journey*

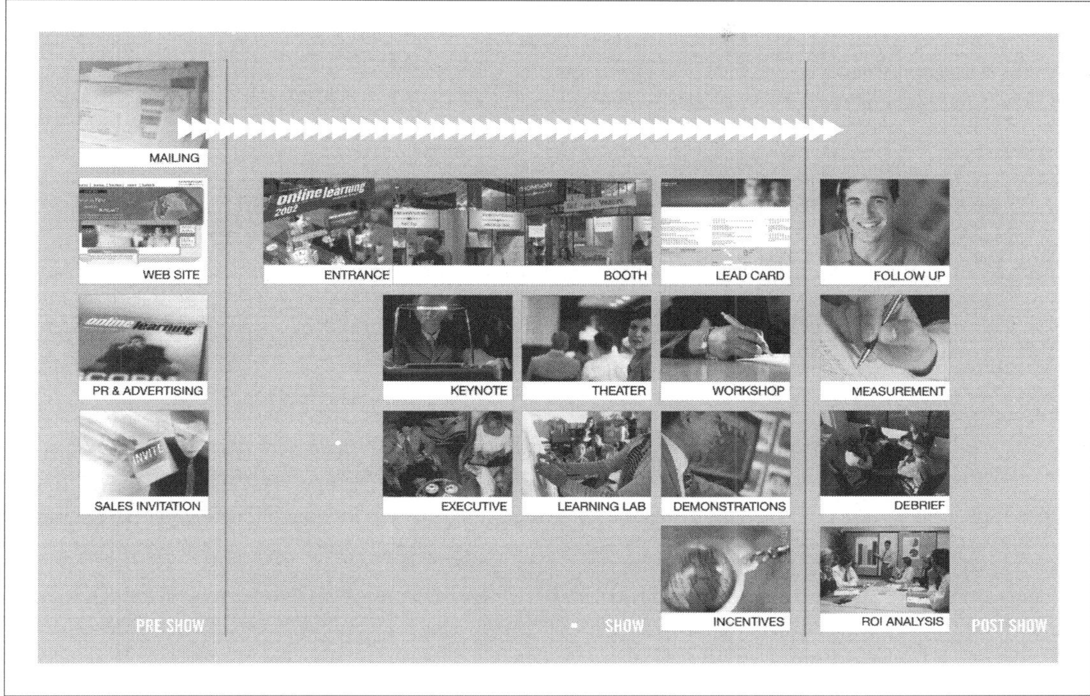

© *White Paper: Building Brand Advocates*
The George P. Johnson Company
Integrated Event Marketing
http://www.gpjco.com

stronger voice. I believe the entertainment industry in Hollywood does this the best, movie releases in particular.

Let us take a look at the "event ingredients" at a movie premiere.

- *Brand Recognition:* The Red Carpet is a standardized logo and there's an international, national, and local press core. The VIP name badges, all signage, promotional items, and multimedia messages feature the movie logo and stars. It's a *"Festival of Branding,"* says Bob Saget, actor, comedian, and director. (And yes, my first cousin and valued member of my event network.)

- *Lead Generation:* Even measurement is in place by calculating weekend box office performance.
- *Thought Leadership:* Celebrities/Stars, studio executives, articles, critic reviews, and topic-driven connections spur current-consumer interests.

When you bite into the EventBLT, you know that independently they'll taste good, but together, it's an entirely different flavor. There is a perception that most event managers provide a very tactile approach and do a great job delivering the pieces. I wish I had a dollar for every time I heard the comment that Event Managers are not strategic but they're great at the logistics. While the back-end logistics are very important, my approach moves beyond the traditional framework into Event Marketing.

"In my current role, I have responsibility for our strategic events plan and I view it as 360-degree program," says Derek Gordon, director, marketing communications, Thomson NETg. "From internal sales empowerment events, to client relationship events, to lead generation/industry events, I feel we've been able to build a program based on the EventBLT system that touches every aspect of the sales cycle (the sales and support teams, current client renewals, and prospect/lead generation). Our program is tightly integrated with all other aspects of the marketing program, including advertising, Web marketing, direct marketing, public relations, promotions, collateral programs, and field marketing." Derek Gordon added, "This tight alignment across all marketing programs ensures that when we engage a client or prospect at one of our event programs, the messaging, positioning, visual cues, and overall tone resonate, and reinforce our core outcome objective."

BEYOND LOGISTICS AND PLANNING

EventBLT—*http://www.eventblt.com*

1. Brand Recognition
2. Lead Generation
3. Thought Leadership

My approach is to mix all the ingredients (BLT) together so it's cohesive. When it comes to events, I believe you cannot separate the ingredients. None of the topics are cut and dry and you can NOT perform one without the other. The ingredients are all intertwined (or buzz word "integrated"). At this point I will provide the highlighted version and will go into detail later in the book. Even if you know this in your heart, it's a good refresher course. If you're at this point for the first time, you'll find I've encapsulated this material in a neat package for you so you can profit from my experience and bypass the 15 years of torture I endured realizing that this is it!

Brand Recognition

When I produce events I always integrate the brand. This could be as simple as the logo or as complicated as the corporate identity—the company name, the product name, as well as the positioning statement. Brand recognition is bigger than just events! It is an integral part of the marketing mix. It runs the gambit and is a long-term initiative. The single, most important piece that is the continuity point is the brand.

Event branding is emphasizing what the image is. Companies, with strong existing brands, find the constant need to maintain dominance and positioning, while firms without brand recognition seek to make a name for themselves within the space. When

> *Tell me and I will forget. Show me and I will remember. Involve me and I will understand.*
>
> – Confucius

> *"Well, it's funny, when I go around and say 'Oh, I produce events for a living,' people are like 'Oh, you throw parties'; and while it's some form of a party celebration, what we specialize in is basically image branding and marketing. And there's a great quote from Confucius that iterates my point."*
>
> Tom Bercu
> Event Producer
> *8 years* owner of Tom Bercu Presents and
> Account Executive for Extraordinary Events

it comes to the event execution, almost everything I create is branded–from the preplanning phase to onsite to postevent activities. It's a formula and I carefully review every "touch point" throughout the event cycle. I will discuss this in detail later in the book.

I actually shake when I see the lack of event marketing. I've attended so many corporate events where thousands or millions of dollars were being spent, hundreds or thousands of people were in attendance, and you look around and you don't know who the sponsor is and what their message is. Plus, you never even meet a representative from their company. By reviewing every touch point, I became an Event Marketing "Brand-A-Holic." I leverage and incorporate the brand every place I can, on any budget! The key is in the approach. Event branding can be done simply by presenting your company or product name in a variety of marketing activities throughout the event.

- *"In-Your-Face" branding.* Everywhere you look you see your company name, your product name, or your graphic image representation (conference brochure ads, hotel room keys, lighting, napkins, cocktail stirrers, banners and signage, ice sculptures, table tent cards, hang tags, and more). A complete list of branded materials is located in Chapter 6 and available on the Web at http://www.eventblt.com.

- *Subliminal branding.* By this I mean "what is it" you want to project about the brand. Most people look at branding as one dimensional: "gotta get the name out there." However, it is so much more than the name. It's also the image. For example, make it sparkle to tell your story. Think logically throughout the process. Match the image to the live presence environment, but remember the detail or logistics because this is where you'll get snagged. Take something as simple as the event venue selection or location to drill home the point. Below are some scenarios that illustrate my point.

Thought Less: A next-generation technology company hosted a preview luncheon for select press and invited analysts to discuss their new product or service, relying upon high-speed Internet access to tell their story.

- *The Problem:* The event was held at the 100-year-old City Yacht Club with only a dial-up phone line in the club's main sales office.
- *The Result:* No product announcement that day and some bad press the following week about how their product wasn't ready, but the food tasted great.

Thought Through: A company hosted a preview luncheon for select press, analysts, customers, executives, partners, and a celebrity guest regarding the announcement of their new product offering. The event was held at a prestigious golf club where the 1½-hour luncheon drove home the key messages through speeches, promotional materials, and signage, along with photo opportunities with the celebrity. After the luncheon, the guests played in a 3½-hour golf outing with a recap at the 19th hole for awards and cocktails.

- *The Result:* Fifteen articles were featured in 2 days and the sales team scheduled 10 appointments within two weeks of the event. Sales and the PR team also hand-delivered each a framed photo to their respective invited guests.

Event branding is something that you can gain in one event. Brand awareness is something that you work on over the course of years. It is important to use events as an integral part of your company's marketing plan.

Lead Generation

Lead generation and lead capture are much bigger than just a single event or event strategy. First, it's about the relationships you build, and then it's supported by the processes you put in place, allowing the event to lead through the sales cycle. In this face-to-face event environment, you become open-minded to what the issues are and allow yourself to find solutions to any obstacles that may come your way.

There are two types of events, and both can yield the same results:

1. The trade show event. This environment provides the audience with an opportunity to explore several potential product, service, and solution providers in a timely manner.
2. A proprietary event. This is hosted exclusively by you and/or your potential partners that allows you to directly focus your solutions in a very efficient manner.

Ken Mortara, president of ShowValue, is a contributor to industry publications, a frequent speaker, and an adjunct professor of business statistics and operations research. He offers, "There are very few places left where there is a face-to-face interaction.

With events, you get the connection (the relationship) and that person-to-person environment is invaluable. It enables the interexchange with someone who is knowledgeable, who can provide solutions, can offer advice, or be someone to bounce ideas against."

With events, you need a process for managing and measuring the person-to-person environment. In 1994, Ken developed an electronic system for trade shows that collects and processes qualifying information from *every* booth visitor, including those who see a company's theater performance. Seeing a similar need for meetings and conferences, the technology was expanded to also evaluate event marketing performance for the overall event, general sessions, and breakouts. This process allows you to identify and evaluate the touch points within an event.

Once you decide whether you are going to sponsor, exhibit, attend, or host an event (see Chapter 4), your lead generation begins with all the various touch points you'll have with those attendees (our buzz word, *target audience*). The touch points, in turn, relate back to brand recognition, lead generation, and thought leadership.

Touch point marketing activities include:

- Pre-event mailers
- Online tactics, sponsorships
- Executive functions
- Speaking engagements
- Educational sessions
- One-on-one time with "the important people"
- Postevent follow-up by your sales force

The EventBLT approach follows the old classic push/pull strategy all the way through the process. The goal is to identify the touch points and think creatively about how to generate that lead. Events let you qualify and quantify. Qualification is for sales,

Understood

Face-to-face sales and motivation are the most important aspect of communication, much more so than a written ad or television piece. With those mediums, you are only reacting to what your eyeballs say. You have no input from anybody else. Simply, it's like watching a game on television alone in your room versus going to the stadium.

With a live event you taste it!

Andrea Michaels
President
Extraordinary Events
http://www.extraordinaryevents.net

quantification is for dominance. I strive to do both, and why not? Because it's already paid for! Remember, you are not measured on the relationships as much, but what you get out of that relationship. Again, it's important to generate numbers.

Thought Leadership

The term *thought leadership* is a buzz word. Many people use the term in relation to claiming their position and the issues they want to convey. When you work in events, it's all about getting above the noise. Events are a great way to position yourself as a thought leader within the industry and to meet with people on a one-to-one basis, so they hear you.

Whether you work for a large corporation or small company, thought leadership is about evangelizing, advocating, and championing the message. By integrating thought leadership into events, you are accelerating the sales cycle. Thought leaders are experts or recognizable individuals. If you carefully craft their message to reflect what it is you want from your target audience, you provide another opportunity within the sales cycle.

If you are using events purely to establish a thought leadership position, your event plan should focus on speaking opportunities; for example, placing your thought leader as a credible source at the conference even if you have to "pay to play." And, once that speaking engagement is secured, then what? Do you simply get up and spew the content or do you engage the audience in a secondary way?

As an event marketer or a vice president of sales or a CXO (meaning a "chief-something officer" in a company; for example: CEO for Chief Executive Officer, CFO for Chief Financial Officer, CMO for Chief Marketing Officer, and CSO for Chief Security Officer), you can reinvent your company's brand recognition, lead generation and thought leadership stature simply by using your marketing materials effectively, by leveraging press coverage you've received, or by distributing whitepapers, research, case studies, and testimonials from customers and partners that have been written or published. The value of thought leadership can be seen through the alignment of business objectives to the conference objectives, and how you marry those two establishes your position as the thought leader when your messaging provides the solution. (Thought leadership is covered in more detail in Chapter 10.)

With events, you can connect with your customer in some physical form on a real level and establish a relationship that you can follow up with a combination of personalized phone calls, scheduled appointments, and one-on-one e-mail communication.

Think of it like this: events personalize a company to its customers. When I look at events, I am most concerned with announcing the existence of the company and the fact that the company is out there providing the solution. I believe that one of the problems with advertising or marketing strategies is that there is so much clutter in the world, we see right past most forms of advertising to the point where the respective advertising becomes invisible.

Events are an expensive proposition and get a lot of visibility within companies because of the price tag. It doesn't matter what size company you work for, no one has the budget today to say, "I just want brand recognition" or "I just want a lot of leads." Reality, sometimes, is hard to swallow. If they are not going to get something out of it on the sales side and have qualified leads, then they are not going to invest the dollars.

As event marketers, it is important to understand that the executive team has expectations when it comes to conferences, trade shows, and customer programs. By using the EventBLT framework and matching it the company's sales initiative and business objectives, you showcase the impact of your event marketing program.

Without the executive view, you have no end result! So, I asked Raymond J. Lane, General Partner at Kleiner Perkins Caufield & Byers, an accessible and forthright executive from America's premier venture capital firm and former president and Chief Operating Officer of Oracle Corporation, what is the #1 lesson he's learned in regard to events. He shared the following: "I think the first thing is probably *sufficient planning . . . and I'm not just talking about the logistics*. Executives tend to expect that events are just going to get done, limiting their interaction. But, if their input into the event is lacking, then it's their own fault if it does not meet their expectations. Whether it's an event planner or they (the executive) themselves, there's got to be a great deal of interaction ahead of time so that the event is actually planned to their liking.

I'm guilty of this myself," Lane continued, "I used to say 'Look, I trust you guys,' but then I'd get on site and shake my head. Now, I expect the event marketer to open the dialog with the executive team by creating a very detailed plan that covers everything from the product messages to the audience we're supposed to meet—down to the look and feel we expect. I always thought it was a waste of my time until I realized that if the marketing team had my input for a couple of hours during the preplanning process, that I'd be a lot happier when I got there."

Insights

Executive Perception: Event Marketers vs. Event Managers

Event managers are like wedding planners, meaning, they do things that are important for appearance, but not thinking about what is it we're trying to accomplish with this event?

Event marketers are thinkers and are in the minority. Event marketers ask the tough questions . . . .

- What messages are we trying to convey to our customers?
- Are we trying to get our audience to buy products?
- How will this impact our sales?
- What are we really trying to accomplish here? Sometimes the journey is convoluted.

Know and understand that the purpose objectives and business objectives are too generic for events. Instead, think in reverse—think about what is it at the end of the day as to why this will have been successful—is it perhaps sales, category dominance, or vision? Then design your event plan around that.

Raymond J. Lane
General Partner
Kleiner Perkins Caufield & Byers

When you use the EventBLT process–you can leverage your event into several key features: building brand awareness, generating leads, and positioning your company as a thought leader so you are able to detect and uncover where the sales opportunities are. The question is why do (or attend) an event unless you are going to do it right–so do all three.

Tip

Position Yourself as an Event Marketer

Have a more strategic view of the marketing events function, instead of tactically focusing on the management/execution of events.

- Learn how strategic events could effectively position the brand within a given market space.
- Communicate the events role as central to the sales cycle and lead generation processes.
- Understand how best to position executives at major events, such that the sales cycle was clearly advanced and their time was effectively used.

Chapter

2

DISCOVERY

Our mantra:
Event Marketing is all about facilitating, easing, opening, accelerating, and shortening the sales cycle. That's it!

Everyone says, "If you have a lot of money, you can do anything." You know what? That's true! But, it's not always about the money, it's how creative you are *using* the money. And with events today, you need to have a lot more creativity with a lot less money.

As an event marketer, you are in the unique position to drive the power of integrated marketing from many sources through a single media. Events allow you to combine all facets of face-to-face marketing to ensure seamless communication throughout the development of the client relationship.

The following factors need to be included in your relationship building:

- *Networking:* Develop invaluable high-level relationships that shorten sales cycles.
- *Awareness:* Forward your message in a face-to-face forum filled with your potential customers.

- *Insight:* Learn about the needs and concerns of your line of business, innovators, executives, customer base, and experts.
- *Leadership:* Position your company as an industry leader for category dominance.

The benefit of the EventBLT model is that is takes you back to basics and sets your foundation firmly into the bedrock of good marketing principles that create results. What I found in my "eventures" is that I kept asking the same questions over and over regardless of the sales initiatives and business objectives—questions such as: Within your target audience who are your top ten customers or prospects? Who are your competitors? And what makes your company unique? It didn't matter what size the company or what they were looking to accomplish with their event or program strategy.

What I also noticed was how difficult it was to get concrete answers to these basic questions, or, even to get time on someone's schedule to ask the basic questions. I'd sit down with our marketing team or the vice president of sales and their feedback would sound something like this: "You perform events—why are you asking me who my top three customers are or what type of revenue opportunity this event represents?" Marketers often underestimate not only the power events can initiate, but also the value of good discovery.

It was at that point that I realized I needed a formula and framework to place events at the top of the marketing chain. I realized that if I was the one who had to assess and integrate each person's vision, opinion, and know-it-all attitude into the event plan, I needed to take control of the program. It was then that I set out to change the way events are approached, managed, and viewed.

For the marketing mix you'll develop an event strategy, however, every program starts with an event marketing plan. Use this plan for communicating with a company's internal departments (usually sales and executives), suppliers, and external agencies. The goal is to communicate every detail of the EventBLT. Most event managers I know have their "own" plan. Just like me, it's something they've developed over the years for themselves, since there is really no industry standard.

Before I create an event plan, I prefer to conduct a "discovery session." I adopted my discovery sessions from Brian VandenBroucke, CEO and Senior Creative Director of articulate creative services, inc., part of my event network, and a strategic agency with rich creative marketing deliverables for trade shows, events, and campaigns, producing measurably better results.

"Discovery is *everything,*" Brian says. "Real discovery—not just asking nice-to-know questions about this or that. Real discovery is the art form of asking questions with intense purpose, curiosity, and enthusiasm. Real questions provide real answers to guide your program as a whole—ultimately ensuring its success! Real discovery provides a program which aligns *both* your strategic *and* creative plans. Without real discovery, you are at risk of creating 'purpose-less marketing.' It's like paddling a canoe from only one side of the boat—you keep going around in BIG circles. Marketing, guided by real discovery, is balanced—the objectives are in line with the creative strategy, and what springs forth from that creative strategy always make sense. The benefit to you? Your investment in creative deliverables is totally justifiable to upper management (or your client if you come from the supplier side.) And in a day of measurable results being the ultimate target of marketing, it's like shooting laser-guided arrows."

Discovery sessions can be formal or informal. Personally, I like to conduct both types. The discovery sessions have taught me to *always* do a follow-up session including an oral review of the strategic/creative proposal. The reason for this (and I have learned the hard way), is that sometimes they just may not understand the proposal. Brian continues, "When proposing your ideas to clients or internal clients, no matter how complete or well composed, the written word cannot fully convey the meaning or passion behind the idea. Only a voice! A person. A living thing, even if it is only a voice on the other end of the telephone, can inspire someone to take a calculated risk. And, as we say here, 'Be good. Be bad. But *never* be boring.'"

A discovery session can happen in any one of the following ways:

- *Formal Discovery:* A face-to-face meeting with a clear-cut agenda, usually 1½ hours.
- *Formalized Conference Call:* Sometimes even better because you can arrange the meeting together faster and thereby spend more time in the preparation process.
- *Informal Discovery:* Out for drinks after work with no set agenda and a more casual atmosphere often provides deeper insight than formal discovery since you are in a relaxed environment where creativity is flowing more freely and political barriers are lowered.

The discovery session is an invaluable tool and should be set up either one-on-one or with a small group of key constituents. Representation may include sales, an executive sponsor, product marketing, research and development (R&D), corporate communications, and public relations—look around your company and select those people that will be engaged with your event program. (Note: Too many cooks in the discovery session can create confusion, however.) Limit your conversations to the key decision makers that will claim ownership of the ultimate result. For example, if you are organizing a customer event, primarily speaking to benefits at the conference, then R&D (the "how something is done" group) may not need to be present.

To explain why, Brian offers, "The biggest challenge working with or within companies, especially in the manufacturing or technology arena, is that they are often too focused on spewing the wrong sales messages to their customer base. Companies who have strong R&D departments or make widgets that go fast tend to focus their sales story on *how* their product or solution works, as opposed to *why* it makes their customer's lives easier, safer, and more prosperous while saving them copious amounts of time. Generally, focusing on the *customer*—their target *audience,* is a great place to focus real discovery. Besides, it gets them talking about something other than themselves. You need to keep uncovering what positively affects their customers' wallet, watch, or ego."

Personally, I'm a fan of the small group and prefer to conduct both formal and informal discovery sessions. There's a higher energy of feedback you get when you're in both environments.

Discovery sets the foundation for your event marketing plan. In order to ask the right questions, I created a discovery template that I use over and over again and fill in the blanks. Based on your program, you'll be able to use some of this information in complete form and/or modify to your needs. Each chapter will delve into further detail about the basic questions that are asked within the discovery session.

Here's an example of how preliminary discovery works:

Steve Zahm, president of start-up company Procore Technologies, makers of custom home building software, decided to exhibit as an entry-level sponsor at their industry's annual National Association of Home Builders conference. It was approximately three months before the actual event date and Steve and I chatted by phone for about 15 minutes. After we caught up personally, he shared that as part of his sponsorship he negotiated for a "free" conference bag insert and that one of the company's board members was featured in the keynote session. He says, "We were definitely in. Our contracts were signed, but we wanted to do more and we had a budget of around $25K." Many companies find themselves in a similar experience to Procore: you're signed up, but what are you are going to do?

Tip

ASK and then LISTEN. Then LISTEN again. And AGAIN. For proprietary events, here's what we like to ask throughout the cycle.

1. If you were a guest walking out of this meeting and/or event, what would be the ONE thing you would want your customer to remember?
2. What did you like best (or totally dislike) at former events you've attended or hosted?
3. What would you have changed?
4. What do you want the experience to be? (This question provides the answer to their expectations.)

Andrea Michaels
President
Extraordinary Events
http://www.extraordinaryevents.com

The first step is to actually schedule a discussion meeting with the key players—on the calendar for 30 minutes to an hour. Give yourself about a week prior to your first discussion meeting so you have time to gather preliminary information about the event. This allows you to research the overall event dynamics and be prepared with the basics so you can conduct a thorough discovery session.

Here are some guides to help you get started.

1. Start with what you know, no matter how basic it may be. Be sure to write it down. For example: Procore is a start-up company. (In a larger company it could be a business unit.) They have first-time entry into the market with a new product and they have a bottom-line budget of $25K to make an impact with their target audience.
2. Review the conference agenda, speakers, sessions, competitors, and sponsors for potential partners or prospects. Use the conference Web site and dig deep through the pages.

Notes: Had this been a proprietary event (one sponsored only by Procore), I would use the same basic techniques for gathering the information, but would first have asked the key players to relate an event similar to what they wanted to accomplish.)

3. Speak directly with the conference coordinator to uncover "what other marketing activities" are available and at what price."
4. Establish relationships at the host hotel with sales, catering, and services contacts.

Take the time to read the discovery template before you actually apply it. Think of three additional questions that you would like to add to your first discovery session. Keep a running list for yourself. Each industry has nuances–bring those questions into the mix.

Through successful discovery, you are able to uncover all customer hot points, company objectives, and tonality that denote the recipe–all the ingredients that are needed to create a successful event.

Executive Perception

What I notice when I attend trade shows or attend events is how companies organize their booths and manage their speaking opportunities. I believe it's viewed as simply a way to convey information and that attendees will sit still to hear their story.

The EventBLT goes beyond. Not only does it ensure that the information is communicated, but the attendees also remember the company, and the brand "sticks" in their head. They recognize the value proposition and key message. These various touch points are uncovered through the discovery session—I've seen it at work.

Steve Zahm
President
Procore Technologies, Inc.

Time Savers

- Creating an executive summary or overview sets the tone for your event program. It's the reason why you are participating in the event. It features details about the big picture regarding the program, including information such as keynotes and speakers, educational sessions, networking, and socializing opportunities.
- Always use existing content and repurpose. If you are sponsoring a tradeshow, conference or seminar, go to their Web site and pull the content for this section. Each event has a purpose for the target audience. Understand it! But read the text, don't just cut and paste. You'll need to modify the content so it reads more personal or tailored to your company when you put together your event plan.
- Get on the phone and speak with the sales representative or account manager from the show's producer. They have an arsenal of information to help you create and manage your event marketing plan.

Through successful discovery, you get a fresh perspective and may even have a different outcome from what you originally had planned. That's the value and the key differentiator. Use this template (Figure 2.1) throughout your discovery session and you'll be well on your way to a successful event for both you and your client!

FIGURE 2.1 *Discovery Session Template*

Use this template to guide you through the discovery session process.

Your Company Name ______________________________

Event Requestor ______________________________

Name of the Event ______________________________

Days and Date of Event ______________________________

Location of Event ______________________________

Address of Event ______________________________

URL/Web site of Event ______________________________

Preliminary Information—Remember to include this on every piece of correspondence regarding the event!

Discovery Template

1. Is this an exclusive Company event?
   - ☐ Yes
   - ☐ No

2. How does this event benefit our sales/marketing plan? Use percentages (%) in your answer.
   - ☐ Brand Awareness
   - ☐ Lead Generation
   - ☐ Thought Leadership

3. Our primary objectives for this event are to: (use strong verbs)
   - ☐ Find and engage new customers.
   - ☐ Generate excitement and favorable publicity about my company or product for my desired target audience.
   - ☐ Build a consistent marketing message that can easily be remembered.
   - ☐ Gather industry and competitive intelligence.
   - ☐ Reposition the competitive landscape.
   - ☐ Make claim to position us as thought leaders.
   - ☐ Other ______________________________

4. What is the Audience Profile for this event?
   Insert: Tell me about our customers or target audience:
   - ☐ Who are they?
   - ☐ How old are they?
   - ☐ Male/Female Ratio (%)

(continued)

FIGURE 2.1 *Discovery Session Template (Continued)*

- ☐ What do they like to do in their spare time?
- ☐ What is their biggest pain? (e.g., the pebble in their shoe)
- ☐ How do you relieve that pain better than anyone else? In other words, how to you modify your pain or make different?
- ☐ How does your product, service, or solution benefit their wallet, watch, or ego?

5. Who are the Exhibitors or Sponsors? ______________________________

____

6. Who are the Media Sponsors? ______________________________

____

7. What is our Product Strategy and/or Launch Plan? ______________________________

____

8. What is our Positioning and Messaging Focus? ______________________________

____

9. Tell me about the overall tonality you want to achieve at this event. ______________________________

____

10. Who are our top three customers attending this event?
    1. ______________________________
    2. ______________________________
    3. ______________________________

11. Who are our top three prospects attending this event?
    1. ______________________________
    2. ______________________________
    3. ______________________________

12. Who are our top three partners attending this event?
    1. ______________________________
    2. ______________________________
    3. ______________________________

FIGURE 2.1 *Discovery Session Template (Continued)*

13. If this is not an exclusive company event, please list the top three primary competitors that are expected to participate.
    1. ______________________________
    2. ______________________________
    3. ______________________________

14. Will we be demonstrating products at this event?
    - ☐ Yes
    - ☐ No

15. Will we require product materials for the demonstration?
    - ☐ Yes
    - ☐ No

16. Is software or hardware required to conduct the demonstration?
    - ☐ Live Server(s)
    - ☐ Computers
    - ☐ Monitors
    - ☐ Internet Connectivity
    - ☐ Other ______________________________

17. Will there be an exhibit component or product showcase component to this event?
    - ☐ Yes
    - ☐ No

18. Is this a Company-only booth or a shared booth or co-sponsored if a proprietary event?
    - ☐ Company Only
    - ☐ Shared Booth/Sponsorship

    If Shared with whom? ______________________________

19. What is the exhibit booth size or the meeting dynamics? ______________________________

    ____

20. Has our Company participated or in exhibited at this event in the past?
    - ☐ Yes
    - ☐ No

(continued)

FIGURE 2.1 *Discovery Session Template (Continued)*

21. What marketing opportunities are available to our Company?
    - ☐ Keynote Speaker
    - ☐ Breakout Speaker
    - ☐ Panel Discussion
    - ☐ Hospitality
    - ☐ Sponsorships
    - ☐ Advertising
    - ☐ Product Description with Logo
    - ☐ Web site
    - ☐ Pre- and/or Post-event Attendee List
    - ☐ Press Release
    - ☐ Product Announcement
    - ☐ Direct Marketing
    - ☐ Affiliate Marketing (e.g., Room Drops, Hotel Keys, etc.?)
    - ☐ Other ______________________________

22. How many NEW opportunities do you expect to generate from this event? ______________

    ____

23. What is the potential revenue associated with these new opportunities? ______________

    ____

24. Will this event influence a specific opportunity?
    - ☐ Yes
    - ☐ No

    If Yes, please elaborate. ____

    ____

25. What existing opportunities do you expect to influence as a result of this event?

    A.) Account Name: ______________________________

    Revenue Opportunity (use $$ percentage to identify the deal size; i.e., $25,000 to $2,000,000 to $25,000,000)
    - ☐ within 3 months
    - ☐ 3–6 months
    - ☐ 6–12 months (give or take)
    - ☐ 12–18 months
    - ☐ 18 months or over

FIGURE 2.1 *Discovery Session Template (Continued)*

B.) Account Name: ______________________________

Revenue Opportunity (use $$ percentage to identify the deal size; i.e., $25,000 to $2,000,000 to $25,000,000)

- ☐ within 3 months
- ☐ 3–6 months
- ☐ 6–12 months (give or take)
- ☐ 12–18 months
- ☐ 18 months or over

C.) Account Name: ______________________________

Revenue Opportunity (use $$ percentage to identify the deal size; i.e., $25,000 to $2,000,000 to $25,000,000)

- ☐ within 3 months
- ☐ 3–6 months
- ☐ 6–12 months (give or take)
- ☐ 12–18 months
- ☐ 18 months or over

D.) Account Name: ______________________________

Revenue Opportunity (use $$ percentage to identify the deal size; i.e., $25,000 to $2,000,000 to $25,000,000)

- ☐ within 3 months
- ☐ 3–6 months
- ☐ 6–12 months (give or take)
- ☐ 12–18 months
- ☐ 18 months or over

E.) Account Name: ______________________________

Revenue Opportunity (use $$ percentage to identify the deal size; i.e., $25,000 to $2,000,000 to $25,000,000)

- ☐ within 3 months
- ☐ 3–6 months
- ☐ 6–12 months (give or take)
- ☐ 12–18 months
- ☐ 18 months or over

26. What is our budget? ______________________________

(continued)

FIGURE 2.1 *Discovery Session Template (Continued)*

27. Are other business units sharing the cost?

☐ Yes
☐ No

If yes, *provide your company's list of business units or divisions below (with funding allocation):*

☐ Sales
☐ Corporate Communications
☐ Global Marketing
☐ Customer Service / Customer Relations
☐ Human Resources
☐ Research and Development
☐ Office of General Counsel
☐ Engineering
☐ Purchasing
☐ Other ______________________________

28. Are partners or channel players sharing the cost?

☐ Yes
☐ No

a. ______________________ $ ________
b. ______________________ $ ________
c. ______________________ $ ________
d. ______________________ $ ________
e. ______________________ $ ________
f. ______________________ $ ________

Chapter

3

TARGET AUDIENCE PROFILE

Our mantra:

Event Marketing is all about facilitating, easing, opening, accelerating, and shortening the sales cycle. That's it!

There's a lot written about understanding your target audience. Standard media jargon (or a definition) is: "A group of people to whom advertising is directed." When it comes to events, your target audience is to whom your message is directed.

This target audience is comprised of "people"–just people. It's what these people do for their companies–their job titles, roles, and responsibilities that become the reason that you want to reach out to this group. These people are labeled as recommenders, influencers, or buyers, and could be a combination of any of the three. Reaching your target audience is a challenge, but by understanding their profile and how to quickly identify whether the audience is qualified or nonqualified becomes the value.

What I've learned in the corporate/business, theatrical, and nonprofit worlds is that there are only so many types of industries and only so many types of people within those industries.

Each person has a specific role they command and many times their roles either overlap others in their organization, or they are collaborative.

Everyone always asks me—where do you start in identifying the target audience for an event? Sales! I start with sales. By tying in your sales force you are able to hit your target audience and desired market. In most companies, the sales team is the pulse of the customer. They are on the front lines. They hear the accolades and take the brunt of the cursing. Salespeople are rewarded based on their understanding of their customer and are fired for lack of understanding customer needs. Marketing can create a great deal of programs, but without sales participation, they mean nothing.

It's important for event professionals to get it in their heads that sales is their "ally" and a huge untapped resource. With their support, input, and buy-in to the event plan, it sets the foundation for *facilitating, easing, opening, accelerating, and shortening the sales cycle.* But to this day . . . I hear it over and over, "Where's sales?" To quickly access how well you know your sales department, ask yourself these three questions:

1. Do you have a territory list organized by name and account?
2. Do you have a main contact from an executive and representative level?
3. Do you know where they sit in your office or are they in a home office?

Sales should be part of the process and have a voice. I believe marketing and sales are codependent. Marketers set the foundation for sales by building the branding, the look, the feel, the messaging, and the content. I think it is critical to get executive sponsorship from sales early in the process, so you do not have any confusion as to what you are trying to accomplish, what the objectives are and at the end of day, or guessing whether you have delivered against the "agreed upon" objectives.

Being intimately involved with the sales team gives you added resources for your event marketing efforts. It allows you to overcome obstacles, personalities, and even budget constraints. A collaborative environment will fuel future projects and make the existing ones stronger and more dynamic. The sales/marketing relationship breeds excitement and should be continuously leveraged.

From my personal experience, I've seen the greatest success in any event when you have the salespeople behind you. Many people believe that no matter what your title or role within your company, you are a salesperson. Why? Because you must know the elevator pitch: "What does your company do?" In 25 words or less you should be able to recite your company's story. With a salesperson or a CXO (a "chief-something officer"), their live performance is critical, whether it's on-site at a trade show, at an executive breakfast meeting, or following a group that's walking up the fairway at a national golf event. They talk the talk! If sales and executive support is not behind you, you'll get out what they've put in! Nothing!

By becoming partners with sales you can use the framework of the EventBLT and define "this is what I can do for you"—brand recognition, lead generation, and thought leadership.

You must ask sales for their support and be clear about what you need from them. Be sure to ask for the following:

- Inside view of the account lists with background profiling
- Commitment by sales to do call-downs to customers and sales
- Customer champions that will speak or be quoted
- Budget support

By partnering with sales for your event strategy, you can offer an account-based marketing perspective—going deep inside the customer profile. "It's beyond what you are selling to them day-to-day and establishing a relationship around how to penetrate the account," says Janice Burg-Levi, Vice President of Global Strategic Marketing, with responsibility for the client reference program at a Fortune 1000 company. She continues, "You may have one key contact and when that contact leaves, oh my goodness, you're in trouble. The premise around account-based marketing is that you have many contacts within that account, both at the decision-making level as well as at the influential level. Within companies it's an extremely fluid experience. Realize that at any point in time these people either move on or move up."

"Let me explain further," continues Janice. "First of all, your target audience becomes a larger list or community. The account-based marketing perspective provides a forum for you to position and market your products, services, or solution. In addition, you can provide ways to educate and leverage your thought leadership. Once aligned, you can then see how you were able to support the sales objectives that have been set and established for the specific client, as determined by the individual sales manager and executives. Therefore, the benefit with the account-based marketing approach is the actual individual relationships themselves. When your competitor is knocking down their door they, or the account, won't think about going someplace else or bailing out, because they now experienced the fact that you have the expertise and you're going to get that next peak piece of business."

Account-based marketing is a great hook from an event marketing perspective. Whether it is with current customers or prospects, it's about uncovering opportunities for sales.

I've probably produced well over 1,500 event-related programs in the last 15 years. During a three-year run in the mid-1990s, I met Suzie Naspo. Suzie has such incredible talent in making it all about the customer and she is part of my event network. It's been 10 years since we first worked together and today she's still my confidante and creative partner. We have a theory when we produce events—no idea is bad, and we both have to like it in

Understood

"You could write a book on the whole sales/marketing dynamics. Before I started using the EventBLT, I never would've thought to work directly with Sales. Now, when I present events to my clients, I insist we open the dialog with their sales team." However, "Be careful what you wish for." The minute sales become engaged and they start seeing results, they are going to be knocking on your door left and right because they are going to see the value. I am already starting to see salespeople figure this out when you pair events with online marketing, for example. There is a huge opportunity to directly reach their customers, prospects, and channels."

Jennifer Bader
McClenahan Bruer Communications
Senior Counsel
http://www.mcbru.com

order to integrate it and implement it. It was with Suzie that I had the opportunity to explore the target audience relationship.

Using the master mind principle and event network as your starting point allows you to leverage your key contacts for the ultimate achievement of reaching your desired target audience. While it is extremely important to take this step back and look at the 30,000-foot view, what Suzie and I have learned is that the sales department "owns" the target audience.

It's your job to:

- Connect Sales to the target audience.
- Find and/or produce the "best" events to match who they want to reach.
- Make the target audience feel excited, interested, and catered to so they want to do business with your company.

It's your job to treat the target audience well so that Sales can do its job—event better!

Tip

Target Audience = Relationships

The event network is the backbone of an effective event strategy and the relationships you build within the network allow you to penetrate your target audience. It reinforces the principles of the "master mind." And it works in all event circumstances. I keep this posted at my desk—Suzie Naspo.

This master mind may be defined as, "coordination of knowledge and effort, in a spirit of harmony, between two or more people for the attainment of a definite purpose."

No individual may have great power without availing himself of the master mind.

Two advantages of the master mind principle:

Economic

Economic advantages may be created by any person who surrounds himself with the advice, counsel, and personal cooperation of a group of people who are willing to lend wholehearted aid in a spirit of perfect harmony.

Psychic

When the minds of two people are coordinated in a spirit of harmony, the spiritual united of energy of each mind form an affinity.

The master mind principle is attributed to Andrew Carnegie whose master mind group consisted of approximately 50 men, with whom he surrounded himself for the definite purpose of manufacturing and marketing steel. He attributed his entire fortune to the power he accumulated through this "Master Mind."

When a group of individual brains are coordinated and function in harmony, the increased energy created through that alliance becomes available to every individual brain in the group.

Think and Grow Rich
Napoleon Hill
Copyright © 1937

IDENTIFYING YOUR TARGET AUDIENCE

Here's an event example.
Who is the target audience?

- *The Scene:* It's your industry's annual three-day conference at a resort location. Your company is a sponsor and there is a small demonstration/display component and you also secured added marketing programs.
- *The Guests:* Prequalified from the membership list, 800 midlevel managers are expected to attend.
- *Overheard:* All content has been prepared by the conference's 25-person advisory council and there are 175 CXO level speakers and six complementary companies (no competitors) have been invited to sponsor.

If you look at the audience profile in this example, the Event-BLT states all four groups are your audience–800 midlevel managers, 25-person advisory board, 175 speakers, and 6 sponsors, which in this environment would probably represent 22 people for at total of 1000+ people–who have a pre-determined vested interest in the topic at hand. The key is to uncover the opportunities with sales and again match it to the business objectives. Think about what this event delivers from the larger perspective and how you should treat them to get to your end goal.

1. *Speakers–The CXO level or "celebrity" audience is widely understood.* There is so much mass information regarding these individuals that it's obvious. It's all about white-glove service and super high-touch dynamics. It's expected and don't think you can fake it. The CXO level group is very predictable and they've got the power. This is the one area that companies put their dollars behind, because the executive is the one that makes the decisions. At every event

This event marketing activity is often called an "Event within an Event."

Tip

How to Reach the Executive Level Audience

"I'll have our executives host a series of private off-site dinners at the finest restaurants in the area. In advance, under the executive's name, I'll send personal VIP invitations to the audience. It's a captive group. Where are they going? So if you contact them six to eight weeks prior to the actual live event, your chances of getting on their schedule increases. On-site reinforcement is mandatory. By sending personal welcome letters with a small room amenity, as well as a voice mail message left during their day in their hotel room, you provide the subliminal branding found in the EventBLT."

Suzie Naspo
Event Producer—15 years

there is someone that fills that role. There's someone at the highest level. Understand the hierarchy and understand it will change within your event program.

2. *The Advisory Council.* You've got be careful. You may want to treat them as CXO level, but you want them embedded in your ongoing product-life cycle.
3. *Sponsors.* This group can bring to you their customers, but have you recognized the partnership opportunities?
4. *The middle-level audience.* It is more about getting them educated, to understand your solution, and getting them embedded into your ongoing product-life cycle. However, white-glove service is NOT the priority here.

To reach this target audience, use the same three principles:

1. *Brand Recognition:* Do a "chair drop" at each session (e.g., a flyer with a candy bar promoting your solutions to the topics at hand).

2. *Lead Generation:* By filling out the flyer and turning it in, the attendee can receive an advanced copy of your new product or white paper, and even win a prize!
3. *Thought Leadership:*
   - Sponsor an entire conference track that will directly reach the group related to your topic.
   - Negotiate to have your company "experts" introduce each session track for 30 seconds of that session's air time.

Each member of the target audience represents different attributes as it relates to the sales cycle. Each one can be a recommender, influencer, or a buyer at any given time. It is the power of event marketing that allows you to "Diana Ross it"—"Reach Out and Touch Somebody's Hand." I think about all the personal touch points when I produce an event and it is these touch points that are invaluable in the sales cycle and sets your programs apart!

My clients ask me this all the time: "How many times do you think you have to "touch" a customer or prospect within the event for it to impact a company's sales?" That's a hard question to answer since I believe that through the entire event cycle you must uncover ways to touch each member of your target audience.

Therefore, if you are working with Sales and your executives and you have the target account and the pipeline list, you may look at the 1,000 people attending the industry conference and break down the framework into who is qualified to who's not qualified.

What you can identify and track here is if you are reaching your desired target audience. The number, 1,000, may actually be a qualified number around 600 just by matching up the target account and pipeline list with the conference's attendee list. Remember: to impact the bottom line, your salespeople have to follow up and close the deal.

With touch points you can reach your desired target audience. It could be 6 or up to 600. "I don't know if there is a magic number," says Lisa Holland, Vice President and Partner, Opts Ideas, another valued member of my event network. "I think that you can have a lot of touch points but they may not be meaningful," continues Lisa. "I think the key to the success of these events is that the touch is meaningful and resonates with the audience."

There are three essential questions that must be answered and then incorporated into the planning of a program in order for it to be successful, no matter what the scope or budget is:

1. Who is my audience?
2. What are the goals and objectives?
3. How will success be measured?

If you create a program that incorporates touch points to address all three of these issues and then execute on it well, then you've virtually guaranteed success. The question is this: Do the touch points map back to the business objectives?

So, from an event marketing perspective, these touch points become the accelerator in *facilitating, easing, opening, accelerating, and shortening the sales cycle. That's it!* You do not want the attendee to just walk in and have one touch point, you want to touch them every place you possibly can with the brand and company messaging, making sure that the look and feel is consistent from start to finish. Yes, it works every time!

Multiple touch points are the key differentiators when it comes to an event and are a viable part of the EventBLT. How many times have you seen a fabulous booth on a show floor and the attendees barely even remember the company's name, except for the 35-cent pen handed to them that they left in their hotel room when they checked out.

"Getting inside the head" of the attendee gives you the path (and the power) to reach them in other ways—and it's through event marketing. When you sponsor an event, like an annual three-day industry conference, for example, think of all the different touch points you have in one of the qualified audiences' hotel room. You can touch them through marketing activities that cost very little money, but in the live presence environment, you have direct impact on your target audience. (See Figure 3.1)

Tip

Touch Points—marketing activities simply in a hotel room.

- morning newspaper drops
- evening turn-down service
- in-room sponsorship of Internet access
- your company literature sitting on top of the magazines and room service menus
- tissue boxes
- TV access channel

Short Cuts to Identifying the Target Audience

- While events allow you to be very focused and get to the audience you want, it is still your responsibility to understand who you are going after. Is it the CEO or the consumer? Is it the doctor or hospital administrator, teacher or superintendent? Each industry has its complete list of titles and roles. To take a look at the target audience in your specific industry, research the top events that are hosted in your industry and review the attendee prospectus offered with the conference materials. Trade publications are a great resource for finding information about your target audience. Schedule meetings with the magazines sales representatives who have qualified research in your arena.
- When you look at a target audience you must look at the account. There's a great deal of discussion today around account-based marketing. This means you go "deep" with the company. It's almost like a site profile that trade magazines provide to advertisers. Understand the organizational structure and know the players. You can then really target the individuals.

FIGURE 3.1 *Target Audience Information*

Please describe the target market/anticipated audience for this event.

Approximate number of attendees at the event: ______________________

General Description or Profile: ______________________

Purchasing ability: ______________________

Customers: from Executives to End Users (sample of titles)

- ☐ CXO
- ☐ Vice President
- ☐ Professional
- ☐ Director
- ☐ Manager
- ☐ Specialist
- ☐ Developer
- ☐ Service/Support
- ☐ Sales/Marketing

Media and Related Community

- ☐ Press
- ☐ Analyst
- ☐ Influencer

Channel

- ☐ Partners
- ☐ Distributors and Resellers
- ☐ Consultants

Competitors

- ☐ General ______________________
- ☐ At the Event ______________________
- ☐ Other (describe) ______________________

Internal Audience and Representation at your event (use a % mix)

- ☐ On-site Staff
- ☐ Attending Conference/Session
- ☐ Senior Management
- ☐ Speakers

FIGURE 3.1 *Target Audience Information (Continued)*

Who are the top three customers you are targeting at this event? (Base this number on percentage to the event you are attending. The company size will determine how many top customers you have.) These are your top VIPs.

1. ______________________________
2. ______________________________
3. ______________________________

Who are the top three prospects you are targeting at this event?

1. ______________________________
2. ______________________________
3. ______________________________

Chapter

4

SPONSOR, EXHIBIT, ATTEND, OR HOST AN EVENT

Our mantra:
Event Marketing is all about facilitating, easing, opening, accelerating, and shortening the sales cycle. That's it!

Deciding whether you should sponsor, exhibit, attend, or host an event could be one of the hardest decisions a company has to make. Just take one variable–look at the financial obligations. Sponsorship is at one level, exhibiting another, even attending the event still costs money, and hosting is a whole other story. Then, look at the overwhelming number of trade shows, conferences, summits, meetings, partner programs, hospitality functions, and charity benefits that are held each year and they all begin to look alike and those old bad habits are creeping up again.

Events are big business. According to StarCite, the leading provider of online meeting and event technology solutions, the industry is a $300 billion business. Events can be the best marketing tool a company can use and if improperly planned, can cause more harm than good–or worse, nothing at all.

Whether you sponsor, exhibit, attend, or host an event, it's important to understand that a well-run program is an investment in the future. The most critical part of any event plan is that it *never, ever stands alone.* It is an integral part of the overall marketing strategy which includes public relations, advertising, direct marketing, telemarketing, online communications, research, and most importantly, personal selling.

In the late 1980s through the mid 1990s, there was a great deal of discussion regarding one-to-one marketing. Books addressed the topic and it was professed at industry events. Research even reinforced the concepts. It changed the way companies approached events. The one-to-one marketing concept has become a "standard way to do business" and is now something that should be innate for marketers.

Today, the discussion centers around Internet marketing. Tomorrow, it will be something else. Look how far it's come along. We have instant messaging and PDAs. We have ways to measure online e-marketing/direct-marketing campaigns. Everything is instantaneous. With events, however, it's about opening a dialogue and a relationship with someone. When you're marketing your products or services you want interaction, or feedback. Events enable companies to have an interaction, a dialogue that is face to face (that is, eyeball to eyeball), with a prospect, customer, partner, or whomever it is that you identify as your target audience.

Trade shows and their value go up and down the ladder. In the early 1980s, they "tanked," but in the 1990s, they blossomed In the early part of 2000, not only did trade shows tank again, but there was a tremendous amount of caution in even hosting an event. I believe the dotcom days and the tragedy of September 11th has definitely changed the dynamics and perception of what these types of events bring to the table. It was at that time the online events became the next big ticket.

So how is it that you decide what to do with your event strategy? Many companies make the mistake of selecting events merely because everyone else in their industry will be present or because it's habit or instinct.

"The goal is to thoroughly research 'events of interest' in general, and then create an event strategy which matches your business objectives," says Wendy Colby, Senior Vice President, Global Marketing, Thomson NETg, and a valued member of my event network. Establishing a set of criteria to evaluate your event program should be in direct relationship with your company's sales initiatives and business objectives. The same set of criteria is used to review previously attended events since times and trends change. An event that was perfect three to five years ago may no longer have the same market appeal due to changes in your company's goals, target audience, or product line.

When you commit to events, it is your responsibility to use and leverage it to its fullest, which I reference as the *own and dominate strategy.* Events are the fastest and most cost-effective way to reach a qualified audience in a controlled environment.

Therefore, before you set out to determine what events you want to sponsor, exhibit, attend, or host, review the specific sales initiatives and business objectives that were uncovered in the discovery session. (I always look for the hook—Why are we doing this and who is interested?)

What I like to do is match the event schedule with the overall marketing plan so they are timed with product releases, customer announcements, or research releases. Sometimes you get a combination of elements. Other times you've got to use your creativity and find the right mix. For example,

- Introduce a new product or present an existing product to a new market.
- Promote the company image to the target audience. Awards and press coverage are great ways to achieve this goal.
- Learn about the competition and industry trends. This will broaden the company's product knowledge and will make the company a stronger player in your industry.

Insights

The Event Principles

Our guiding principles in producing events require that we strategically identify the objective, the market, and customer opportunity, and then build a fully integrated program that enables high touch with our clients and prospects.

We focus on the full experience—from first point of contact with our team, our solutions, our brand position, our unique value differentiation, the perception, and the impression we create in the minds of those clients. Those are the essential elements. And we know that what moves an event from good to great, beyond the obvious rigor needed in the business development upfront. It is the thoughtful consideration and planning that goes into every detail, every opportunity—whether it is an invitation to our booth, a promotion, a hospitality suite, a special guest speaker, a workshop, or a keynote with one of our executives.

We constantly aim to shorten the sales cycle, build awareness of our offerings, and carry that experience through to the training, skill, and passion that our people exhibit.

Finally, we build our presence and our program on what makes us unique and delivers value to those we serve, and we track our progress in the form of leads, meeting with the right decision makers, new sales, and general activity levels. We test out new products. We demonstrate a spirit and an atmosphere of being the "right" choice.

Wendy Colby
Senior Vice President, Global Marketing
Thomson NETg, a part of the Thomson Corporation
(NYSE: TOC)

Wendy Colby is strategically responsible for all marketing, product management, business development, and alliance activities at Thomson NETg, a leading provider of Internet-based learning solutions to corporations, institutions, and consumers.

- Conduct market research on new products. Feedback on features, price, and packaging can be gathered. This research can reveal open niches.

Let's take a closer look at trade shows. These shows are designed to increase sales by generating leads and increasing awareness of your product and/or company. The trade show selling environment is unique. It combines knowledge of the product and the market with the personality and individual selling techniques. Because of the nature of trade shows and proprietary events, a great deal of thought and effort should go into selecting the right shows and planning all of the necessary elements. A well-planned event with a clearly defined strategy and set of objectives will almost always yield better results than an event hastily thrown together at the last minute. In every industry, the same mistake is made over and over—once the event has been chosen, the sponsor sets up a booth, prints new collateral and signage, and shows up on site. It's amazing to watch, and then they question "why has this trade show yielded nothing?" The key is maximizing the event marketing investment opportunities.

It is important to put together an event strategy no matter the size of the company. People often ask, "How does one decide whether to sponsor, exhibit, attend, or host an event?" I start with the core. I actually equate this to mall shopping.

Tip

Make The Most of Your Event Strategy

Today, events are positioned as both physical and virtual. There is no reason why an event has to be just physical. Our world evolves and the dynamics and the communication process always changes.

- For example, take your event and simulcast your keynote address on the Web during your conference, *basically augmenting the physical with the virtual.*

Think about the layout of a shopping mall. There are anchor stores, boutiques, a food court, and an information kiosk.

Anchors. Major department stores are usually located one on each end of the mall, drawing in the largest walk-in traffic. Use this analogy to your advantage. In other words, place an anchor event in your strategy. Anchor events are your starting point, whether you work for a large or small company. When you select your anchor events, remember the following:

- The dates of the event will impact sales. Create a master schedule and match the event to the quarter so you know where the activity falls in the sales cycle.
- Events held the last few days of the quarter are tough. The sales department is busting their humps to close deals. Will the basic element like selecting the event date either help or hinder the opportunities? Consider instead using events to accelerate closing the business. If you know the sales pipeline and you use account-based marketing and your prospect is based in Chicago, and so is the next industry conference, think about how you could leverage the EventBLT in the accounts' own backyard.

Boutiques are the small shops and cool trendy venues that line the corridors and aisleways. Many are fashion forward and others cater to service needs. Industry conferences, summits, forums, and hospitality dinners are all examples of boutique events. Each has its own specialty and a specific target audience.

Food court, a splish-splash of back-to-back eateries designed to get you in and out appealing direct to a specific target audience. Each eatery has a different flavor. Field marketing events are like the food court—they host their customers and prospects on a regular basis. Many do this work themselves and some companies have a built-in program that addresses their field marketing efforts.

- For instance, let's take pharmaceutical sales representatives. They constantly entertain hospital administrators and doctors. The local region will sponsor the area hospitals' seminar at a fine restaurant or hotel. The cost of the event is usually handled by the region's budget. While you may not plan field marketing events, you can contribute to their overall success. Simply understanding what field marketing is doing in the "food court" can leverage your overall event strategy.

Imagine if a major anchor event was being held in a region where they had already scheduled an executive breakfast with their partners that same week. Think of how you can marry the two events to better leverage your overall event plan.

Information Boards and Floor Plan Layouts. It's simply a list of what's available in the space. You may look at it quickly or pass it up all together. The events that equate to information boards is everything that doesn't show up on your original research, but is still out there. The choice is either evaluate everything (go into every store), or decide to consider it next time.

> ■ **Hint:** Conferences' account executives are eager to speak with you to pitch their marketing sponsorships; in turn they also can provide you with very detailed information about the audience and market. Try to encourage the conference organizer to provide you with a complimentary conference pass for one of your sales representatives to conduct an audit of their event (see event audit form later in this chapter).
>
> If the conference organizer provides you with the free pass, feel encouraged. If they can't provide the complimentary pass due to their regulations, ask them the following: "How could I possibly decide to

FIGURE 4.1 *Faster Way to Close the Deal*

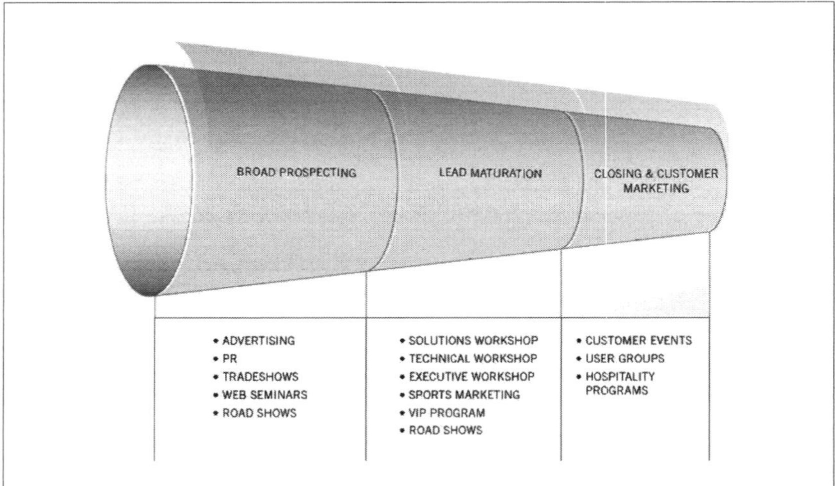

© *White Paper: Five Trends to Watch (2003 edition of MPI/GPJ Event Trends Study)*
The George P. Johnson Company
Integrated Event Marketing
www.gpjco.com

sponsor or exhibit at an event if I've never attended it or heard of it?" If you don't get the pass, you may consider sidestepping the event until the next evaluation time.

To sponsor, exhibit, attend, or host an event is completely a function of who the attendees are and what the business objectives are. Will you reach your target audience? That's why you initially should conduct a discovery session so you fully understand what direction to go.

Take a look at the *"Faster Way to Close the Deal"* illustration created by The George P. Johnson Company (Figure 4.1). The company published an excellent white paper titled, *"Five Trends to Watch."* Besides a great source for information, the graphic in their white paper depicts where events fit in the cycle, I use it over and over to illustrate what it is that events can do for *facilitating, easing, opening, accelerating, and shortening the sales cycle.* Before I set out to determine the event strategy, I reference this material. It helps me stay focused on how to match up what we should actually sponsor, exhibit, attend, or host, and in what stage of the sales cycle.

Whether you are a small start-up company or a large company in an established market, you should strive to develop a comprehensive event strategy. Events are a critical component in the marketing mix. If you are not taking the time to seek every branding opportunity and every opportunity to establish a relationship with your prospective customers, you have a flaw in your marketing program. Proficient event marketers create all of the "props" that you need to give a great performance at the event and it's the "props" that match to a leveraged investment. When you set out to write an event strategy, here's the process you'll need to follow.

AUTHOR A COMPREHENSIVE EVENT STRATEGY

- Select the best events for your company to sponsor, exhibit, host, attend, or speak at to achieve marketing goals and objectives.
- Maximize event budget through creative spending and tactics such as:
  - Custom programs
  - Speaking opportunities

Three-Phased Approach to a Comprehensive Event Strategy

Phase I. Develop baseline information to measure performance and to use in new opportunity analysis, as below:

- Establish criteria
- Decide audience profile (and relevance to your company)

- Compile event history and summary
- Select educational program content and speaker depth/knowledge
- Obtain press and analyst support
- Decide event direction

Phase II. Use an industry audit of event opportunities, as described below:

- Create a short list of events relevant to the market (based on industry knowledge and past experience).
- Reference others in your company for their perspective on the proposed events.
- Design a final list of events featuring competitive information, participation details, and rationales.

Category	Date	Event/ Location	Description	Fiscal Year	Number of Attendees and Audience Profile	Competitors, Customers, and/or Partners	Secured Opportunities	Web Address	Cost
Internal: Sales Meeting									
External: Customer Conference									
External: Industry Trade Show									
External: Press/Analyst Relations									

Phase III. Define the final event plan recommendations. For instance,

- What is the relevance to your company's initiatives?
- How does the event selection map to specific objective(s)? Provide a description of the conference content/agenda.
- What is the recommendation as to participation at the event (exhibit, sponsorship and/or speaking)?
- Who supports the rationale behind the recommendation?
- Where does this event sit as far as priority ranking in your marketing program?
- When are the deadlines?
- Who are the competitors and who will gather on-site competitive intelligence?
- What are the exact logistics? (location, dates, exhibit, and conference contact information)

SPONSOR OR EXHIBIT AT AN EVENT

When evaluating whether you should sponsor or exhibit at an event, you must uncover the value-added marketing activities available to you. When authoring your comprehensive event strategy, match this list to what you want to accomplish. This allows you to detail how you envision the EventBLT working within your event program.

What marketing opportunities are available to your company?

- Brand Recognition
- Lead Generation
- Thought Leadership

Tip

Helpful information when researching a conference:

- Conference name and URL
- Organization managing the event
- Start and end dates
- Location
- Overview of the conference—three to four sentences (erase all marketing hyperbole)
- Speaking—submission deadline date (if available)
- Speaking—submission guidelines
- List of last year's topics
- List of themes/topics under consideration
- Advisory committee members
- Audience demographics
- Organizer's contact information
- Sponsorship information
- Exhibiting information

Things to consider when evaluating a conference or opportunity:

Relationship Potential

- Is there relationship/business development potential by participating in the event?
- Is there an existing relationship that the company would like to maintain or develop?

Co-association with Organizer

- Is this a "blue-chip" conference/forum/symposium that we want to be associated with?
- What is the reputation of the conference organizer? Are they known for high-quality events?

Platform for Speaker's Specialty

- Is the overall content of the conference consistent with our promotional objectives?

Franchise Visibility

- Is this a strategic sector we want to promote?
- Does the event have a prominent reputation within the industry?

Audience Reach

- Will the speaking opportunity be aimed at the appropriate audience?
- How deep or wide will the reach of the speaking opportunity be?

Networking Opportunity

- How can we benefit from our co-association with other participating companies?

Cece Lee, Account Director and Conference Strategist
Blanc and Otus
http://www.blancandotus.com

Branding

- Sponsorships Level—Event organizers will find some sort of designator to describe the various sponsorship levels. Here are some of the most common:
  - Platinum
  - Gold
  - Silver
  - Bronze
- Advertising
- Show Guide
- Web Site Banner Ad
- Product Description with Logo
- Web Site
- Affiliate Marketing (room drops, hotel keys, etc.)
- Product Announcement

Lead Generation (see Chapter 8)

- Pre/Post Event Attendee List
- Direct Marketing
- Hospitality Functions

Thought Leadership (See Chapter 10)

- Keynote Speaker
- Breakout Speaker
- Panel Discussion
- Moderator
- Session Introducer
- Press Release

ATTEND AN EVENT

As an event marketer, you will be bombarded with requests from sales representatives, executives and other internal groups who will insist that they "must be at this event." Maybe they should attend the event, but it's wise to recommend an event audit first. In other words, you register a representative from your company as a conference attendee and then they supply you with their opinion as to whether or not your company should participate. The audit provides a level of accountability and helps you control your budget. An "Event Audit Marketing Form" (Figure 4.2) can help with developing an event strategy-comparing horizontal to vertical events, regional versus national, or international. This event audit is different from an independent show audit that an organizer would commission to see how an event was received.

Taking the time to audit or evaluate the quality of an event helps you with three major elements in event marketing:

- Should my company participate in this event next year?
- Determining the return of investment (ROI).
- Obtaining information for history and archive purposes.

A great way to find out whether a show is worth your while is to audit the event. In auditing the event, you need a template for your sales team and executives. Once the event is a go, e-mail the designated representative. This representative should also be prepared with additional information (for example, branded apparel, a set agenda, what sessions they will attend, and scheduling meetings with other attendees, speakers, or the press).

Determine the Value That Your Company Brings to the Events

Refresh yourself with the reasons why your company should have a role in specific events. Remember, it is important to communicate with Sales what it is that brings you to your decisions regarding events as it relates to the marketing mix. You can reference this framework before you create the event strategy.

- *Can you think of anything else that your company brings to conferences and events?*
- *Can you own and dominate what you set out to do?*

What does your company bring to conferences and events?

- Market context and a next-generation solution
- Opportunity to introduce and/or present the product, service, or solution

FIGURE 4.2 *Event Marketing Audit Form*

Your Name: ______________________________

Name of Event: ______________________________

Dates: ______________________________

Location: ______________________________

Your role at event: ______________________________

Attendee Profile

Gender Mix: Male: ________ % Female: ________ %

Average Age: Show Attendance (from Web site): __________

- ☐ 18–30
- ☐ 31–49
- ☐ 50+

Type:

- ☐ CXO
- ☐ Vice President/Director
- ☐ Manager
- ☐ Specialist
- ☐ Consultant
- ☐ Developer
- ☐ Service/Support
- ☐ Analyst
- ☐ Press/Media
- ☐ Sales/Marketing

Where to find info:

- Badges
- Showbook
- Conference Schedule
- Show Web site

Purchasing Authority:

- ☐ Decision Maker
- ☐ Recommender
- ☐ Influencer
- ☐ Unable to Assess

International ________ %

USA ________ %

Local (in state) ________ %

(this will tell whether the attendance tracks with the company's target market)

FIGURE 4.2 *Event Marketing Audit Form (Continued)*

Content

Please List the Main Topics ("hot buttons") Covered: ______________________________

____

How many presentations related to our company and our message?

☐ None
☐ 1–3
☐ 3–5
☐ 5–7
☐ 7+

What was the most beneficial presentation? ______________________________

____

Was it due to one or more of the following:

☐ Content
☐ Speaker
☐ Promo
☐ Other

Outline the content tracks or attach the event program agenda and guide: ______________

____

Was it easy to attend the tracks you were interested in?

☐ Yes
☐ No

Number of Speakers:

☐ 1–3
☐ 3–5
☐ 5–7
☐ 7+

Who did you speak with the most?

☐ Delegates
☐ Exhibitors
☐ Speakers
☐ Other

(continued)

FIGURE 4.2 *Event Marketing Audit Form (Continued)*

Logistics and Format

List the main sponsors of the event: ____

____

Did the show floor have a buzz . . . was it crowded? *(Use your gut feeling here.):* ____________

____

Describe the layout of the show floor (select all that apply):

☐ Large booths—20' × 20' and over
☐ Small or pop-up booths—10' × 10' to 10' × 20'
☐ Table top—6' or 8' display area
☐ Each exhibitor has the same booth, only signage is different
☐ Not applicable

How did the majority of exhibitors display their products and/or services:

☐ Theater presentation
☐ Demo pods and/or stations
☐ One-on-one meetings
☐ Promo or Giveaway Materials

What type of sponsorships where available:

☐ Meals—breakfast, lunches, breaks, dinners, special events
☐ Printed materials—program guide, newsletter, online
☐ Signage—taxi flags, banners, etc.
☐ Other: ______________________________

Can you recall the sponsors for specific areas? If so, please provide below: ____________

____

Were there social events? Please write your comments if you participated.

☐ Golf outing
☐ Sporting event tickets
☐ Dinners
☐ Dancing
☐ Other: ______________________________

Comments: ____

FIGURE 4.2 *Event Marketing Audit Form (Continued)*

Competitors

Which of our competitors exhibited?

1. ______________________ Booth size _____ × _____ Presentation ☐ Yes ☐ No
2. ______________________ Booth size _____ × _____ Presentation ☐ Yes ☐ No
3. ______________________ Booth size _____ × _____ Presentation ☐ Yes ☐ No
4. ______________________ Booth size _____ × _____ Presentation ☐ Yes ☐ No
5. ______________________ Booth size _____ × _____ Presentation ☐ Yes ☐ No

Did any of our competitors have speakers at the sessions or keynotes?

	Name	*Session*	*Title*
1.			
2.			
3.			
4.			
5.			

ROI Observations

What ROI would our company obtain from the show?

☐ Closed deals
☐ Solid leads
☐ Soft leads
☐ Waste of time/money/energy

Would this show be beneficial for our company to participate?

☐ Yes
☐ No

Why? ____

Overall experience of the show:

☐ Great
☐ Good
☐ Moderate
☐ Bad
☐ Never Again

(continued)

FIGURE 4.2 *Event Marketing Audit Form (Continued)*

What areas were the best? *(check all that apply)*	What areas needed improvement? *(check all that apply)*
☐ Attendance	☐ Attendance
☐ Content	☐ Content
☐ Sponsorship	☐ Sponsorship
☐ Exhibitors	☐ Exhibitors
☐ Presentations	☐ Presentations
☐ Quality	☐ Quality

Your Recommendation

Next scheduled occurrence of this event? Date: ____________ Location/Venue

☐ Exhibit at next event
☐ Audit next time before making decision
☐ Do not exhibit at this event

Why? ____

Other comments about the event: ______________________________

____

- Expertise in the area
- Evidence to backup your claims
- The ability to reference customer metrics when applicable
- Your *Presence–present your products*
- Economic profit (conference producers make money from sponsorship fees, so sponsors should use and leverage to fullest)

Own and Dominate. Invest in a limited set of events. It's the fastest and most cost-effective way to reach qualified audience in a controlled environment. Why?

- A target audience is the decision driver.

- Delegates use conferences to gather information as part of contemplating the buy.
- Peer-to-peer interaction creates a forum for validation of their decisions.
- Media organizations and analyst firms have intimate relationships with their customers.
- Executive participation proves highly valuable.
- Executives have insights and stature.
- Scheduling "often requested" one-on-one time is now available.
- Sales leads often result from preliminary executive meetings.
- Your company can set the stage for leadership.
- Events are a good environment for relationship building.
- Delegates are freer to discuss what resonates and what does not.
- Your company goes to exceptional lengths to touch the conference audience.

Event Strategy—GO DEEP

Create the one-on-one relationship.

- **Partner with Media Orgs and Analyst Firms**
    - Intimate relationships with subscribers and customers
    - Leverage editors, reporters, analysts, and your sales representatives
- **Target Accounts**
    - Touch a prequalified decision driver
    - Match prospects to delegates

Focus on *their* reason for attending.

- Gather data as part of contemplating "the buy"

    - Peer-to-peer interaction creates a forum for validation of their decisions

- **Your Company sets the stage for leadership**
    - Executive and board participation are valuable hooks
    - Scheduling "often requested" one-on-one time now available
    - Sales leads often result from preliminary executive meetings

It's great knowing that you need to create an event strategy, but if you don't understand the terminology for the different types of events, it's hard to get started. Today, you're finding a great deal of focus on ROI and what events bring to companies. Basically, if an event is performed correctly, you will see a greater response to a company's product; that is, through a product launch. Internally, it could be a boost in sales, a boost in production, a boost in morale, a number of things. Match the items under "Event Types At-a-Glance" (below) with the graphic on a *Faster Way to Close the Deal* (See Figure 4.1 earlier in this chapter). This will help you to categorize events into the appropriate buckets when you build out your company's Event Strategy.

EVENT TYPES AT-A-GLANCE

Trade Show

Trade shows are programs in which space is rented for exhibits/booths/stands to showcase product offerings to horizontal or vertical industries. Costs vary based on nature of participation, which includes size of space and booth property. There are a variety of complementary sponsorships or added-value marketing associated with these events. Every industry has trade shows.

Seminar

Seminars are often two-hour, half-day, or full-day programs. This is typical for vertical events for industries such as financial services, healthcare, and technology, just to name a few. The agenda or content is the draw.

■ **Hint:** Food and beverage should complement the seminar function. Consider hosting a breakfast or lunch with the day's activities or a "happy hour" reception immediately following the afternoon sessions. This allows a networking opportunity to further discuss the topics at hand and further define relationships.

Conference (a.k.a. Summit or Symposium)

- *Industry Conference/Summit.* Usually a vertically focused event that features content delivered by guest speakers. This could include a co-sponsorship opportunity. There may be a mix of both hospitality and business sessions within the format. The content is focused on education.
- *Industry Conference with Exhibition.* Similar to above, but also includes a demonstration area.

Product Launch/Road Show

- *Product/Services Launch.* This event is designed to introduce a new product or service. There should be a speaking opportunity. In most cases, there will be a mix of hospitality, exhibition, advertising, direct marketing, online communications, and public relations.

- *Road Show.* A customer-focused program presented in multiple cities. It promotes brand and product awareness to current and prospective customers.

User Group and Exhibition

This is an industry event in which your company will participate as attendee, exhibitor, and/or presenter. Such events may be usually sponsored by an independent association, your company, or another organization, and you graciously attend alongside other companies.

Forum

- *Executive Forum.* These special events target CXO level executives from among your customers, prospects, and partners. The event provides a unique relationship building opportunity within the target audience.
- *Peer-to-Peer Forum.* These events are designed as soft-sell programs and encourage a dynamic dialog exchange, usually on visionary topics. The approach should be "white glove," and the sessions should be hosted in convenient locations, such as a briefing center, top-rated restaurant, or hotel. Peer-to-peer forums are most successful when hosted in conjunction with an existing event.
- *Roundtable.* Attendee size usually ranges in 8 to 16 people and the content is especially topic-driven. There is no sales pitch in a roundtable but a dynamic exchange of information. It's a listening opportunity. It's important to talk with attendees, not talk at them. Food and beverage selections should follow the guidelines of a seminar.

- *Birds-of-a-Feather.* These events are usually held within a trade show, conference, or summit. They are topic-driven and it is common to have participants hold discussions for approximately 1½ hours. It is best to pair this concept with a meal function.
- *One-on-One Briefings.* These are programs in which sponsors and delegates meet one-on-one through prescheduled appointments arranged by the show producer using an Internet site. There is no exhibit component and no signage is allowed. One or two senior-level managers or executives would represent your company when they meet the prospects. Some of these types of events are held in a remote resort location or a cruise ship, so there is a captive audience without any distractions.

■ **Hint:** To brand this event, place a decal sign across the center of your presentation laptop. Bring a sales collateral kit and an executive promotional item (see Chapter 6).

Meetings

External meetings:

- *Annual Stockholders Meeting.* As a public company, a meeting is held for shareholders. The voting of board members and the amendments are the content.
- *Financial Analyst Meeting.* Held with members of the financial community, usually by the CFO or CEO.

Internal meetings:

- *National Sales Meetings.* Held annually or quarterly, the focus is on product and positioning education, networking, and team building.
- *Incentive Programs.* Held to recognize outstanding efforts such as a sales quota club results.
- *Executive Retreats.* Held by senior-level management, traditionally at a remote location for strategic planning and team/relationship building.

E-Seminar/Webinar—(Online)

Think of an e-seminar or Webinar as a live meeting but hosted on the Internet. Your message is conveyed via an audio and/or video stream. The presentation is typically archived for continuous use. It's a cost-effective medium that is simply a venue to convey information. With online seminars you are replacing the live classroom environment.

■ **Hint:** Online events are great for education. You can dive deep into your product or services without pulling people out of their office structure. With these types of events, you are on and off in a couple of hours. But remember, there's still follow-up. Did you promise to send a report after your event? Make sure you have a call-to-action when conducting an online event.

Technology Enablers

- *Video Conference.* Participants are linked through technology and can see each others' faces. So it appears that you are all in the same room even if you are connecting from

"Blogging is just completely taking off and is a huge opportunity yet very controversial. There are many marketing people out there who do not really buy into blogging, but I think that is very short-sighted. Marketers need to understand about blogging and how to leverage it. You need to be careful not to abuse it. You can get a lot of information and insights about competition, about what customers are experiencing—it is definitely growing in the industry.

So the next question is this: "How will events and blogging work together?" From what I've uncovered it will play a significant part in the next wave of online events."

Jennifer Bader
Senior Council
McClenahan Bruer Communications
http://www.mcbru.com

different areas of the world. Currently, voice, video, and data applications can all be viewed via video conference.

- *Teleconference.* Participants are linked through technology and can hear one another's voices using the telephone or other type of PDA. Participators usually dial in to a central conference call number that includes a password for security purposes.

Venue Enablers/Backdrop

Meal function. These functions bring an opportunity to experience the culinary delights of a fabulous area restaurant or dining experience within a hotel.

- *Breakfast.* Set early in the morning either in a restaurant or private room.
- *Lunch.* They don't say, "let's do lunch" for just any reason.
- *Dinner.* Usually for your VIPs with an added opportunity to entertain and network.

Networking reception. These generally do not feature a sales pitch, but there a great deal of "schmoozing" and subliminal positioning of your message.

Hospitality functions. Hospitality/cultural events are programs generally associated with entertainment, sports, or cultural events. The invited audience can range from 2 to 100 or more, and includes senior-level executives or qualified customers, prospect, and partners. In many cases, the events include attendance at a sponsored event, an activity program, and an evening event.

Sports marketing. Reflects major sports marketing contracts or addresses business relationship needs, revenue opportunities, or internal activities. Local or regional venues such as tickets or box seats at professional sports arenas would fall into this category.

Golf outing. Hosted in a corporate environment as a scramble-style tournament. Players are strategically paired in foursomes by job title or role and responsibility. Tournament time ranges from four hours to a full day. A prestigious club is traditionally selected as the venue.

- Enhance the golf outing by hosting a breakfast on the green with a motivational address.
- Arrange for special "treats" on various holes (hole-in-one prizes, deduct a stroke if you can answer a product-related question, etc.).
- Create and design a custom scorecard and include it on the cart.
- Create name signs for the cart with your company logo.
- Brand the beverage carts and the cart driver with logo clothing.

- Distribute a golf pack from your Promotional Inventory Package (PIP) purchase that includes:
  - Golf balls
  - Visor/baseball cap
  - Towels
  - Pencils

Theme parks. A great spot for entertaining a large group of end users. For instance, an evening "buy out" of such venues as a Disney property, provides a way to associate your brand with a first-class organization.

Chapter

5

POSITIONING AND MESSAGING

Our mantra:
Event Marketing is all about facilitating, easing, opening, accelerating, and shortening the sales cycle. That's it!

After you've decided what event(s) your company will sponsor, exhibit, attend, or host, you should begin to identify what it is your company really wants to say. Deciding on what the message is and what it is that you want your target audience to walk away remembering, are key ingredients within the event cycle. By starting with your sales initiatives and business objectives, you now know why your company is performing this process and what to measure your success against.

When you work in events, your job is to communicate your company's message in 25 words or less (and much less). I profess this concept over and over as an event marketer. Events represent a live presence environment and within those walls, the target audience is bombarded with so many stimuli, how do you as a company break through? That's why it's important to stay focused on just 25 words. These words become your message and how you conduct your efforts in the live presentation environment.

Tip

Events are an open format for communications. When you set out to write the positioning and messaging, know why you are doing this, how the success will be measured, and who the target audience may be.

Knowing the basics can help you craft a message that will hopefully resonate with your desired target audience.

To be clear, I am not stating that your direct mail pieces or your sales collateral/literature, press announcements, or multimedia presentations are 25 words or less.

I like to model event thinking after what I learned in principles of advertising. In the book *How to Advertise,* by Kenneth Roman and Jane Maas, they write that creative strategies differ in form and terminology, but a good one must cover five key points: objective, audience, benefit, support, and tonality. I've taken their advertising framework and adopted it for events.

1. *Objective.* What is the purpose of the event?
2. *Target audience.* Who is your audience profile?
3. *Key benefit.* Why should the target audience buy your product?
4. *Support.* Give one good reason to believe in the key benefit.
5. *Tone and manner.* Provide a statement of the product's "personality."

Jennifer Bader, senior counsel for McClenahan Bruer Communications, a boutique firm that is an integrated advertising and public relations agency, explains her company's approach to positioning and messaging through:

- Message Storming
- Brand Vision

Message Storming

It is a physical and structural process, and we go through it with every client. We will not start messaging until we have a brand. In some cases, the company has identified their brand, and that's awesome; in others they start from scratch. By doing this exercise with every client, we can determine what the positioning and messaging should be.

Our firm just hosted an exercise for a client where we had the executive management team say, "Oh, we do not need to do the branding exercise, we know what we want our brand to be." We ask them to humor us and let us just do a quick little exercise. So we pose five questions about branding, personalities, and the attributes. We had each person fill out their answers on a sheet of paper. We reviewed their feedback collectively, and every single person from the top down (CEO's and Vice President's of Marketing, Research and Development, Corporate Communications, etc.) all had varying viewpoints and wording. There was no consistency. They all had a different idea.

At McBru, we create messaging documents. Then identify the positioning and messaging. The key is consistency.

Brand Vision

With the McBru mode, there are four quadrants that companies fit into. Within each quadrant you have power brands, explorer brands, icon, and identities. So on the bottom right hand corner would be the power brand and the bottom left hand is explorer. Top left would be identity and top right would iconic.

For example, an identity brand at a consumer level would be Harley Davidson or Porsche. People identify themselves as a Harley Davidson person. People identify themselves as a Porsche driver; it is like you are part of a club.

It takes about a month to go through the process. Our McBru team looks at competitive landscape. We go through and review their current customer base; we speak to employees; we may conduct focus groups and outline where the company is at today and where would they would like it to go in the future.

Jennifer Bader
McClenahan Bruer Communications
Senior Counsel
http://www.mcbru.com

Once the messaging process is in place and you have an understanding of what your company is, now comes the fun part where you get to find your voice. At McBru, they use "message storming" in finding the company's voice. So if you go through McBru's message storming, you'll figure out the rational and emotional connections between the brand, message, and audience.

If you look at it from an event standpoint, it's leveraging that voice within the live presence environment. It's the emotional connection that will set you apart—hit them in their heart. It's important to create a positioning framework, a document that features company information, tag line, key messaging, and supporting points. Does your company have one?

When it comes to events, I needed a way to work with my teams in order to match what we were saying directly to our target audience. Why? Because there are so many branding opportunities available to you when you sponsor, exhibit, attend, or host an event, the positioning framework becomes the core for the branding in the EventBLT.

Getting consensus on your three main messages can be quite painful at times. But it is one of the best attributes you bring to the table when planning an event. I actually remember folks getting into screaming matches over event messaging. When you're involved in an event, remember that everyone thinks they can do that job and wants input. The field organization believes the message should say one thing, the corporate communications team another, product marketing something else, and executives (the approvers) are actually off somewhere else. Therefore, the positioning framework also provides you with the content for an Event Messaging document that can be circulated for approval.

Once approved, how do you get to those key points that you want to have communicated and train your teams? With the positioning framework you also have a "cheat sheet" to use so everybody knows their lines, so to speak. It provides a common set of talking points. So when you share the logistics, such as the dress code and the name badges, your job is to communicate the message. Whether you actually present the content in the positioning framework is up to you and your company protocol.

Engage other members of your team. For example, a senior executive presenting the messages to your team is much stronger than you would be as the event marketer. Look at what will provide you with the most retention and leave your ego at the door. Senior execs have people's ears–take advantage of it! The net-net (bottom line) here is to communicate your company's key messages in a consistent, repeatable fashion.

Think of it like this:

- *The Scene:* A product launch occurs on a Wednesday evening after work. There's a cocktail party held approximately 45 minutes before guests are invited to view the presentation. Afterwards, drinks continue to pour and the networking cocktail reception continues for another hour. There are some who stay around longer, probably another hour or so.
- *The Guests:* 1,000 hot pipeline customers, press, and analysts
- *The Message:* Preview your next line of products.
- *Overheard:* What Do I Say?

If you look at the audience profile, you're right on the money. But as you look closer, there are two open dialog periods (pre- and post-presentation) where representatives from your company will be interacting with your customers, prospects, press, and analysts. Does your team know what to say? Have they been given tools to communicate effectively? Are their statements supporting what your speakers, demo, and collateral reflect?

Imagine this: The same prospect speaks with a sales rep from the Midwest who also happens to be his old college friend and 20 minutes later is introduced to his new rep based on the East

Coast. What starts off as a random conversation, gets into one of the key messages presented at your event.

- The Midwest rep hits the nail on the head and reinforces the story based on details provided in the positioning framework. His call-to-action is to suggest a follow-up meeting at the customers' headquarters, as well as introduce his friend and now company prospect to the new territory rep. The introduction is made within 15 minutes of the evening's demo and presentation.
- The East Coast rep introduces herself and then fumbles through the story and never highlights one, two, or three of the key benefits, because she's has nothing to contribute to the conversation. She starts relaying past experiences when working for her last company. The prospect is a bit confused and walks away bewildered instead of asking for more scheduling time on the calendar to discuss further.

To get started, it's your responsibility to be a sleuth. Take a look around you. This positioning framework only takes about 60 minutes to work through the first time. Try at least three to five revisions within the cycle for each event. The time you invest on the front end will prove invaluable when it comes to actually executing the materials needed for the event.

Here are the three steps for the positioning framework:

1. Use your external Web site and the information contained on your Intranet. Use the materials created by your product marketing, marketing, public relations, and corporate communications teams. The content has already been approved. *(20 minutes)*
2. Read articles published about your company and the product(s) you are featuring. A simple online search via Google, Yahoo!, Ask Jeeves, etc., can provide you with

some great gems. It also gives you punchy copy that can be repurposed for your event materials developed within your marketing program. In large corporations, secondary sources include your human resources and/or your legal departments. *(20 minutes)*

3. Get the story straight! One way to jumpstart your program is to schedule ten-minute "discovery sessions" with Sales and Product Marketing. Through customer testimonials and awards the company's recently won, there's a wealth of great material to use. *(20 minutes)*

In my Marketing 101 class sophomore year over 20 years ago, I learned the "three legs to a stool rule." You only get three—how simple is that! I've taken that basic principle and applied the rule: you only get three main messages at the event. Take a look at Figure 5.1, the quick-start outline called the Positioning Framework and Messaging, a document that captures company information, the tagline, and three key benefits and supporting points.

It's one of my favorites and helps me set the tone for what messages will be featured throughout the event. It's really easy to work with and is something I use over and over again. A completed version featuring Procore Technologies, the company I mentioned in previous chapters, is also included.

Now it comes to the actual live event. How do you figure out what words to use on your signage and banners, copy for the event program guides, Web links, and online ads? The key is consistency, consistency, and consistency.

Figure 5.2 shows my "Positioning and Messaging Copy Guide." I create one to complement the event plan. It saves me so much time. Look at your event cycle. Within each industry, cycles are held at certain times, so by reinforcing your event messages throughout your entire event program, you are one step further in *facilitating, easing, opening, accelerating, and shortening the sales cycle.*

FIGURE 5.1 *Positioning and Messaging Framework*

Company Name: **Product Name:** **URL:** **Stock Symbol:**			
Position/Vision Statement:			
Tag Line/ Sub-Statement			
Acronyms:			
Target Audience Profile:			
Benefits:	1.	2.	3.
Value Points	a. b. c.	a. b. c.	a. b. c.

FIGURE 5.1 *Positioning and Messaging Framework (Continued)*

Company Name: Procore Technologies **Product Name:** SitePro **URL:** www.pro-core.com **Stock Symbol:**			
Position/Vision Statement:	SitePro is powerful project management software for custom home builders. SitePro enables builders to keep accurate project schedules, improve project team communications, and accelerate responses to requests-for-information (RFIs). SitePro's Web cam service allows builders and project owners to log in and view live video of the project site from any Internet connection.		
Tag Line/ Sub-Statement	"Our Builders Know"		
Acronyms:			
Target Audience Profile:	Custom Home Builders—99% men, ages 34-65. Typical technology experience is limited to e-mail and Web browsing.		
Benefits:	More accurate project schedules	Improved project team communications	Accelerated RFI responses avoid project delays. Critical project information is communicated in time to keep project on schedule.
Value Points	• Project schedules kept online, available for viewing by all project team members. • Changes to project task dates are made online by project superintendent from any Internet connection. • Reasons for schedule changes are automatically documented and archived online.	• SitePro online communications module centralizes project team e-mails and comments in one location. • Project team members can comment and share information on any topic, with full record of every communication saved to provide a project history. • SitePro eliminates lost communications from separate e-mail systems and provides the whole team insight into on-going issues.	• Requests-for-Information (RFIs) are automatically dated and numbered, eliminating confusion over RFI dates and sequence. • Each RFI is e-mailed to the respondent, as well as to any other individuals on a distribution list. RFIs are not lost via fax or postal mail. • Every RFI has a due date, after which reminder e-mails are sent to the respondent and the distribution list. Reminder notices eliminate "forgotten RFIs" and speed up closure of issues.

FIGURE 5.2 *Positioning and Messaging Copy Guide*

For signage, banners, event program guides, Web links, online ads, and more.

Description	Copy
Headline and three bullet points	Product Name Start sentence with action words
25 words	Elevator Pitch
50 words	Elevator Pitch with one Key Benefit
75 words	Elevator Pitch with two Key Benefits
100 words	Elevator Pitch with three Key Benefits
250 words	The Full Story
500 words	The Full Story with In-depth Product Info
Appropriate URL	Your call to action—don't forget to include it

POSITIONING MESSAGE DELIVERABLES

An interview with someone who knows what it's like.

Brian Vanden Broucke is articulate creative services, inc.'s Chief Executive Officer and Senior Creative Director with 17 years of marketing experience. He has orchestrated high-profile productions for Harcourt Achieve, Thomson Learning, Baker-Hughes, IBM, Xerox, Siemens, Bentley, Lucent, Life Fitness, and Convergys, to name a few. Having won numerous industry awards, he is also a popular motivational speaker in the United States and abroad.

AS: We talked about the essential role of discovery and focusing *everything* around the customer, really spending the time to *profile* the customer deeper than one would think. But what's next? How do you begin to figure out what to *do* as it relates to the EventBLT?

BV: When you were growing up, the things you remember more than anything else in your life are stories. Grandfathers, Auntie Jane's, whoever, telling you a story about when they were 12 running through the streets at midnight without their shoes on when it started to rain, and how cool it was between their toes. And because it was framed as a *story* instead of just "something that happened the other day," it is remembered. That is the job of a marketing deliverable. To get the message (story) not only told—*but remembered.*

AS: How does the process start?

BV: Let's start with your "B" part in an EventBLT. You have to get that brand out there consistently and with punch. We are so over stimulated in our society. In bars, we see video, TVs everywhere; things are going off, video games screaming, Blackerries ringing, even cars have DVD players. Because we are so over stimulated with messages, we need to keep our customers' minds moving forward in a clear path to understand a clear message.

AS: How do you articulate it? No pun intended.

BV: (with a chuckle) I love the name of this company, because that IS the product. We *articulate.* First of all, the story part of it has to be very simple. It should not have more than one consistent major message and at the most three sub-messages in the whole deal. You ought to be able to whittle it down even to one succinct sentence.

Next. What is the *compelling* part of your story? What are the *benefits* of this compelling story to the audience? For example, if you are selling a new type of Web browser that optimizes the time people spend on search engines, you may consider typifying what their *lives* look like. Scouring the Web into the wee hours of the night for the right information with dark, deep circles under his eyes and cobwebs hanging from the computer monitor, his aged, arthritic fingers have become worn down past his first knuckle due to all of the savage typing. The keyboard has turned yellow and brittle. There are beer bottles everywhere, and Clinton was still President the last time he went outside. He has no love in his life. He has NO life whatsoever, because he spends ALL of his time looking for information where it cannot be found. Whereas with "opti-search," he has already found a date for the next 20 years, a place to get the circles under his eyes removed, and has booked a vacation in the Bahamas for less than the cost of his monthly antidepressant meds.

You can *feel* the compelling story and *see* the dramatic pictures as this story ran through your mind. That's how good creative event marketing can make a brand so memorable. It turns your brand into a three dimensional, full-on emotional experience. So many people write bad or boring marketing communications because they focus on features—not on the ramifications of how the audiences' lives will be positively affected by their product, service, or solution in a visceral way.

Look at the guy who founded Wendy's—Dave, okay? He became the greatest spokesman in the history of American advertising by speaking directly to his hamburger-chomping public in a way he *knew* they would understand. And even though the real Dave was purportedly *nothing* like the character he portrayed on TV, it was powerful. Why? Because he told stories. And he told them in a way that touched the customer.

AS: What is the next step?

BV: With good brainstorming on your objectives and target customers and a team of creative and marketing people, you have now come up with a viable strategy and abstract storyline. Next, a script must be written, even if the communication is only ten seconds in length.

AS: Why can't you go right to selecting the compelling pictures that tell the story?

BV: Because words need to come before pictures. You don't illustrate a book before you write the story. The illustrations are invaluable mind you, but this is the correct order of worship. Besides, it wastes time and money. So, if you want to waste time and money, place the pictures first.

AS: Got it.

BV: So, let's assume you are branding at a trade show. Once that has gone through the approval process, a storyboard of visuals that support the script eventually begins to take shape and turn your compelling story into a visual and audio experience as well!

AS: What about the human element?

BV: I'm *getting* there. Nothing communicates your brand better than a live scripted presentation with powerful visual support (not merely PowerPoint), but a good storyline professionally executed. Especially at a trade show. Nothing. Period!

A scripted, yet very natural, story being told by one or more people who represent the company on some level. The live presentation. We are all in the business. We have *all* been witness to dumber than *dumb* live trade show presentations. You know the kind. Somebody doing something just embarrassing enough to draw attention. But *what kind* of attention does it draw? Does it "brand" you? Yeah. It brands you as someone with no clue!

You should work with your team or with a creative agency to present yourself to the outside world in a Brand Appropriate (BA) manner. That five-minute branding message could be seen by a sizeable chunk of the invited audience at a trade show. For goodness sake, don't make it the wrong one!

We just finished a project where there were 21,000 attendees at the show. The live presentation mechanism remarkably processed and gave a tight brand message to over *8,300 people,* who spent more than a half an hour at the exhibit in just three days (it can be done!). And, even if they only give you five minutes, you had better make that a worthwhile and *appropriate* five minutes.

It's got to go through a scripting process. It will need professional visual support. You will need to have a good position in the booth near a busy aisle. It's got to be short. It's got to be filled with benefits. It's got to be aimed at your audience—not too high, not too low. It's got to be engaging, not necessarily just entertaining, and it has to be memorable. It's got to be interactive. You've got to ask them some questions, provoke some thought. And you've got to execute it extremely well. Do *not* go on the cheap now that you have gone this far and think that you are going to find a couple of local models to pull this off. Your spokespeople and people handlers need to be professional, well-paid professionals. They are worth it. Anything else is like launching the space shuttle and asking a temp to push the liftoff button.

AS: Can you use a company person to do your pitch? Can they be trained?

BV: In some cases, a *special* individual with higher-than-average communication skills at the company is capable of delivering a consistent and compelling presentation, but having the endurance to do it 12 to 14 times or more a day is a lot to ask. They may be more valuable in a selling role or as a tag team.

AS: Tag team?

BV: Sure. A professional presenter teamed with product specialist. Create a synergy between them that is professional and with a "real efficacy" to it. A good professional presenter, however, should blend into your company—unless they are playing a goofy character or something very comedic.

AS: What about getting a Leadership message out?

BV: So many customers spend too much time talking about what they do, not what they do for their customer. It is a fundamental problem in most business communications. If they do not articulate their message with their audience forefront in their minds, if you do not examine every single word you say and how you say it as it relates to your audience, you are going to miss the boat. You are going to create something that is just aimed at a very broad spectrum of faceless drones.

AS: The executive mouthpiece?

BV: As you state, the executive thought leader. Your thought leader must be committed to what they are saying. And, the *only* way you are going to find out how committed they are is to talk to them about it. Ask them specific questions. Why are you committed to this product? Why do you work here? Why is this important to you? What would you like to change about how you are perceived? Are you comfortable giving this message? Why or why not? What is different about this? Then listen and listen some more. You will get some pretty interesting answers if you go deep enough and more than that, you will get something very, very personal. And when you get something personal from that executive, now *you have a story.* Not a dumb joke, but a story. Now you have something that is completely individual, contains the corporate message, and is delivered in a compelling way by a live human being of some stature.

Nothing builds efficacy more than a leader who can communicate. Look at JFK. Reagan. Clinton. Pee Wee Herman.

AS: You build their content and compelling visual support. What's next?

BV: A famous designer or architect once said, "Life IS details." People only remember the last 5 percent. The content is a given and as in Vegas it's your ante chip to get into the game. But it is the ease, the personality, the wit, the humor, the engaging style of the executive that makes their *leadership role* come alive in a palpable way.

If you think that an executive has nothing on his mind except that speech to be delivered on May 1st at your all-important conference and that they will study and work on it themselves to do a professional job, you are naïve. What makes you think that executives are going to be able to step out of their high-pressure roles long enough to hone an effective message-based presentation for your product or service?

Even Michael Jordan had a coach. You need a *professional* speech coach. (Forget the resume; ask to hear your coach speak for five minutes themselves as the interview.) They should be able to break down barriers. Meet with them eye-to-eye in order give them positive, yet *honest* support. Help them along.

> *"Management is three parts positive and one part criticism."*
>
> ***–G. Daniel Lumpkin.***

Do this right and in most cases they will start coming alive. They start becoming human and more accessible to your audience. And *that* is a winning way to get a leadership message out to a targeted crowd.

That is what makes really good executive speakers so good! A good story! Good refined content. Good visual support and good coaching.

AS: How long does it take?

BV: Most of the time you should allow from the time a client would come to us and we want to produce this executive presentation from cradle to grave . . . I would say between six to eight weeks is ideal.

AS: For my last question, you've talked a lot about powerful visual support. How is that created and how does it contribute to the EventBLT?

BV: OK. For example, you need to support a "growth" message visually that will be elucidated by your professional spokesperson or your executive. You *could* show a chart with an arrow going up pulling the image from clip art or creating it in Excel. Or, you *could* provide an image that makes a statement, a metaphor on growth that is more compelling.

For example, use time-lapse photography of seedlings sprouting from the ground as a .wmv file imbedded within PowerPoint. Or, you might use three children standing next to one another, one at a one-year-old, one who looks preadolescent, and one with a diploma in hand. Now, with either of these choices, you have evoked a *feeling* of growth that is far deeper and more communicative than just an abstract chart with numbers on it.

Is multimedia effective? Absolutely! Multimedia, dollar for dollar, is the most effective deliverable you can use to stop people in their tracks—on the Web, as a PR initiative, at a trade show, as an opening module for a keynote address, etc. You can do so much more with multimedia today. It can be produced affordably compared to the old days and repurposed (when non-rights-managed images are used) and digitally streamed over the Web. It can be projected, high-definition on indoor projection devices á la Times Square. That will stop them in their tracks at a trade show if combined with a professional and an *incentive to participate.* NOTE: Don't ever underestimate the power of winning something or getting something for nothing. You need that at a trade show to get them to stop.

AS: How much do you need to spend to communicate the message in multimedia?

BV: There is no limit to it. The question is: what is the *best* investment in your multimedia dollar? For most cost-effective multimedia, first you have to have a clear concept and some words. Then you start putting concepts together, words and pictures on *paper* before you start putting pixels onto anything. It is a process, and the process must be in alignment with the usage and reusability factor.

For example, if you are spending thousands of dollars to create a five-minute video loop to run by itself at a trade show you are *wasting* your money. But, if you preordain *how* you want to use the media throughout the year, you may use it for:

- Executive briefing intro
- Sales presentation intro
- PR communication
- Trade show
- Opening module for the national sales meeting
- Web stream

Now you have multiple filet of media. You've carved out creative ways to maximize the investment of the video and parse it out as needed in a cost-efficient, responsible, measurably better way.

Chapter

6

CREATIVE MATERIALS, PROMOTIONAL ITEMS, AND GIVEAWAYS

Our mantra:
Event Marketing is all about facilitating, easing, opening, accelerating, and shortening the sales cycle. That's it!

Close your eyes for a minute and think of all the events you've planned or been to in your lifetime, from industry trade shows to customer dinners to a kid's birthday party. I actually believe kids' birthday parties do branding right. It's such a simple example, but is one that when I discuss it, people "pooh-pooh," but it then visually evokes some sort of recollection.

Kids' parties start with a theme (think "Sponge Bob," the "Muppets," "Finding Nemo"). You go to the party store or online to order all the materials–and they match, such as the invitations, plates, napkins, and tablecloths. You plan party games that are in line with the theme, and the giveaway (party favors) are in a plastic bag filled with candy and inexpensive toys. Do you get the picture? The key in this scenario is the consistency, and it's the fundamental principle that I apply in branding events.

As you are building out your event strategy, deciding what event(s) your company will sponsor, exhibit, attend, or host and you've established the framework for positioning and messaging, it is your responsibility to really maximize the brand throughout the event cycle. You'll be working in a parallel path within the event cycle which reflects the pre-event activities, on-site and postevent marketing. Within the cycle, your efforts will include:

- Direct attendee mailings
- PR
- Advertising
- Online communications
- Speaking engagements
- Hospitality functions
- Demonstration or product showcase
- Education and training sessions
- Giveaways and promotional items
- Incentives
- Telemarketing
- Followup (sales calls for appointments, thank you letters, invitations to upcoming events)

With events, it is the constant reinforcement of your message that will set your company apart. Through visual materials, you have a plethora of ways in which to get your message out! The same look and feel provides you with consistency and consistency is what resonates with your target audience. The key here is how creative you are within your event program and how you leverage what you've produced at not only one event, but at multiple events.

Tip

Think 25 words or less

(The cornerstone includes logo, tag line, URL, and elevator pitch.)

From event to event, it is important to recognize that many of the materials you create can be repurposed or reused. When I recognized that option, it's when I became an "Event Marketing Brand-A-Holic." I looked at every surface within the event as a touch point to reaching my target audience. It became a challenge for me as to how creative I could get with our visual materials. I was so hooked, I couldn't get enough. I realized that no matter what type of event (see "Event Types At-a-Glance," Chapter 4), there were basic materials that I could repurpose, no matter who the target audience was.

So how do you actually take your company's position or message and bring that to life at an event with the type of materials that you produce? There are a variety of ways, however, to leverage materials across all events. It comes down to budget and maximizing that "spend" actually puts money back into your budget. Here are some quick tricks to maximize your marketing spend.

- When you produce events, it makes so much more financial sense to design materials that are a little bit more generic so they can be used across the board for an entire season or year than to do individual one-offs. Because one-offs, no matter what, are always going to be more expensive unless it's a program of a specific event that it needs to be dated, or you have a sponsor and you need to have that sponsor name indicated. You can also supplement a dated print run with generic materials.
- For executive events, let's use signage as an example. Produce a poster on foam board and laminate it instead of being locked into using items like unsightly vinyl banners. With just a small modification in the physical materials, your look and feel has more class.
- Keep an inventory of all your branding components—items like table tent cards, name badges, hangtags, and banners. By producing them in bulk, using them multiple

> times, and consuming them as you use them, you've extended the power of your brand. You have to pound it home. Don't save it!

Events require a significant amount of visual materials. The creative materials you produce for events are different from giveaway and promotional items, as well as sales literature and collateral. I'm a big organizer and in order to keep straight what it was we actually needed for our programs and how it aligned to our budget buckets, I developed the "Event Marketing Creative Materials Tool Kit."

Think of these items as your decorations. It's a way for you to identify who you are and what you do. Really look at the event. Remember the Hollywood movie premiere example outlined earlier in the book. It's a formula, and yes, the content and the people change from event to event, but the thinking about the creative materials and execution process is all the same.

This tool kit provides you with all the items you need to brand your event. It's what you put into the tool kit that makes all the difference in the world. I view this kit as my "toiletry bag." It carries the fundamental things I need to survive.

The materials you create to form your own tool kit will help reinforce your brand and image. The design elements should mirror that of your sales collateral and advertising campaign. When you use this system, you will find that you will save time and money.

The first step in building your own tool kit is finding a printer or production house that can produce the items. Your relationship with a print and production vendor has a lot to do with what you'll get in your final product. Your company probably already has suppliers that they've worked with, so tap into your internal resources first. If none are available, ask friends and colleagues in product marketing, corporate communications, legal, or human resources for references.

This relationship is extremely critical, especially under deadline. I like to look for printers and production houses that are customer focused and solutions-oriented. Their services may include design, artwork, copy writing, photography, production, printing and distribution. A creative agency on the other hand may specialize in marketing strategy, name/identity development, branding, advertising, copywriting, and design. A creative agency may produce deliverables such as logos, brochures, stationary packages, signage, sales tools, and collateral, and may even do the interface for you with the printer and/or production house.

Another good thing about partnering with your vendor is trust and that trust innately breeds a little bit more quality. I've also noticed that there's an "even-ing out" on price. Some projects may be a little bit more expensive, some projects may be a little bit less expensive. If you always shop on price though, you're never going to build that relationship!

As part of my event network, I work with Lynn Hughes, an account executive at Visual Resource, a print and production company in San Francisco. This company creates and develops print

Look for simple ways to save money!

Tip

Vendor Management

"A good vendor that you're partnered with will be able to offer you more value. If you are producing easel-back signage and it's a funky size, we'll tell our clients by reducing the size by two inches you can save $100 per piece. If you produce four signs, that's $400.

Part of the conversation when you initially talk to a client is, what are your plans and what are your goals? It's our job to offer suggestions and provide you with affordable solutions."

Lynn Hughes
Account Executive, Visual Resource
http://www.visualresource.com

window and in-store signage for Gap, one of the world's largest specialty retailers with three of the most recognized and respected brands in the apparel industry: Gap, Banana Republic, and Old Navy. Gap Inc. has more than 150,000 employees supporting about 3,000 stores in the United States, United Kingdom, Canada, France, and Japan.

In retail, there is constant changing of in-store signage. There's a short shelf life to the signage, and the messages and graphic images are succinct. Lynn has been instrumental in creative solutions for my event programs. By working with such clients as the GAP, she provides a perspective in the live presence environment that one might not normally see.

One of the most fun and biggest opportunities Lynn and I faced was a special event during an end-user conference for 5,000 people at Disney World in Orlando, Florida. "It was interesting for me because it was such a large venue and so well known a venue to rent out (exclusive buy-out). Try to brand at Disney World. I thought it was going to be an impossible task. The other component that was just as important . . . getting it all organized, shipped there, and actually going on-site, and seeing how it all turned out to make certain it met our clients' objectives. It was probably one of my favorite events we've ever done," admits Lynn.

We worked together for about three months to put our touch on the park. We also spent a great deal of time with Disney's special events team working out the details. Talk about customer-service focused and no failure rates. Our end result? It was a brand-fest!

Here's what we did:

Pre-event:

- Created a "By Invitation Only" postcard prepromoting the company and its special event. The postcard was glued to the front cover of the pre-event conference brochure mailer.

- Developed special online banner ads that ran on the conference Web site.

On-site:

- Negotiated a full-page ad in the conference program.
- Purchased bus seat covers promoting the company and upcoming event.
- Decorated park entranceways with our company colors and placed welcome signage in archways with a red carpet logo.
- Hung more than 30 banners with logos throughout the park.
- Produced over 2,500 tabletop signs that were placed in every restaurant seating area and condiment bar.
- Replaced all cocktail napkins in the restaurant with our logo item.
- Distributed all soft drinks in logo paper cups.
- Designed jumbo hot-air balloons with our logo and strategically placed them in key passageways throughout the facilities.
- Set a presentation time at the end of the evening where our executives spoke and roused the crowd while lead coordinators handed out logoed 3-D glasses.
- Designed a logoed 3-D firework display at the end of the parade over Cinderella's castle.
- Gave away co-branded sports bottles on the buses headed back to the hotels.

Postevent

- Posted event photos on our Web site that attendees could download.
- Sent a follow-up survey to measure brand recognition.
- Featured a story in the following quarter's newsletter.

I took away a lot of experience after our company did the buy-out of the theme park. In my opinion, Disney has a seamless approach to event execution, and I modeled much of my "get it done" attitude on this after seeing how they produce an event.

■ **Hint:** Find companies outside your specific industry that you feel do it right. Liquor and soft drink companies are heavily into branding at events. Watch their approach.

It was after that event that I designed my "Creative Materials Tool Kit." This tool kit keeps me organized and helps bring my panic level down. I've learned that something will always go wrong in production, and having a backup with this kit allows me to stay focused on the customer experience.

Most events will require some sort of customization to the generic materials you'll have produced. This is where things go wrong. Running for approvals at the last minute, and not giving enough time to the vendors contributes to errors. Realize it's inevitable; changes in copy, content, and graphics. They happen, so just face it. Be flexible and solutions oriented! Remember, nice over nasty. Good vendors won't point fingers; they'll just fix it, get it to you as fast as possible, and worry about the rest later.

Tip

Inevitably something will go wrong—there's always a "creative" solution

I remember arranging a "VIP Customer Golf Outing" in Florida. We had 18 different sponsors, and as part of our program we printed a complete signage package as part of their participation.

Our number one sponsor's materials were lost on-site. We had the tracking numbers, we knew who signed for them but they were gone.

It was early Sunday evening and we were setting up for our Monday morning "Breakfast on the Green" event, when we discovered the mishap. Everyone started to panic and people were all over the place. Nothing was open, and the nearest 24-hour printer was too far away to give us what we needed.

Figure 6.1 is my checklist of items in my own tool kit. It's currently up to 55 items. I use this every time I do an event. I also build inventory at the beginning of the year and look at my schedule to bulk order items at the same time. It's really just looking at each touch point, and then determining what kind of printed branded item you can add to enhance that. There are little things that you can do without being obnoxious. The materials in the tool kit are subtle, add-on reminders that feature the brand and the message. Can you think of other visual materials to add to this list?

I found a local printer whose shop was closed but had left an emergency number. When we spoke he said he was at a party and would not open. I told him I'd pay him $1,500 to open his print shop to print 10 signs by 6:00 AM, delivered, and guess what? He opened the print shop and delivered by 5:30 AM. By thinking creatively and using the power of the dollar, we got what we needed.

GIVEAWAY AND PROMOTIONAL ITEMS

While the tool kit houses a company's visual materials, the Promotional Items Package (PIP) is a list of fundamental "tchotchkes, swag, or trash and trinkets"—as they are so lovingly referred to in the event world—that you can purchase to enhance your brand. It's a list that's complementary to what's included in the tool kit.

Coordinators to executives love putting in their two cents about what to give away at an event. Items you choose should have a purpose and match your message. Promotional items should be tied back to your business objectives but usually much of the selection of these items are based on gut instinct, budget, or on "Ooh, I like that" types of remarks. That's why it's important—as outlined in previous chapters—to understand your company's brand and your business objectives and to integrate the components accordingly.

FIGURE 6.1 *Creative Materials Tool Kit*

For the electronic version of this list go to http://www.eventblt.com.

Description	Event Name	Copy and Content	Vendor	Date Due	PO Number	Quantity	Cost
4¼' × 5½' Table Tent Card							
4' Easel-back, Stand-alone signs (foam board)							
4" × 6" Table Top Sign							
8½" × 11" Table Top Sign							
11" × 14" Table Top Sign							
17" × 24" Easel-Back Sign							
A4 Conversion of all materials							
Agenda Sheets							
Banners, 2 sizes: (5' long and 10' long)							
Ballot Boxes/Fish Bowls							
Belly Bands for Binders and Newspapers							
Binder Insert Side							
Binder Insert Slip Sheet Back Cover							
Binder Insert Slip Sheets Front Cover							
CD-ROM Packaging							
CD-ROM/DVD Disk							
Envelope Seals							
Event Envelopes							
Event Program (like a playbill)							
Event Stationary							
Flyers							
Gift Cards							
Generic Business Card							

FIGURE 6.1 *Creative Materials Tool Kit (Continued)*

Description	Event Name	Copy and Content	Vendor	Date Due	PO Number	Quantity	Cost
Hangtags							
Hotel Room Key Cards							
Lead Generation Card							
Literature Display Holders							
Logos (easily downloadable and viewable) .eps; jpeg; .tif							
Memo Pads							
Menu Card							
Name Place Cards—Boardroom Style							
Name Place Cards—for Individual Seating							
Notepads							
On-site Note Cards—for last-minute handwritten invitations, etc.							
On-site Pocket Guide							
Penguin Signs							
Personalized Stationary							
Promotional Offers and Tie-in Packages							
Registration Area • Press Only • A–M • N–Z • Coat Check • Directional Arrows							
Report Cover Sheets							
"Reserved" Signs							
Room Drop Card							
Small Business Card Holder							

(continued)

FIGURE 6.1 *Creative Materials Tool Kit (Continued)*

Description	Event Name	Copy and Content	Vendor	Date Due	PO Number	Quantity	Cost
Stickers (with logo and tag line only—various 1", 2" or 3")							
Stickers: Compliments of "Your Company Name"							
Survey Cards							
Survey Collection Boxes							
Survey Form							
Tablecloths—6' table							
Tablecloths—8' table							
Tabs							
Thank You cards							
Ticket Holder Serve Hospitality Program							
TV Tent Cards							
Vinyl Decals							

Over the years, I've always ended up with the promotional items responsibility, from purchasing to distribution. I view promotional items as a means to deliver the call-to-action. You can use the items themselves for your call-to-action. ("View our Webinar and we'll send you a complimentary white paper, and if you're among the first 50 to register, we'll also send you a complimentary product sample and tee shirts.") Giveaways have a lot of power and using the "right" items at the "right" time is the opportunity.

I noticed that I was constantly ordering the same primary list of items; such as pens, tee shirts, and cocktail napkins. You can build your inventory based on your sales initiatives and business objectives. Eventually, you'll get a "marketing closet," an on-site storage area that's under lock and key. A couple of people in your office will have a key to this closet. In larger companies, online stores have become the marketing closet, but if you ever look in a sales rep's garage or basement, you'll know what I'm talking about. All the items are logoed and sales reps bring these materials with them on sales calls.

For events, when you are developing your promotional and giveaway program a significant amount of it has to do with budgets. In the late '90s and until 9/11, companies had looser purse strings. Today, companies pinch every penny, budgets are scrutinized, and you will be held accountable for all the dollars that go out. By leveraging your promotional item spending, you again put money back into your budget.

To come up with ideas, I rely on my vendors, research, and attend many events, from fundraisers to corporate executive events to Hollywood premieres. I save or jot down what I think is a good idea and keep it in a tickler file. Consider keeping a drawer filled with magazine articles, catalogs, and suggestions from colleagues.

If you need a promotional supplier, look for those that are members of ASI (Advertising Specialties Institute). ASI is set up primarily to help suppliers (manufacturers) and distributors (selling arm for end customers). By putting these groups together, it makes it easier for both to create relationships and work together to ultimately make it a better experience for the end customer.

There are many promotional items companies and you may have multiple suppliers based on your needs. There are so many ways to buy today. Pick a style that's comfortable for you. Establish a relationship with a reputable company. For events, I believe in the old-fashioned way. I like full-service suppliers and I've used the same two for basically ten years now. I like service and quality with "mishpukah" pricing. In my event network I have Kent Larson, president of M.A. Apparel, a Minnesota-based company, and Susan Roth, from Trims Unlimited, based in California.

"We're not just here to sell merchandise. Our goal is to make your event successful. It's about the big picture. Establishing a relationship with the customer first and foremost, and that creates the snowballing effect to create other potential customers. So you make one person happy in the smallest way. It can also be the biggest way for certain people.

Here's a kind of a case in point about our embroidery shop, Twin Cities Embroidery. We'll take somebody that walks in off the street and wants a name put on their jacket that they're wearing. A lot of places like us, being kind of an industrial embroiderer, would not do something like that; but by doing that, you must again take the "one-offs" to get the good, and you're establishing a relationship not based on what can you do for us, but what can we do for you first. And that's the key objective."

Kent Larson
President
M.A. Apparel
Twin Cities Embroidery
http://www.maapparel.com

There's a perception in the marketplace that there are only two types of suppliers. The traditional model is low-cost/high-volume, and the other is high-cost/low-volume. You'll find the model while it does provide a generic reference, full-service means just that. While both cross over into each other's arenas, each event is different and thus you may need or want different services.

Figure 6.2 is my basic PIP. I use this for every client. It's so easy and it allows me to add items as needed. Everything you need to know is right here, and you never have to think about it again. Just check off what's needed, place an order, and ship to the event.

So now that you have my list, how do you make it better? Try a hangtag from a tee shirt and feature your company logo and 25 words, or your current positioning and messaging. Logos are great, but remember what your company does is critical.

FIGURE 6.2 *Promotional Inventory List–Standard Items*

All of these items should include logo, tag line, and URL, if space permits.

Description	Vendor(s)	Date Due	Quantity	Item Number	Branding	Cost
12 oz. Paper Coffee Cup						
16 oz. and 32 oz. Stadium-Size Plastic Cups						
8 oz. Plastic Drinking Cup						
8 oz. Paper Coffee Cup						
Belly Hot Bands for Coffee Cups (like coffee houses do)						
Baseball-style Cap or Visor—one structured and one un-structured crown; tag line embossed on back; logo on front or under the bill						
Candy Dishes/Bowls						
Chocolates						
Coasters (doubles as hangtags)						
Cocktail Napkins						
Coffee Mug—travel type						
Engraved Brushed Metal Name Identifiers, Pins						
Executive Gifts: *Suggestions*— • Leather Goods • Electronics • Desk Set • Personalized Stationery • Crystal						
Fish Bowls						
Glasses (great for themed functions) • Margarita • Martini						
Gift Cards						

FIGURE 6.2 *Promotional Inventory List–Standard Items (Continued)*

Description	Vendor(s)	Date Due	Quantity	Item Number	Branding	Cost
For Field Sales Golf Pack—includes: • Golf Balls • Visor/Baseball Cap • Towels • Pencils • Complimentary Tickets to a tournament						
Infant "Onesy"—employee/ customer baby gifts						
Jacket—lightweight—logo embossed left chest						
Kids' tee shirt						
Women's cotton knit shirts (crew and V-neck, possibly long/short sleeve with cardigan)						
Lanyards						
Lapel Pins						
Laptop/Attaché Case						
Laptop Bag/Attaché Case						
Leather Portfolios						
Luggage Tags						
Men's cotton button-down shirt or three-button/V-neck style sweater						
Men's polo shirt—embroidered logo left chest						
Mouse Pads for Demo areas						
Name Tag Holder or Neck Wallet						
Name Tags for Wine Glasses						
Notepads						
Pencils						

FIGURE 6.2 *Promotional Inventory List–Standard Items (Continued)*

Description	Vendor(s)	Date Due	Quantity	Item Number	Branding	Cost
Pens						
Plates—Plastic or China with Stem Holder						
Stir Sticks for Cocktails						
Sticks for Bar Fruit						
Tissue Boxes						
Tote Bag—deluxe						
Tote Bag—trade show (cheaper handout)						
Tee shirt—screen printed (basic/simple)						
Tee shirt—screen printed with a loud and sassy design—we can come up with!						

Here's an example of how to use the Creative Materials Tool Kit and the Promotional Items Package together. When using promotional items with visual materials you are now touching that same member of your target audience.

FIGURE 6.3 *Event Marketing*

Description	Person Responsible	Deadline Date	Status	Cost
Package Includes:				
Participation Fee Payment/Check				
Logo—Sponsor name and logo on select conference materials				
Logo on conference Web site with link to company URL				

(continued)

FIGURE 6.3 *Event Marketing (Continued)*

Description	Person Responsible	Deadline Date	Status	Cost
Speaking Engagement—board member or executive has a keynote address • Scripted text to include in speech for maximum message impact				
One copy of preconference attendee lists • Call Downs • E-mail Invites • On-site Meeting				
One copy of postconference attendee lists • Cross Reference with Leads Received at Show				
Two full conference registrations—online (complimentary)				
Roundtable Discussion • The roundtable sessions are informal, but attendees will have information about the roundtables in their materials, a private meeting space, allowing 30 minutes to each sponsor. • Develop and script a basic 15-minute presentation on SitePro for use in our roundtable; 15 minutes for Q&A, leave with next steps.				
Display as a tabletop exhibit in the Sponsor Resource Center • Giveaway: Construction Pencil • Print Materials: Collateral Folders, 3 Article Reprints, 4 Data Sheets—100 total • Print Materials: Signage use 24" × 36" logo sign; will mirror the online ad—need to create a backdrop • Personal Identification: Logo Clothing • Logistics—Internet Access Wireless confirmed • Equipment: Laptop, Monitor, Cables, Power strip provided by Procore • Presentation: Web site video to play on computer and sales rep's personal interaction				

FIGURE 6.3 *Event Marketing (Continued)*

Description	Person Responsible	Deadline Date	Status	Cost
Value-Added Program				
Conference Bag Insert • Quantity: 750 • Giveaway: Tee shirt will feature logo without tag line on front left chest pocket with URL, and back of shirt in MEGA size will feature logo and tag line only • Print Material: We will produce a Hangtag which will double as a coaster for our hospitality events				
Guest Room Internet Connection • Quantity: 750 • Print Material: Table Tent Card—featuring giveaway and "We Pay 1 Day Connection Fee"—turn in the card for lead generating opportunity • Logistics: Coordinate delivery of materials with hotel				
Guest Room Evening Turn-Down Service • Quantity: 2,000 (1,400 per box) • Giveaway: Two Dark Chocolates per night for Friday and Saturday, features logo • Print Material: Note Card with tie-in copy • Logistics: Coordinate delivery of materials with hotel				
Hospitality—Late Night Drinks in the Hotel Bar • Giveaway: Drinks are on us—we pay the tab • Print Materials: Small VIP Ticket for Procore sales team to give to high-level prospects for our private evening activity in the hotel bar; ability to write notes on back • Print Materials: Table Tent Cards—logo only • Logistics: Secure Reserved Tables with hotel • Personal Identification: Logo Clothing				

(continued)

FIGURE 6.3 *Event Marketing (Continued)*

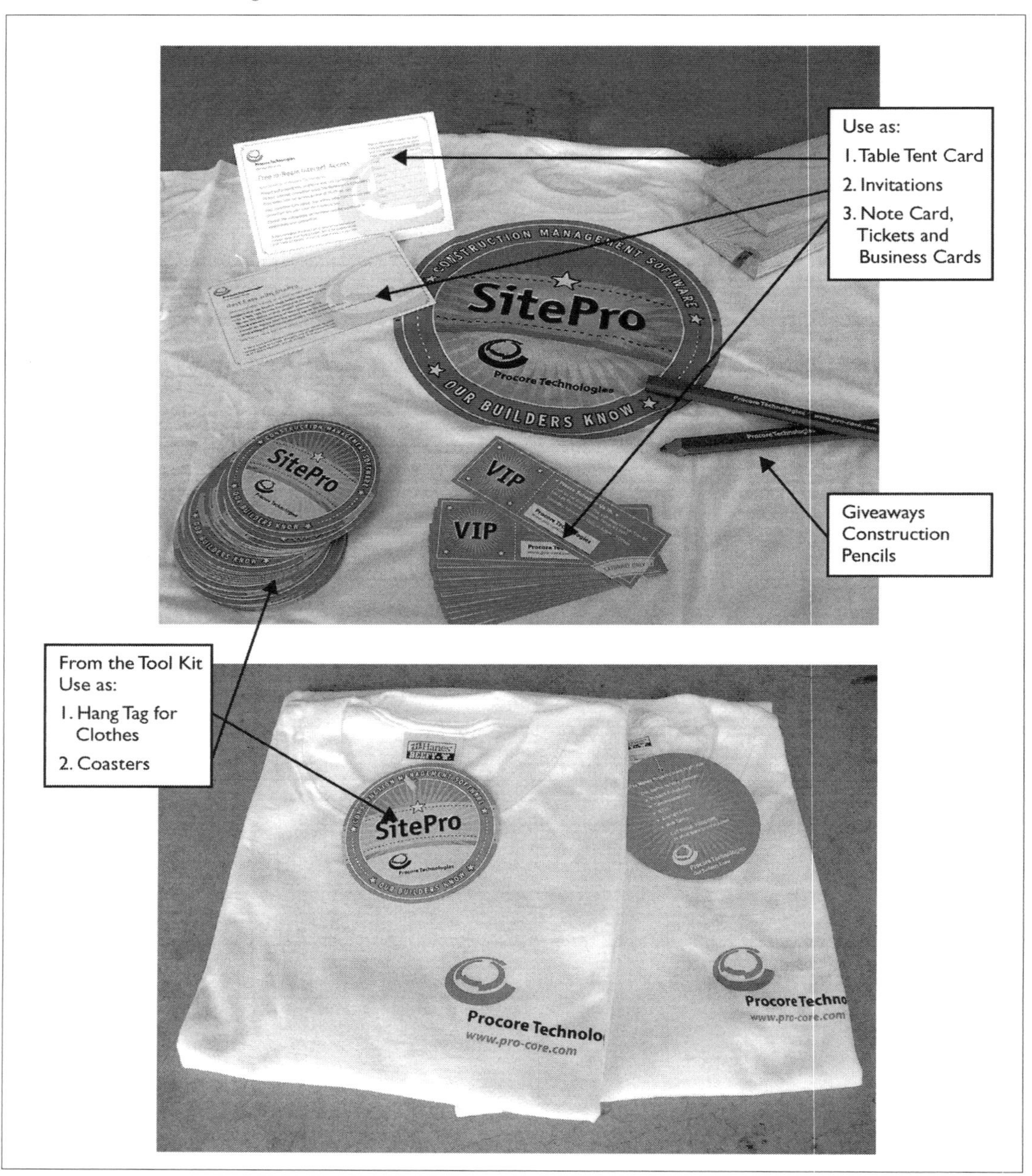

Photo credit: Garth Humbert, Carom Visual Communication, http://www.carommedia.com.

Chapter

7

SALES COLLATERAL

Our mantra:
Event Marketing is all about facilitating, easing, opening, accelerating, and shortening the sales cycle. That's it!

The advantage with events is the face-to-face interaction for communication. The networking, or talking, that people get on-site with their peers, customers, partners, press, and even competitors, is vital. In the live presence environment, you can feel the energy that attendees are there for the same purpose. They get to "talk shop" and/or "comparison shop" to find the latest and greatest, or reinforce that their prior decisions were correct.

Besides the face-to-face interaction, your target audience will also get information about your company through its written and multimedia communications, from print to online.

These forms of communication are often put under the umbrella of either of the following categories:

- Sales Tools
- Sales Collateral/Sales Literature

Within the two categories you will find everything from ad and article reprints to brochures and catalogs to return on investment (ROI) calculators and white papers. It is important to understand that your sales tools/collateral must be integrated into your event marketing plan as well as reflect your company's brand.

Let's take a step back and look at the larger picture. In business and as consumers, it's become natural for us to go to a Web site to look for current or updated information. Even within your own organization you probably no longer just print documentation but you are using some sort of technology to share "internal only or confidential info," which is usually behind your firewall and may be known as a portal, common server, or the Intranet. Realize that the content is still the same, whether it's a print brochure or a landing page on your company's Web site or an automatic download direct to your iPod or mobile phone. For sales tools/collateral the content is the key and it's here to stay!

What I have found in my career is this constant: I basically used a variation of the same types of print materials or online communications at each and every event.

Interestingly, the names of what the collateral or literature is called is what varies, a "data sheet" for one company is a "fact sheet" for another and yet a "sell sheet" for another. The way in which you distribute the material also varies, which is either in hard copy (print material) or soft copy (electronic–Web, a PDF file, etc.).

At this point, you've hopefully identified a qualified target audience and developed your event strategy. It's time to plan and decide what sales tools/collateral to bring and distribute at the event, and even at what time. This is a strategic and tactical decision.

When you work in marketing you naturally play a role in everything from the content development to distribution. As an event marketer, you are also charged with uncovering innovative ways to get your message out. Take a look around. Who exactly is responsible for designing and deciding what sales tools/collateral should be incorporated into the event program? What is your role and responsibility in the process?

- *Content and concept development.* Typically provided by product marketing/management, marketing, corporate communication, sales, research, engineering, legal, etc.
- *Design.* Typically created by graphic artists, marketing
- *Wordsmithing and editing.* Typically performed by a copywriter, marketing, legal
- *Distribution.* Typically supported by marketing and sales

With thought-through planning, events can increase the impact and effectiveness of the sales tools/collateral by presenting your company and its product line in the best possible light.

First, look at the target audience and determine the following: What will they want to bring home with them? Will they read it? What will they read? It's really a tough question. I've realized it is specific by industry, and it's about distribution of how one receives the communications that is different. For example:

- Teachers and school administrators will keep everything from books to single flash cards. They need and want materials, and they can never have enough.
- In technology, CDs, memory sticks, and business cards are in, brochures and folders are out, and it's always too much! Many companies also only offer "on demand" Web-based communications.

Sales tools/collateral is meant to be used. If you're hitting your target audience to the tee, then why back off when you are that close. One of my constants at events is creating a printed piece specifically to that event. It's a low-cost way to increase the impact of your initiatives. For distribution it becomes an inventory game and how you manage it.

Include in your Event Positioning and Messaging Framework (see Chapter 5)

Tip

Acronyms and buzz words are great attractors at events

Stay on top of the most current terminology and trends in your industry. Think about how quickly things change.

What's hot now

- Education: ELL (English Language Learners) AYP (Adequate Yearly Progress)
- Technology: SPAM, BLOG (Web log)

What's not

- Education: ESL (English as a Second Language or Balanced Literacy)
- Technology: eBusiness

Here's an example of extending the value of your print collateral.

When I worked for the e-learning company, DigitalThink, I had responsibility for determining what events we sponsored, exhibited, attended, or hosted. At the time, we had a catalog of e-learning courses that featured around 500 titles. We had a full series of sales tools, but from an event perspective, I wanted to create and distribute a piece of literature that could be used for multiple purposes and worked directly with product marketing, sales, and graphics to produce the additional collateral. We collectively agreed to a 3" × 3" pocket-size catalog. It was inexpensive to produce but had considerable impact:

- *The Scene:* Sponsor and exhibit at four industry conferences and marketing activities that include a "Lunch and Learn" program at each show

■ **Hint:** Lunch and Learn is an extension of a speaking opportunity and, it's also a way to reach most or all of the attendees.

- *The Guests:* 25,000 training managers
- *The Objective:* Drive prospects to the Web site to learn more about the product line and to sign up for a complimentary course.

Preevent

- Designed and printed 30,000 pocket-size catalogs about 3" × 3" (the size of a baseball schedule). The call-to-action was a free course if they used a specific promotional code.
- Promoted sponsorship on show Web site and in preshow conference brochures sent to the organizer's database list.
- Updated the events landing page on the company's public Web site with details.

On-Site

- Purchased 25,000 six-pack can coolers that served as attendees "lunch box." The company logo was centered on the front. These replaced the standard boxed lunches that included a sandwich, chips, and fruit that came with our sponsorship package.
- Attached a two-sided corporate hangtag with logo, URL, and elevator pitch to the cooler strap *(selected stock items from Creative Materials Tool Kit, PIP, and Sales Tools).*
- Inserted the 3" × 3" pocket-size catalog with four branded chocolate squares, and wrapped the utensils in a logo paper dinner napkin which was inserted into the new lunch box *(selected stock items from Creative Materials Tool Kit, PIP, and Sales Tools).*
- Monitored session attendance via badge swipe as attendees entered and left the room

Postevent

- Sent thank-you e-mails to session attendees

Tip

KISS (Keep It Simple, Stupid)

- Messages need to be consistent with image; use an appropriate tone and be clear and concise when presenting an idea.
- Make it easy for the customer to read and the sales force to use.
- Don't just show features and benefits; show advantages.
- Stay away from long-winded tales.

- Tracked activity for free course–8,000 people registered for the course via a link through the events landing page in a two week period
- Increased print-run of pocket-size guide and used for all events

Here are some other ways in which to expand the power of your sales tools/collateral.

Create an event specific piece—a one-page, two-sided postcard or flyer.

- *Side 1:* Feature all your on-site marketing activities, such as speaking engagements, promotional incentives, hospitality functions, and an action regarding the product info (schedule an in-depth demo, buy now, etc.). Never include confidential meetings on this piece.
- *Side 2:* Feature the benefits and advantages from the positioning framework.

■ **Hint:** Out of time? Use an article reprint or the ad that you placed in the conference program or that's currently running as part of a current campaign in a magazine.

Tip

Package It Up!

Take your sales tools and marry them to the creative materials and promotional items.

If you're hosting an evening cocktail reception for your top 50 prospects, avoid handing out data sheets or sell sheets.

- Use a company logo folder to house a new brochure, a customer testimonial flyer, most recent press coverage, and a sales rep's business card.
- Tie a self-contained pen and pencil set with branded ribbon to the folder and insert both items into a logo gift bag with complementary tissue paper.

Quick Fix. Find a creative and fast way to promote a recent award that your company received by the editors of your industry's trade magazine to their "Top 100 Products to Watch" list. There's a major industry conference in 1½ weeks.

- Get the "Top 100" logo from magazine publisher, print stickers, and affix to the cover of brochures you're distributing at the next three events.
- Produce tabletop sign that you can display at upcoming events.
- Use quotes from happy customers or industry experts who use your products to validate your story at events.

Demo first—distribute during. As your sales reps are speaking to the attendee have them hand the collateral piece to them with their business card. Usually, the reaction from the attendee is to briefly look at the piece and pull out their business card.

Be selective, not rude. If it's expensive to produce a specific brochure, bring a limited quantity and set up a criteria, such as only conference attendees are to receive it and not other exhibitors, or instead bring no brochures and use them for followup.

Have materials that you can distribute. Why print them and then not distribute them? At most trade shows for example, you'll find that each exhibitor is handing out some sort of print materials. If you walk around the exhibit floor here's what you'll observe.

- *Company A:* Provides complete literature folders and promotional items to every attendee that walks by.
- *Company B:* Hands out a mini CD and a one-sheet flyer after their theater presentation or demo.
- *Company C:* Directs people to their Web site and hands out a generic business card.
- *Company D:* Hides everything they have and after a two-minute conversation will go into a locked cabinet to hand them either a brochure, flyer, or promo item.

Fulfill requests. If you tell an attendee that you will send literature after the event, make sure you do it and have it arrive within ten days. Using literature for follow-up purposes is a good way to extend the "B-branding" within your program.

> ■ **Hint:** Before you send anything out, work with Sales. Customize a letter or personal e-mail from the appropriate territory representative or the CEO from your company. Get granular. Reiterate what the attendee spoke about or saw. Attach the letter, literature, and business card . . . and send!

There is no right answer to how each company provides communication tools at events. Look for the combination of the right materials. But you always get snagged on the detail of how much to send. How much is too much? Keep an eye on how much you ship out and how much is left.

The costs for shipping print collateral to the actual event can get costly. So, I created this guide so that I would remember to send or recommend the right amount of material required per event.

Event Size—Number of Attendees	High-Tech Company Quantity of Sales Tools	An Educational Company Quantity of Sales Tools
125 and below	50–125 pieces	150
500 and below	100–500 pieces	600
2,500 and below	250–500 pieces	3,000
5,000 and below	500–1,000 pieces	5,500
10,000 and below	1,000–1,500 pieces	10,000

Electronic distribution of marketing collateral is a viable way for companies to manage costs. Documents-on-demand, print-on-demand, and downloads to PDAs are all included as the "call-to-action" deliverable in the event cycle. The call-to-action mechanism keeps your company connected to the attendee. Electronic communication is a complement to what you do on-site. A company's Web site becomes the central storage area for the sales collateral. A link will take the viewer to a landing page in which they will find a list of "on demand" collateral. It's like a store. You look at the list of items, see the descriptions, place your order, and it ships (downloads) to where you designate.

The other benefit to a company for on demand collateral distribution is storage space. Available square footage costs money and those dollars can be invested elsewhere. Could on demand eliminate the always locked marketing closet? Never!

Electronic distribution of marketing collateral is high-tech and a viable way for companies to manage costs. Besides the creative materials and promotional items, the marketing closet usually stores the sales tools as well, so companies have moved online to address the issue of space and current information.

Tip

20 years of Technology

Stay ahead of the curve. In just 20 years, here's what changed:

Intern 1976: Worked for an Advertising Agency. We used a Telex machine for direct-mail programs, a campaign targeted to 2,000 consumers; took two weeks to send out (each label had to printed, affixed to an envelope, stamped, and mailed); two months to get responses.

Account Manager 1989: Worked for a corporate software reseller. We did fax broadcast campaigns for Microsoft and IBM targeted to 2,000 consumers; took two days to fax out; two weeks to track responses.

Director 2002: Worked for a large corporation. We launched an e-mail blast targeted to 20,000 consumers; took two minutes to send out; 20 minutes to begin tracking responses.

Figure 7.1 is the list that serves as a reminder for the sales tools you have available. Matching up the deliverables to the event cycle is the fun part.

If you start with the "B" in the EventBLT, you can really make an impact. It's all about the touch points. I'm a big fan of the added value marketing sponsorships (see Chapter 4, "Sponsor, Exhibit, Attend, or Host an Event") at trade shows, conferences, and summits to reach my target audience. Also, in a defined industry, if you take a specific program and sponsor it consistently you further expand the event branding!

For example, sign up for a meal sponsorship at a trade show or cosponsor a meal with a partner. Depending on your budget, choose one is most appropriate. This includes breakfasts, lunches, dinners, breaks, and hospitality events. The value of a sponsorship such as this is that it allows you to use visual materials, giveaways, and promotional items and sales tools, which puts you on the path for *facilitating, easing, opening, accelerating, and shortening the sales cycle.*

FIGURE 7.1 *Materials Kit*

Sales Tools	Event Name	Quantity	Shipping Information
Ad Reprints			
Analyst Reports			
Annual Reports			
Article Reprints (keep yearly list)			
Award Announcements			
Books			
Booklets			
Brochures • Capabilities • Corporate • Product • Technical			
Business Cards • Generic • Personal			
Calling Scripts			
Case Studies			
Catalogs • Print • Online • CD versions			
Channel, Distributor, and Partner Communications			
Commercials • Radio • TV			
Customer Quotes and Testimonials			
Direct Mailers			
E-mail Blasts			
Events Calendar			

(continued)

FIGURE 7.1 *Materials Kit (Continued)*

Sales Tools	Event Name	Quantity	Shipping Information
FAQs • Company • Product • Technical			
Fax Broadcasts			
Flyers • One-Page • Four-Page			
Folders			
Full Product CD			
Literature Memory Sticks			
Magazines • Custom Publishing Supplements			
Newsletters			
Product/Services Coverage • Data Sheets • Fact Sheets • Sell Sheets • Spec Sheets			
Postcards			
Posters			
Presentations • PowerPoint • Multimedia			
Press Kits			
Press Releases			
Price Lists			
Proposals			
Research Reports			
ROI Calculators			
Trial CD			
Web site • Landing Page			
White Papers			

Chapter

8

LEADS

Our mantra:
Event Marketing is all about facilitating, easing, opening, accelerating, and shortening the sales cycle. That's it!

Lead capture, also known as lead generation, goes hand-in-hand with brand recognition. People buy your product because they recognize the brand and there is a benefit match.

In a broad sweeping generalization, there are only three hard objectives you can expect to accomplish at most events: Brand Recognition, Lead Generation, and Thought Leadership. The surrounding objectives that support these efforts include customer relations, public relations or simply entertaining your guests. As you build each individual event marketing plan, you'll be faced with the decision on which objectives are most important in a descending order of importance.

This hierarchy of objectives will guide your creative marketing approach. So, please note that not *every* company classifies leads as the number one objective. But, if lead generation is even tertiary on your list, you MUST integrate a lead generation strategy into the plan early. Lead generation is absolutely essential, and it's why a cohesive approach is so attractive.

Lead generation goes outside of the realm of straight marketing and moves into the realm of sales. In marketing and sales, it is widely appreciated that leads are company assets. Leads generate sales and provide valuable information to you about that company or person. Leads can also be referred to as *inquiries*.

When it comes to events, take a step back and look at the built-in opportunities. By constantly reminding yourself of these opportunities, you give yourself the framework for building out the strategy. It's also what I use when I speak with others in the company about their intent when it comes to the event components.

- *Opportunity knocks once:* How can your company create deeper relationships with prospects and customers?
- *Opportunity knocks twice:* How can your company effectively analyze the success of the campaign?
- *Opportunity knocks three times:* How can your company manage a systematic follow-up after a prospect response?

■ **Hint:** Knowing within your company the right person to feed the information is half the battle.

- *Opportunity knocks four times:* How do you take control of your own targeted direct-marketing programs with limited in-house resources or your in-house telemarketing and sales support teams?
- *Opportunity knocks five times:* How can your company use Web data collected in the past to create new strategies for the future?

At the risk of sounding redundant, in order for lead capture/generation to be effective you MUST have your sales team involved all the way through the process. You would be surprised how many clients of mine never get around to asking their sales team about what THEY would like to accomplish sales results or HOW. But this is certain, for this to work, the sales team must be ready to actively engage prospects and customers on the frontlines and follow through on leads that are generated on the back end. It is a way to common practice at events where tons of leads are generated, but they are not then taken to that next step.

The sad truth is that half the sponsors do *not* even use a lead retrieval system on-site. Others do *not* even take advantage of the pre- and post-attendee lists offered by the show organizer. Pre- and post-attendees are usually offered as part of a sponsorship package and typically require a third-party bonded mail house to facilitate the direct mailer. Make sure you request that these lists be sent to your mail house; if you don't have one, use theirs, but take advantage of the program.

Events uncover the opportunities; they open the dialog; they create a perceived need of the role of Sales to further define and more importantly CLOSE. An event marketer can only do so much, but when you begin to bring the often diametrically opposed worlds of sales and marketing together at an event, you have the potential of real power.

"The Exordium Group estimates that 75 percent of all exhibitors and sponsors do not take advantage of the value-added benefits offered in their sponsorship package. By simply fulfilling the fundamental marketing benefits, you can increase your lead generation efforts by 15 to 20 percent."

Ronda Thomas Farrell
CEO
The Exordium Group, Inc.
http://www.exordiumgroup.com

The Exordium Group is a leading international sponsorship strategy consultancy and specializes in sponsorship marketing for the IT industry.

Tip

Event Marketing Supports Sales

"The left hand needs to be empowered by the right hand. We marketers need to be humble enough to understand that marketing must *support* sales. As difficult as it is to swallow, event marketers need to accept the fact that without *sales* there will be no resources to pay for marketing. If we operate in an adversarial or exclusionary way with Sales when planning, we are going to create beautiful events with minimal results that will ultimately lead to changes up and down and across the lines, and they won't be pretty ones."

Brian Vanden Broucke,
CEO and Sr. Creative Director,
articulate creative services, inc.
http://www.articulatecreative.com

It is my belief that no event marketing program should even take place without a strategy that has the full blessing of Sales.

Here is a simple *how-to* list from articulate creative services, inc., to get the sales integration ball rolling. Ask yourself or Sales:

1. HOW does Sales identify and profile the target prospect in their normal way of doing business?
2. What pieces of qualifying information DO they capture but what MUST they capture?
3. HOW can you, the event marketer, capture the MUST HAVE information in the shortest period of time possible at the event? (30–45 seconds)
4. HOW can you creatively and cleverly weave this information-gathering process into your event strategy as a normal outgrowth of the event strategy?

As I said before, an effective event marketing strategy integrates lead generation into the plan very early. Your objective is to outline exactly how the leads will be followed through in a meaningful way. It is important to understand the various lead capture initiatives and mechanisms prior to deciding how to execute a lead generation strategy.

LEAD CAPTURE INITIATIVES

Objectives

- Generate a minimum X number of leads, of which X number are deemed qualified opportunities
- Outreach to top accounts or prospects
- Move from the current situation to broad market awareness

Strategies

- Develop and execute awareness and demand generation programs based on customers' and prospects' most urgent needs
- Target audience of decision makers

Key Tactics

- Execute event marketing programs
- Direct marketing

LEAD CAPTURE DATA COLLECTION TOUCH POINTS

There are a variety of lead capture solutions to help you increase the number of qualified leads gathered from your event activity. Everything from paper to electronic media can be used. Some prefer the old-fashioned way of just taking a business card and writing notes on the back. I like to use a variety of lead capture mechanisms and do *not* rely on one over another. Each is specific to an event. I also prefer to interact with the staff working the event to get a general sense of the hot leads on a daily basis.

Here are the three most common choices for effective lead capture.

1. *Paper.* Name or business card attached with qualifying information manually entered by sales reps in an organized, fast query. Have a temporary employee place them into your database later.
2. *Electronic.* Magnetic strip or barcode readers. These can customize questions that can capture answers electronically, but can cause a bottleneck if you are busy or don't have enough machines. These include handheld, wireless, or static.
3. *Combo high-tech/low-tech.* Nothing beats the simplicity of this system. Just get the basics printed out with an electronic solution, staple the readout to a paper form, and marry qualifying info later.

Every touch point with an attendee is an area for potential lead capture. For branding-only purposes, you may only want to capture a person's name, state, and e-mail address. If your objective is more complex, complete information from salutation to purchasing timeframe could be critical.

- If you are an exhibitor, focus on demo areas, your theater presentation, hospitality events, and speaking engagements.
- If you're hosting an event you can use this same methodology. Ask yourself, "Of the qualified guests or customers I've invited, what is their interest level compared to what I am promoting or selling? And how do I measure that or capture their interest in something new?" Just because you've got the customer already in house, doesn't mean the lead capture information stops.

Let's look at the lead capture mechanisms. The at-a-glance definitions are my interpretation of the touch points for events only.

LEAD CAPTURE MECHANISMS AT-A-GLANCE

Capture Data

- *Badge swipe.* At trade shows and conferences, attendee data is housed through either a barcode or magnetic strip. Exhibitors, sponsors, and session track monitors use a device to scan the attendee's card.

■ **Hint:** Radio frequency identification (RFID) technology is making headway in the badge and lead capture/retrieval market for its ability to store and track attendee information. Expense, deployment, protocols, and privacy issues are currently some of the barriers.

- *Registration.* For a proprietary event, this is your opportunity to collect general demographic information as well as product interest and purchasing time frame. It's a way for attendees to sign up for an event and it's typically done online. For a trade show or conference the preshow attendee registration list is provided by the show organizer and is negotiated as part of your value-added marketing sponsorship.

■ **Hint:** Paper may be used on-site. You can ask everything from company name to tee shirt size.

- *Business card delivery or exchange.* Also known as a calling card, this 2" × 3½" (sizes will vary by country) staple is still the easiest way to have information on an attendee. The card is rarely thrown out.

■ **Hint:** You can use a business card exchange by making on-site luggage tags. Take two—one for you and one for them.

- *Interactive kiosks.* Stationed throughout the event venue, attendees receive a user name and password to pull personal agenda. Touch-screen technology is often found at an interactive kiosk.
- *Laptop/PDA/notepad.* Integration from event direct to database. Attendee data may be loaded in advance.
- *Lead form.* Asks personal data as well as product interest level, purchasing authority, and time frame.
- *Raffle ticket or card.* Used for prize giveaways. Customize to include personal data name, organization e-mail. This should be cross-referenced with the event database you are maintaining.
- *Web inquiry capture response.* Attendees ask questions online and you respond via e-mail.
- *Direct mailer.* A printed piece sent directly to the attendee usually pre- and post event. Reinforces your key messages and should feature a business reply card (hard copy).
- *Direct-marketing campaign.* An initiative that includes e-mail marketing, tele-connecting, and direct advertising. The goal of direct marketing is not only to make money but find other ways to make money. This seemingly simple statement has far-reaching effects for companies looking to grow through the development of proactively generated leads. The objective is to stimulate a response that can be developed into a lead and ultimately into a new customer.
  - Pre-Invitation: Save the date
  - Invitation RSVP Methods: Online; direct attendees to a specific Web site, phone; set up a specific voice mail box, monitor daily, track and post. Card: may include prepaid postage
  - Follow-up: Confirmation notification

    - Premailer: Use lists provided to you by the show organizer, or your sales team, or purchase lists from a third-party vendor; such as a list broker or industry magazine.
    - Postmailer: Use lists provided to you by the show organizer and cross-reference with your actual attendee list, if possible.
    - E-mail Blast: Pre- or postevent
    - Tele-connecting Campaign: Calling to invite, lead follow-up (pre- and postevent)
    - Advertising Program
- *Lead coordinators.* Professionals who know how to engage prospects can be one of the best investments you can make, dollar for dollar. Lead coordinators provide added value and are especially helpful at larger events if you are short on resources; usually costs about $500 to $1,000 per person with a per diem.
    - Properly briefed and secured from an appropriate agency
    - Not necessarily fashion models, though they can be attractive and engaging

■ **Hint:** *Too* attractive in some industries sends out the wrong message and attracts people for the wrong reasons. Be sensitive to ethnicity as well as gender.

    - Professional "people-handlers" or "lead coordinators" can prequalify interest in your product or service and save your reps from exhaustion, or stretch the reach of a smaller sales force on-site.
    - Lead coordinators are trained to understand your company's elevator pitch as well as to ask the attendee simple qualifying questions.

■ **Hint:** In the old days, "Demo Dollys" were hired—attractive young women in short skirts with great cleavage. Today, some of that still exists.

Technology Enablers

CDs and Memory Sticks. Sales tools/collateral is preloaded on the media.

- Place a hyperlink that launches to your Web site.
- Items should be branded with your logo.

The key in lead capture is to know what questions to ask, almost like a reporter. In my event network is Ken Mortara, president of ShowValue, Inc., an event measurement firm that helps companies determine how well they've performed and the value they receive from participating in an event(s). Their focus is in corporate event-marketing measurement including business impact analysis, meeting and conference evaluation, trade show lead processing, and Web surveys. They have built systems and solutions providing the metrics around lead capture information.

Tip:

E-mail: Opt-In

"Remember to ask an e-mail opt-in question if you intend to contact the attendee via e-mail after the show. It is good business practice and anti-spam laws are becoming more and more draconian."

Ken Mortara
President
ShowValue, Inc.
http://www.showvalue.com

Ken and I regularly discuss in detail how lead capture must meet business objectives. Ken says, "basically there three things you need to know about the *attendee*":

1. Attendee demographics.
2. Attendee's qualifications as a prospect.
3. Attendee's interests.

Once you know your sales initiatives and business objectives, you can build your lead capture form.

Figure 8.1 is an excellent lead form questionnaire guide that was developed by ShowValue. I find this information extremely useful for all types of event programs. Figure 8.2 offers some lead capture questions that may help in creating the guide.

LEAD QUALIFICATION

I am often asked about the role of Event Marketing in *qualifying* leads and facilitating them through the system, and at what point does the role start and stop. I believe the role of the event marketer is that he/she understands their organization and knows the appropriate people to leverage the information.

Event marketers cannot qualify the leads. They must, however, understand a qualifying system that is approved by the sales team. Some of the value designators are 1, 2, 3, or A, B, C. Each company has their own system.

When you engage the sales team early in the planning stage, they will do the qualifying work for you–actually, they will *want* to do this for you. This is where they will see the value of events as long as you *show them* the value of events. You can build big-time points with sales and build your ROI/measurement opportunities if you design your program around the sales objectives. Seems fundamental, but can so easily be forgotten in the heat of marketing. Leads are for deals!

FIGURE 8.1 *Creating Lead Form/Questionnaires . . . That Work*

Background

There are three fundamental reasons most companies invest in event marketing:

1. **To Inform**—People attend events to learn about companies; their strategies, products, and services, as well as industry changes.
2. **To Demonstrate**—Studies show that over 75 percent of people attend events to actually see what products look like and what features they offer, both yours and your competitors. Over 60% attend specifically to evaluate competitive products.
3. **To Capture Leads**—While most event personnel enjoy talking about their company, they especially enjoy demonstrating the features and capabilities of their specific products. More often than not, capturing lead information is simply not a high priority. This is often a training issue (they have never been told the importance of capturing leads), but is usually a function of the lead capture process itself. Demo personnel do not want to interrupt their presentations to ask and record the answers to qualifying questions. And if there are several people watching the demonstration, it is often impossible to capture information about each person—one at a time. The problem is even more difficult if the presentation is given in a theater environment. However, given the audience (studies indicate that as many as 50 percent of the attendees are final decision makers with purchasing authority) and the expense associated with exhibiting at a show, lead capture, and qualification is generally not a priority to your on-site personnel.

Salespeople often complain that the leads they get from events are not as good as those they receive from other sources. They are usually right! It is generally because there hasn't been enough emphasis placed on lead capture. Also, the process in place doesn't support quality sales prospecting. Capturing good lead information must be made a priority and as simple as possible for personnel. And, it must be both easy and nonintrusive to the "inform" and "demonstrate" objectives of the event.

What Questions to Ask

Lead capture questions can be categorized into four general classes:

1. *Prospect Qualifiers.* Salespeople generally are interested in three basic prospect attributes:
   a) Is there a funded project?
   b) When will the purchasing decision be made?
   c) Is the person the final decision maker?
2. *Product Interest.* Which of your products and services are of interest to the prospect?
3. *Business or Industry.* Into which business category does the prospect's company fall? How many employees are there, how many locations, annual revenue, etc.? If the company is involved with the government, are they Federal, State, and Local, a special agency, etc.?

FIGURE 8.1 *Creating Lead Form/Questionnaires . . . That Work (Continued)*

4. *Marketing Questions.* An event can be used as a focus group to ask various marketing questions. For example, interest in potential new product features can be measured. However, it is vital to recognize that the primary purpose of lead capture at events is qualifying leads and generating sales opportunities. Be certain to limit the use of marketing questions on questionnaires (see How Many Questions Can I Ask, below).

How to Ask Questions

Attendees recognize that there is a tradeoff when they attend an event. You tell them about your company, your products and services, and answer their questions. In return, they provide information about themselves and their companies. Generally, if they are unwilling to provide this information, they are not real prospects for you. However, and this is an important point, they are free to ask as many questions as you permit, but you can only expect a certain limited amount of their time answering the questionnaire. Of course, you can ask as much as you like while talking to the person, but the questionnaire must be reasonable in length.

People are asked to fill in a questionnaire at virtually every booth; for example, they visit, usually with very similar questions. If it's a hosted event, there's usually a postevent questionnaire. Your ability to make filling in the form as easy as possible for the attendee increases the probability of getting a complete questionnaire with answers that are generally more accurate.

The event environment is different from other forms of selling. You have very limited time with each person. Ask only those questions required to determine if the person is a real prospect. The ideal questionnaire is a tool to decide whether to contact the person after the event ends. It is definitely not a tool to gather full sales information. That can be done in a telemarketing follow-up or in a sales call.

Answers should be designed so attendees can easily select the appropriate answer for themselves and their companies. It is easier when the answers are multiple-choice rather than the fill-in-the-blank variety. Instead of asking for a discrete answer, it is much easier for the attendee to answer a question in the form of a range. For example, the purchasing timeframe may be "less than three months," "three to six months," "seven to twelve months," and "over one year." When constructing answers to questions, you need to ask yourself if there is a real difference between a purchase timeframe answer of "four months" or "three to six months" when the lead is placed in the hands of a salesperson. If a question is easy to answer, it is likely the question will be answered and the answer will be more accurate.

Keep the wording of questions brief and direct and, where possible, use correct English sentences. Differentiate questions and answers by printing the question in bold typeface. If you must use a fill-in-the-blank question (although we discourage this approach), provide lines on the form to encourage neatness and to limit the length of the answer (some people are novelists).

How Many Questions Can I Ask

As discussed above, you can reasonably expect a limited amount of time from attendees for answering questions on a questionnaire. Most attendees believe you are there for their convenience. Once

(continued)

FIGURE 8.1 *Creating Lead Form/Questionnaires . . . That Work (Continued)*

they tire of answering questions, they will stop, period. You lose valuable information. We recommend placing questions on the questionnaire in the order of importance. What do you need to know versus what would you like to know.

Only you can decide how many questions are required to qualify a prospect. However, we recommend limiting questions to a total of six to eight. Similarly, questions requiring only one selection should be limited to about five answers. There are, of course, exceptions, but it is rare that an attendee will make the effort to accurately differentiate among many more possible answers. The list of answers can reasonably be longer if multiple selections can be made; for example a list of products and services. But, generally, fewer is better.

Layout of the Questionnaire

Make sure your company name and logo are at the top of the questionnaire. This form is marketing material and should support your branding strategy. You may want to put the name of the show on the questionnaire as well.

Place any messaging next, especially if you have a promotional giveaway or are using a paper lead card as entry in a drawing. If there is a drawing, be sure to indicate any rules such as a requirement to be present. If the drawing is for something of great value, you may want to consult your legal department for guidelines. You may need to check with show management as well.

For paper lead forms, leave ample room for the person's name, title, company, etc. Legibility will be affected by allowing too little room for this information. At ShowValue, we have The ScanQuest system. From the system you can print a label so the attendee does not need to write this information. It is more accurate, speeds the process of filling in the questionnaire, encourages the attendee to answer the questions, and is always readable.

Place the most important questions first. If the attendee has limited time (or attention span), at least these questions have a higher probability of being answered. Leave enough space between questions and answers. A busy-looking form can be intimidating and reduces the probability of the attendee answering all your questions.

If your on-site personnel frequently write comments on the questionnaire, display a "comments" input area. On paper lead forms, provide a "comments" section. If you don't, people will write all over the form. The use of lines in the comment area will help keep the comments neater.

The size of a paper lead form is a function of the number of questions and answers. It should generally be no larger than 8½" × 11" and usually no smaller than 6" × 9". Paper can be white or colored. If you use colored paper, make sure the color is light enough so the printing is easy to read. Use a minimum of 24-pound stock. A 67-pound cover stock is easier to write on. Lighter stock may require you to supply a clipboard if the person is expected to fill in the lead form while standing. You may also be required to make copies to distribute.

FIGURE 8.2 *Lead Capture Questions to Create a Form*

Salutation ______________________________

First and Last Name ______________________________

Title ______________________________

Organization/Company/Firm/School, etc. ______________________________

Address ______________________________

City ______________________________

State ______________________________

Zip/Postal Code ______________________________

Country ______________________________

E-mail Address ______________________________

Phone Number ______________________________

Fax Number ______________________________

Cell Phone Number ______________________________

Hotel ______________________________

Here are some general questions. Pick 3–5

Ex: "Have you ever done business with our company?" would be a great question for an objective of "identify more than 100 visitors who are not current customers."

☐ Which of the following products/services/solutions are you interested in (select all that apply)

- Put your list of products/services or solutions here.

☐ Do you have a funded project?

☐ What is your budget range for this project?

☐ What is your time frame to purchase?

☐ What is your role in the purchasing decision process?

☐ What stage of the buying process are you in?

☐ Please have a salesperson contact me.

- There's no better indication of interest.

(continued)

FIGURE 8.2 *Lead Capture Questions to Create a Form (Continued)*

- ☐ May we contact you via e-mail?
  - These days, you cannot send e-mail without it.
- ☐ Which method of contact do you prefer?
- ☐ How important is this event in helping you make purchasing decisions?
- ☐ Before visiting our booth, how familiar were you with our company/products/services?
- ☐ Have you ever done business with our company?
- ☐ How likely are you to do business with our company?
- ☐ How helpful was the presentation?

Questions for the lead capture form have been provided by ShowValue, Inc.

Attendee Rating Scale:

Here's an easy way to identify the action for the leads. By designing an effective, qualifying process you will be *facilitating, easing, opening, accelerating, and shortening the sales cycle.* When you work an event there's usually "typical" responses to the attendee's view of your product offering. In order to explain the attendee rating scale, I've incorporated a typical response to the value designator—meaning, all attendees will be rated on a scale. You can use the value designator or 1, 2, 3, but remember to meet with Sales to match their value designator.

1. Hot (Extremely interested in your product or service. "You know you should speak with my boss about this and "Let's talk on Tuesday," are often said by the attendee.) Lengthy discussion occurs with the prospect, and the prospect displays considerable interest in your company, or looks to schedule further visit from your sales team or executives. Multiple lead capture mechanisms usually occur with a

hot lead (both the business card exchange and badge swipe). The attendee has the following:
- Buying authority or influence
- Budget approval
- Defined purchase timeline
- Strong interest in product or service

2. Warm (Interested. "Maybe we'd consider this in the future, but just not at this time.") This is a good prospect to maintain a teleconnect. Ask more questions to qualify needs. The attendee has the following:
   - Some buying authority or influence
   - Budget is under consideration
   - Purchase timeline in the future
   - Some interest in product or service
3. Cool (No action. "Thanks for the light-up pen; my kids will love it.")—Made five-second branding connection with your company; attendee shows little interest, nodded head and smiled, picked up a giveaway item in exchange for the badge swipe or just turned back and walked away. The attendee is:
   - Unable to determine buying authority or influence
   - Shows little or no interest in product or service at this time
   - No budget or timeline

LEAD MANAGEMENT

In the planning stage, as you are developing the lead generation strategy it is important to define a standard contact rating and lead tracking process for ALL events in which your company invests money. The lead management program should establish a contact rating criteria that includes telemarketing followup and revenue tracking if possible.

As an event marketer, you are the owner or key contact of the program. Once an event ends, it's really not over, it's still in process. Quite frankly, the challenge as the "owner" comes from having to move onto other projects and trusting that your hard work will not be lost in the shuffle.

By setting up a simple internal procedure pre-event, the lead value increases and measurable if tied to sales. How involved should you be? As involved as you need to keep the momentum moving forward. You can't close the business for them but the last thing you want to do is have management scratching their heads regarding next year's budget because you have no plan in place to assist Sales in the conversion of new business.

- Define a consistent method for lead capture and followup.
- Process inquiries and leads for fulfillment and followup based on the designated qualification system.
- Develop an "event influenced" sales report, tracking against your company pipeline.

You must understand the intent and objective for the lead.

Goal

- Garner sales management support
- Disseminate qualified opportunities to the field
- Track opportunities

Action

- Develop methodology for lead capture and order tracking
- Develop close loop tracking
- Use in direct marketing campaigns

Business Impact

- Determine an ROI for every campaign
- Establish company's best practice for processing

When I work with sales, I use the phrase "you are a talking brochure for the company." You must be able to convey what the company offers, what the value is to the prospect, and how the prospect goes about buying it.

If you are going to an event in a part of the country where it is more likely that local attendees are going to be there, make sure that your sales staff at the event are from that local region and make sure you have executives, if needed. In other words, do not bring in the West Coast sales team to an East Coast sales function if you believe the attendees are going to be from the East Coast. A geographically based sales team at a hospitality function as your partners can be directed to the appropriate salesperson immediately, and can establish the relationship.

■ **Hint:** One great tip is to create a pocket-size map with rep name, region, and phone number and give it to your on-site staff and executives. If your salespeople engage with someone outside of their territory, they can then provide the prospect with the correct information.

Empowering the staff is key! I engage them to think about what "just one more sale" from each event would mean to the company's bottom line. I also explain that value of events comes from their ability to follow up. It's challenging, because even when you host an event, remember your competitors probably have some type of program scheduled directly behind you. The followup and followthrough are critical throughout the event strategy.

In a small company, you are going to be much more hands-on with the lead capture/generation approach (as opposed to a big company where you may have Customer Relationship Database, or CRM, such as salesforce.com, Siebel, or a homegrown application) in the way in which you forward the lead process. If you are not using an online application for lead management today, you are behind the times. What is the outcome of the event? The advantages are obvious, but I'll reiterate the value anyway.

- Access to online leads
- Access to online distribution of reps and partners
- Monitor followup
- Track pipeline and forecast
- Measure closed business
- Measure ROI

The lead generation strategy is broken into three stages:

1. Pre-Event
2. On-site
3. Postevent

Finding a strategy that fits your needs for a specific event is a bit of a fact-finding journey. Use what makes sense and throw away the rest.

Pre-Event Lead Management

Prior to the opening of any event, I recommend a run-through with the entire on-site team and those in the office that will be supporting the program. With each event, it is important to review with your on-site staff the designated attendee rating scale. Make sure you announce the type of lead capture mechanisms you plan to use. It is important to house this information and maintain it in a central repository, also known as event database, or the company's approved online application. Make sure you reiterate from where you are seeking to gather the information.

■ **Hint:** Create an Events Database (even if you have a CRM system in place)

Tip

The Power of Pre-Event Mailers

Most event programs should include direct mail. Pre-event direct mailers can be especially effective if leveraged correctly.

Hot List. Spend the time on the front end putting your "list" together and get complete profile information. Use lists from past events.

Simplicity. Keep your copy to one message as chosen from your Positioning and Messaging Framework.

- You can inform and educate the attendee about your product and services when you meet one-on-one.

Appeal. Make sure you integrate the visuals into your message and corporate identity. The pre-event mailer sets the tone and spirit for your event and does a double duty when branding. The more impressions the better.

TMI (too much information). Focus on the *benefits,* not the features and the call-to-action: Register today or Meet with us. (Stay away from information overload.)

Quiz question:

If we were selling a pen with a clip, is the benefit of the clip the fact that we won't lose the pen?

No. That is the *advantage*. The benefit always should logically follow an advantage and always be preceded with the word therefore. *"Therefore, you don't have to BUY another one." (Remember, benefits are all about wallet, watch, or ego.)*

Creative. Be clever and clean. The goal is to meet with you. It's not about winning a design award.

Humility. Be friendly, not arrogant. Focus on the why *they* should want to learn more about your product and services. Focus on things that mean something to *them.* Save the bragging rights for later. Use awards and customer testimonials to reinforce your key benefits.

(continued)

Timing. Establish a schedule to release mailers.

- "Save the dates" should release three months to a year in advance.
- "Looking forward to seeing you" notes should drop about 15 days before the actual event date.
- Match the timeline to the budget and gang together print runs.
- If you are using a list from the show organizer, make sure you understand their guidelines and limitations.

Action. The mailer should have a purpose. "Bring the mailer with you to redeem a free gift or for VIP access to special events; have it stamped, fill out a form, visit four product stations, etc." Make it easy for your recipient. Giving them specific instructions as to what you want them to do works in certain markets and for certain audiences.

On-site Lead Management

Event marketers must process information quickly and efficiently.

- Schedule an on-site briefing. For example, the success of the event and the value you will gain from your investment will depend on the professionalism, training, and discipline of your team.

■ **Hint:** Kent Emeson, Events and Exhibit Manager for Harcourt Achieve, a educational company that provides customer-driven learning solutions for teachers and children ages K-12, insists that his salespeople working trade shows be thoroughly prepared for "doing battle." He makes it fun, though, and explains, "I always make sure they have some food in them or drinks if it is the appropriate hour, to make the pre-event training seem more valuable and enjoyable. But I ALWAYS make sure that the trainer that I use is not only professional, but familiar with how to talk in a 'non-professorial' mode to my people. These people fall into just two categories: veteran professionals that are very good at what they do, or stone rookies. And no matter which, they need the training to focus and perform under pressure and in a tight timeline when it comes to sales. They need to practice shorter, more benefits-driven ways to engage prospects. And, they need drilling on what is new, what may be problematic in their industry, and *how* each other is selling benefits before they ever set foot on the show floor."

- Meet with your team on a daily basis to get a sense of with whom they are speaking.
- Keep an ongoing list or hand out a Contact Profile Summary form (Figure 8.3).
- Don't forget. Salespeople have big egos, too. Make them compete! Use incentive programs built into the fabric of the event to reward the best performers. Metrics could be most leads, best leads, or biggest sale on the show floor.
- Use a lead-retrieval system.

■ **Hint:** Personally, I've worked for some companies that could not care less about following up on leads at all. In those cases, I never throw away the information immediately; I just keep it as a reference for future projects.

Figure 8.3 is an example of a handwritten form. It is your job as the event marketer to get this adapted and translated into a lead-retrieval system with the ability to decipher the good leads from the bad.

FOLLOW-UP LEAD MANAGEMENT

To ensure those measurable postevent results, the sales staff absolutely has to do the call-downs on every single lead, and those call-downs have to be done in a timely matter. I would say within 14 days of the event, and they have to be done by the territory

FIGURE 8.3 *Event Contact Profile Summary*

Date ______________________________

Sales Person ______________________________

Company Name ______________________________

Event Manager ______________________________

Event Name and Date ______________________________

Meeting Attendees ______________________________

____

Discussion Points ______________________________

____

____

Opportunities ______________________________

____

Objections ______________________________

____

Competitive Information ______________________________

____

Follow-Up Activity ______________________________

____

____

Follow-Up Date ______________________________

Estimated Revenue Forecast ______________________________

Estimated Closing Opportunity (Rank)—(Circle)

1 2 3 4 5 6 7 8 9 10

Estimated Closing Date ______________________________

representative who wishes to establish that relationship. They should be called first, then a personal e-mail or note should follow. Strangely enough, upon my return from most events, I am contacted three to four weeks afterwards via mail, but no phone call. It is really amazing!

Take a proactive approach when you return from your event. Many companies use technology that will update their database in realtime while others may still do this manually. It doesn't matter, don't get hung up in the "how," just make sure it gets done! I've been hired by companies and walked in the door to see leads from three months ago still sitting in a box on the floor with trash on top. That is where the meeting and events industry always carries a heavy heart. DON'T LET THIS HAPPEN TO YOU!

- Make a commitment to yourself to process the leads in your system within three to five business days, maximum.
- Send your vice president of sales the downloaded leads immediately. Make sure that your plan to get the leads out the door and off to sales is fully engaged before planning gets too far.
- Every time you return from an event, download the leads into your own files; what type of files varies from company to company. It can be as simple as an Excel spreadsheet or by using an online application.
- Save lead capture information somewhere, because it will come back to haunt you when you either have to validate why your company is doing the event or for funding in the future.

"I think it is interesting for us as another start-up company," says Steve Zahm from Procore Technologies. "What I am finding is that the percentage of actual physical standard mail I get is limited to two things: it is either a bill for services from one of my vendors or a direct mailer which I briefly look at and toss in the

Events
Action Process to Maximize Investment

Pre-event Activity to Target Audience

- Use your complimentary conference passes as a way to entice the prospect or customer to join you at the event.
- Offer one-on-one meetings with your executives.
- Encourage Sales to accompany their customer(s) throughout the event.

Pre-event Communications with the Registered Attendee List

- Telesales makes an introduction promoting your on-site marketing. activities such as, "come to our break-out session."
- Marketing sends "visit us" correspondence via e-mail.
- Handwritten note from Sales
- Register list—Sales reps introduce all your marketing activities; reminder two days prior phone in evening; sales reps leave cell phone number

On-site Relationship Building

- Attend the conference sessions and interact with delegates, speakers, partners, press, and analysts.
- Introduce yourself to clients and prospects at all hospitality functions.
- Schedule meetings between your customers and your executives.
- Work the event at all times. Outline what they should be doing; show vested interest in the dialog and sales, and then walk away.

Postevent Activity

- Forward new contacts to appropriate channel with follow-up communication plan and summary of your communication, telemarketing direct mail, scripting
- Telemarket to list generated at events.
- Send a series of follow-up correspondence to attendee list.
- *Followthrough*—Sales conversion leads to sales
- Offer opportunity workshops or one-on-one demos and decide how are you plan to offer this workshop.
- Give them a hook or call to action for the next step.

garbage. Therefore, I do not think that you can just make contact through direct mail for a buyer who is looking for a service nearly as effectively as you can with a phone call. We have directly seen it and that's why events are a key marketing component for our sales efforts. We are very selective in the events we sponsor or exhibit. We know our target audience. Our success postevent has come from the introduction and connections we made on-site and then calling up to speak with the contact directly to get us to the next step."

EVENTS AND THE ATTENDEES' PERSONAL PRIVACY INFORMATION

Privacy is an extremely hot topic and ranges from everything from HIPAA (healthcare) to identity theft. With events, it's important to realize that the data you collect from a conference, trade show, road show, or partner dinner must be held and processed with the utmost care. Lead capture is critical to the development of your company's business, especially in the current competitive or uncertain market environments.

Rules and regulations are changing every day. Currently, each company has different privacy policies. Look on any Web site and you'll find different statements. Basically, they all say the same things, "we will not resell, reuse, or share your information." Check to see if your company has a global privacy policy for personal data. If you're a small company, search around the Internet and adopt language for your company but adhere to what you claim. Treat your attendee data as if it contained your own personal social security number or ID number. Regardless of the company size, every company has some type of legal representation. Go through your proper channels and use the Internet as a guide.

As a company, you should be committed to privacy and data protections for your customers and prospects throughout the

Tip

Lead Generation Now

Two more sweeping generalizations: Salespeople should, by nature, be focused on money (greed is good) and are unfortunately inherently lazy and tend to place blame elsewhere when the sales are not coming in. So, make it a slam dunk for them. They will be your champions down the line.

1. Create an event database file to house leads, allowing you to cleanse for duplication and forward to Sales.
   - At this step, you may also have the ability to assign leads by rep, region, or distributor. Assign each event a specific code so you can track where the lead came from.
2. Schedule a 15-minute conference call or meeting to discuss the "attendee list" with the sales teams processing the leads from the database.
   - Play the "match game" and know if any of the leads captured are current customers. This quick review can prove invaluable in further identifying the quality of the lead inquiry.
3. Develop a call guide for use in contacting the number two or "B" leads. Companies with inside sales or telemarketing teams usually give B leads to this group. The number one or "A" leads are given directly to the rep. Content should include "nice meeting you," "thanks for coming," a one-minute reiteration of product or service highlights, next steps, a call to action, etc.
   - You may want to write and approve the script. You may find that a parallel direct-marketing campaign could increase the ability for your sales reps to open the door to warm or cool leads.
4. Execute a Direct Marketing Campaign
   - *Number One or A*—Sales reps should followup with a phone call immediately, send an e-mail and a personal letter. Closing the deal should be tracked back to the database.
   - *Number Two or B*—If you have the person's e-mail address, send a personal note and reiterate the points discussed in your conver-

sation. Sales reps should call these individuals. Some examples may be to look to schedule a future meeting, or flag the results of the discussion to the database.

- *Number Three or C*—If you have e-mail addresses setup, an e-mail blast with a "thank you for stopping by, your URL, a contact person, and phone number should be sent. If you have anything to offer from a catalog to a white paper, here's the place to include it. If you don't have the e-mail addresses or you are using the show organizers "postevent attendee list," do the same content but create a postcard.

5. Marketing owns it—Host end-of-quarter reviews by phone or in person. Walk through the quarters events, discuss the followup, and update the event database with any missing info. Personally, I feel the best time to do this is around 4:00 PM on Friday afternoons with a glass of wine in hand.
6. Reporting—It's got to be done at some point. Pick critical times that match your company's goals; for example, end of quarter.
   - Be prepared to have this information ready when asked. Some companies use what's called a marketing dashboard to input all metrics.
   - Events create leads and leads are considered part of how you define metrics. Make sure you roll event data into the proper buckets. You can also create your own chart.
7. Create a simple tracking report. Reports should be cumulative over a determined time span and an annual rollup should also be provided from the event marketing group.

event process. There are some quick and easy reminders for you to use, so that when acquiring this info it has already complied with your company's privacy program. Fortunately, the public is aware of this issue and often now asks, "What are you going to do with the information you just swiped from my badge?" or, "...now that I registered to attend your golf outing?"

At a conference organized by a major analyst firm, for instance, many professionals believe that once a delegate has registered for a conference, this automatically grants permission to the sponsor to use that name once they have scanned the delegate's badge. Is this a true or false statement? Well, it depends on the policy of the analyst firm. To be safe, advise your on-site staff of your company's policy prior to the event. Include a brief paragraph of information in their training materials.

Take a look at the following scenario. There is not a right or wrong answer. This is just something to consider in regards to privacy rights when you are involved in an event.

Your company and its number one business partner have just released a new cobranded product and want to host both a seminar and a Webinar to a select group of top prospects in ten cities throughout the country. Take a look at the snowball effect with contact information.

1. To promote the events to three different audiences, the marketing team sent out an e-mail invitation and a print invite with RSVP, it set up a registration site, and ran a telemarketing campaign.
2. At the first seminar, a prospect handed her business card to a sales rep and said, "Feel free to e-mail me with that information we were discussing." The prospect was not invited to the event but came with a colleague (she's the boss).
3. All the seminar attendees receive an e-mail thank you letter. Does receiving a business card from a prospect mean the personal data from the business card can now be entered into your event database? Can the marketing department now send an e-mail thank you letter to this prospect?
4. The seminar is sponsored by a partner. What information, if any, does a sponsoring partner receive?
5. The Webinar attendees receive a postevent e-mail thank you that promotes the next event. Some send back a response that they are not interested in attending. Do you remove them from your event base?

6. How does your company treat the prospect's information?
7. How many times can you send an e-mail to a prospect or a customer? What kind of marketing communications can you use?

Cosponsoring events runs into some challenges as it relates to each company's contact information. Here's a way to get a handle around how an attendee's privacy rights interact with your event strategy.

Your company, a partner, and an industry trade magazine (each a cosponsor and collectively, cosponsors) agree that it may be mutually beneficial to jointly promote and market their respective products and services through a series of two-day conferences with followup seminars and a Webinar that explains the combined benefits of their offerings to prospective customers.

Each of the three companies will issue its own invitations to a list of their customers and prospects to attend the events. The invitations will direct the attendee to a Web site developed and hosted by your company. The Web site will house the agenda, content, and logistics information regarding the event. The attendee registration will be confirmed via e-mail notification. Other materials such as conference brochures regarding the conference may be sent to the registrants by e-mail, direct mail, or telemarketing. Each cosponsor will have access to the attendees, contact information in order to initiate followup activities, either individually or in partnership with (an)other cosponsor(s).

Marketing Campaign

The conference and seminar series will be held in a hotel and is aimed at attracting a middle-level management target audience from major corporations. The industry trade magazine will serve as a neutral third party and will develop the content and secure the speakers. Your company and your partner will have a series of sessions where they will copresent their new solutions.

Interested parties will register for the conference by visiting a Web site and completing an online registration form.

Mailing Lists

Your company will send invitations by traditional country mail and e-mail to primary mailing lists. Your company will obtain the primary lists from your in-house event database. All external lists will be provided by the industry trade magazine which has the greatest target market focus. Cosponsors plan to send invitations by traditional mail and e-mail to secondary mailing lists that they obtain or maintain on their own. (Note: If you plan to use lists from third-party providers, make certain that these providers are reputable and reliable.) Make sure you only purchase opt-in contacts or use by permission only databases. With any communication executed off the mailing list, confirm that the recipient has an opt-out mechanism, otherwise known as "get me off this list" (under the Data Protection Act).

To streamline efforts, one company should take control of the creative materials. For example, your company can create the primary invitations and approve all secondary mailing invitations for overall consistency with campaign messages and themes, proper identification, and opt-out info. Cosponsors would review the materials and be responsible for any claims they make in conjunction with their own communications.

At the end of the campaign, the lead company agrees to compile all of the attendee contact information from all lead capture mechanisms and provide a copy to all cosponsors. The privacy information and usage previously agreed upon would be in effect.

Web Site

The Web site will need to be paid for and administered under one company for consistency as it relates to content and design and should be protected behind a firewall (a secure area). You can share costs or include it in as part of your funding contribution. All e-mail communications generated from the Web site should go to and come from a specific e-mail address. This mailbox will need to be monitored and updated as needed. Set an agreement for any loss of service or even a crash of the World Wide Web or telecom equipment malfunctions. The domain name for the Web site should be properly registered.

Resource Allocation

It is important to determine how each company's resources will be allocated in producing the conference and seminar series. The components include but are not limited to Web site development, invitation creation and approval, primary invitation distribution, logistics management, event facilitation, content and presentations, lead management, reporting, and followup.

Expense Allocation

Agree on how related expenses will be covered for the two-day conference series. The components include but are not limited to: Web site development, logistics, creative logistics, food and beverage, travel expenses, promotional items, mailing costs, and communication materials.

Reminder:

Data Collection Touch Points

- Have you complied with your company's privacy policy?
- What is the process for collecting personal data (e.g., name, mailing address, e-mail address, telephone number, Social Security or insurance number, etc.)?
  - How does the personal data get transferred?
  - Does the personal data get transferred outside of your home country?
  - Who will have access to the personal data?
  - How will you be using this personal information (e.g., targeting ads, telemarketing, e-mail, sales calls)?
  - Will someone else in the company use or have access to this personal information again at a later date?
  - How long you will keep the personal data?
  - What happens if the user fails to provide all personal data requested (e.g., access denied; can't download software, etc.)?
  - In what countries, states, provinces, or cities will the attendee's info be located?

Events and Data Collection

Figure 8.4 reflects the event types at-a-glance and matches it to the lead capture mechanisms outlined in this chapter. The table reflects the various touch points for data collection that may be involved, no matter what the event. Think of the chart as an airline route. Airlines routes crisscross and get you where you want to be.

Make a matrix or menu for your touch points for each event. Create policy definitions to reflect both paper and Web-based initiatives.

FIGURE 8.4 *Touch Points for Data Collection*

Event Types at A Glance	**Lead Capture Mechanisms**
Trade Show	Registration
Seminar	Badge Swipe
Conference and Summit	Business Card Delivery or Exchange
Forum	Direct Mail
Webinar	Pre-Invitation (save the date)
Live Meeting (internal and external)	Invitation
Video Conference	Followup
Teleconference	Pre-mailer
Roundtable	Postmailer
Meal Function	E-mail
Breakfast	Pre-Invitation (save the date)
Lunch	Invitation
Dinner	Follow-up
Networking Reception	Premailer
Sports and Hospitality Function	Postmailer
	E-mail Blast (pre- or postevent)
	Business Reply Card (hard copy)
	Telephone Solicitation
	Calling to Invite
	Lead followup (pre- and postevent)
	Response to Web Inquiry
	Raffle Ticket
	Lead Generation Card
	Flash CDs
	Interactive Kiosks
	Laptop/PDA/Notepad
	RSVP Methods:
	Phone
	Hard copy
	Online

What's in Your E-Mail

THE CAN-SPAM ACT went into effect January 1, 2005, restricting unsolicited commercial e-mail and imposing stiff penalties for violations. The Act defines "unsolicited e-mail" as "any electronic mail message the primary purpose of which is the commercial advertisement or promotion of a commercial product or service" (including seminars, sponsorships, conferences, educational materials, membership drives, etc.).

While the CAN-SPAM Act is clear about how commercial e-mails must be treated—they must be identified as an advertisement or solicitation, provide an opt-out mechanism, and include the sender's physical address. Only recently has the Federal Trade Commission issued regulations defining the criteria for determining the "primary purpose" of an e-mail.

What happens when your e-mails contain some commercial content and some transactional content? (E.g. those sent to complete a previous commercial transaction; those that provide information regarding subscriptions, memberships, accounts, or similar ongoing relationships; or those that provide information related to an employment relationship—these are not subject to the Act's requirements.)

That's exactly what the FTC's new "primary purpose" regulations explain. Here they are, effective March 28, 2005:

1. If an e-mail message contains only the commercial advertisement or promotion of a commercial product or service ("commercial content"), its primary purpose is commercial.
2. If an e-mail message contains a mix of commercial content and transactional content, it is considered commercial if:
   - a recipient interpreting the subject line would likely conclude that the message contains commercial content; or,
   - the e-mail's transactional content does not appear in whole or in substantial part at the beginning of the message.
3. If an e-mail message contains both commercial content and content that does not qualify as commercial or transactional, it will be deemed to be commercial if either:
   - a recipient interpreting the subject line would likely conclude that the message contains commercial content; or,

- a recipient interpreting the body of the message would likely conclude that the primary purpose of the message is commercial. Relevant factors include the placement of commercial content at the beginning of the message; the proportion of the message dedicated to commercial content; and how color, graphics, type size, and style are used to highlight commercial content.

The Act prohibits the use of fraudulent or deceptive subject lines in any type of e-mail.

Organizations should establish a format for both commercial and transactional messages, and institute policies to ensure that the proper format is used for every e-mail that is sent out on an organization's behalf. Additionally, an opt-out system must be instituted, effectively managed, and integrated with an organization's customer/client database.

Jed Mandel is a partner in the Chicago-based law firm of Neal, Gerber & Eisenberg, where he heads the trade and professional association practice. jmandel@ngelaw.com

Let's summarize here. This important chapter may save your job someday. It saved mine more than once. No matter how you do it, if the objective *anywhere* in the marketing plan has the word "prospect" in it, that is your clue to address the needs of the sales team in order to "tee up" their efforts. And, you will need to deal with these strategies throughout the lifecycle of the event marketing initiative.

- Pre-event
- On-site
- Postevent

Don't be seduced into thinking that your brilliant event strategy or creative approach won't or can't be derailed by a halfhearted effort in this area. It is a "necessary evil."

Chapter

9

EVENT MEASUREMENT AND ROI

Our mantra:
Event Marketing is all about facilitating, easing, opening, accelerating, and shortening the sales cycle. That's it!

Advertising and PR does a great job of metrics. It's easy for most people, from the CEO to the college intern, to understand advertising terms like *frequency* and *reach* and PR's *column inch* for word space. These buzzwords provide consistency and measurement for the advertising industry which lives and dies by the numbers, and PR which hangs onto every word and measures every placement. It's tangible. There's also the fact that you have independent audit bureaus supplying the information.

Events do not enjoy the same ease in which metrics and ROI (return on investment) information is communicated. The issue is that senior-level executives in most companies have been through business school either at an undergraduate or graduate level, and all have taken courses in marketing. These courses covered direct marketing, advertising, promotion. I've never come across anyone who's said they've taken a course specifically in event marketing. Finally, at the college level, many schools now offer hospitality and event courses and degrees.

Today, there is no set metrics for event marketing. Companies like ShowValue and Exhibit Surveys have made great strides in this area. Pop-up organizations, like the effort being led by Carat called the Technology Event Marketing Strategy Committee or TEMSC, has been formed to address the event measurement arena. The TEMSC strives to build the model for standardized cross event auditing and measurement, developing and monitoring event industry standards, and creating an industry voice and strong negotiating lobby.

For metrics, ROI, and measurement, event marketers are forced to provide market data like "number of leads" acquired at an event. For me, this term alone is confusing because there are "qualified leads" or "inquiries." The process begins in lead capture and pulls through to what Exhibit Surveys refers to as an *event measurement program*.

Like lead generation in the previous chapter, event measurement in some shape or form has to be done. From my perspective, I find it quite difficult to actualize what is real ROI because I believe events are *all about facilitating, easing, opening, accelerating, and shortening the sales cycle.* This is a soft metric.

The typical definition for ROI is a measurement of the return against the investment made. The investment might be money, but for your company, it might be time or resources that could be leveraged elsewhere. It all depends on how you define it and what you want to accomplish. (See Figure 9.1)

Buzzword	**Measurement Definition**
ROI—Return on Investment	Assesses long-term financial benefits and ties to the sales process.

ROO—Return on Opportunity (or Return on Objective)	Summarizes short-term goals (such as did the target audience learn about your product).
ROE—Return on Experience	Focuses on the immediate reaction to what has just been learned or communicated.
ROR—Return on Relationships	Centers on customer loyalty and is measured with an account-based marketing approach.
ROR—Return on Return	Ongoing and endless justification of why you are doing an event program.
ROS—Return on Smiles	In the moment measurement, gives you a feeling, a buzz, or an energy.
LOL—Laugh Out Loud	Releases stress while you are working on your event measurement initiatives.

In the *Change of Events, 2003* white paper, from The George P. Johnson Company the following is reported:

> *"Events continue to lead sales promotion, public relations, and online initiatives. Twice as many businesses are utilizing the skills of independent measurement companies as they did the previous year and they are utilizing specialized measurement tools internally to a greater extent."*

"I typically advise event marketers to pick one or two objectives, measure it, and then come back into the meeting with results," says

FIGURE 9.1 *Event Types with the Greatest ROI*

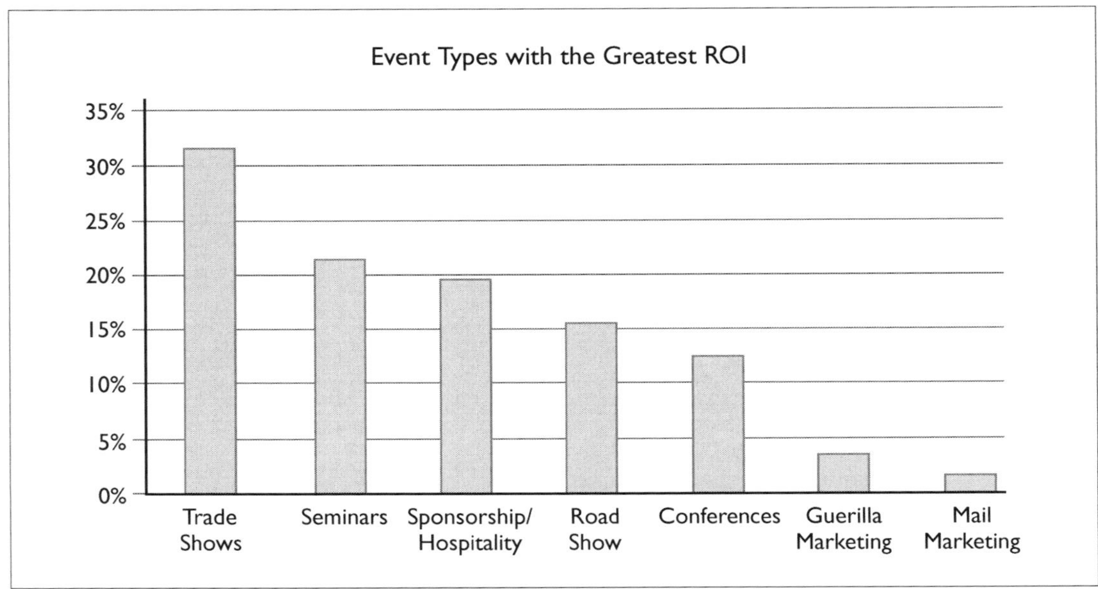

* Respondents: 350 senior marketing executives (vice president, director), companies: $500m+, automotive, healthcare, financial services, high-tech, telecom, consumer, and manufacturing.

© *White paper: Change of Events, 2003–The MPI Trends Report Reveals Changes for Events in the Marketing Mix*
The George P. Johnson Company
Integrated Event Marketing
http://www.gpjco.com

Ken Mortara of ShowValue. "If you try to measure 20 metrics everyone is going to look at you questioning what any of it means. Get one or two things that you can really explain—that you can demonstrate to some degree of success with, and start building a program, find out what is important to your company and start reporting on those kinds of metrics," continues Mortara.

For another angle on Return on Objective, Brian Vanden Broucke says, "Measurement is the bastard child in the industry—we wish it would just go away and let us live our lives and spend our budgets however we wish. Grow up!"

Metrics are here to stay and because they are a long-term strategy, a good starting point is to weave into the creative strategy a real-time survey on customer perceptions (ROO or ROE) right on the show floor or at your event reception. Handled much like a mini-market research campaign, you can assign one or more attractive, engaging, communicative people, dress them in something neutral (not company-sponsored clothing), ask five to ten *mostly* close-ended, non-sales related questions in exchange for a small incentive. Close-ended questions are easier to graph. It should be fun! Do it in an informal but professional manner. Why? Because it provides a snapshot of how people perceived your efforts NOW and gives you something tangible to take back to management that can steer the most noticeable elements of your strategy. For example: "What is it exactly you think we do here at ____________ ?" "What do you think of the event today or our booth experience?" "Are you planning to view our Webinar in two weeks? "How clear was our message during the reception or in the exhibit?" In this way, you can verify your marketing assumptions, decisions, and branding efforts with live human beings, and not spend a fortune assembling a simple report. Be careful of what you wish for! Sometime, your results are not as positive as you may like. And, please, don't ask anything that you can't use like: "Do you like the color of our logo?" If they said no, could you change it anyway? You want to ask intelligent questions for feedback on *actionable* items.

In a nutshell, there are two types of methods for capturing attendee data that support the RO (Return On-something)

- Qualitative Research: focus groups, interviews
- Quantitative Research: pre- and postevent surveys conducted by phone, mail, optical scanning or online

What you want to do is start with your sales initiatives and business objectives. It's deciding what to measure that is the challenge. The key is defining the objectives in order for you to measure them.

Tip

Event Measurement

- Profile demographics and buying power of attendees/visitors.
- Determine needs, expectations, and reasons for attending.
- Review overlap in attendance between events.
- Assess value received (ROI/ROO) from events.
- Measure tactical and logistical elements.

Exhibit Surveys
http://www.exhibitsurveys.com

- It's not enough to say to "increase market share." It needs to be more definitive: "increase market share by five percent in this particular environment," for example, is something that you can measure. An objective to increase market share alone has no goals.

- You'll ultimately ask questions about their overall experience: were they treated well, how did you like our graphics, etc. A trick I learned from Ken Mortara was to include on a survey a question that relates to a tag line which may belong to one of your competitors and asks: "What company do you associate this line with?" Just to find out how much the individual who is being surveyed knows about the competition in the industry. So there is some marketing information that can be drawn out as well.

It's back to Sales again. Sales should be included in the measurement and ROI process. Make no mistake, this is done for a very self-serving reason. *Accountability!* As mentioned before, get Sales involved and keep them involved. Ask Sales, "Please explain to me what the profile of a hot prospect is." It transfers some responsibility for asking the right questions to the sales organiza-

Tip

Performance Measurement—Driven by Objectives

Knowing which event measurement tools to use and to what extent, is determined by your own set of business objectives.

Objective	Measurement Method	Tools
Increased Brand Awareness and Preference	1. Audience quality and delivery 2. Message effectiveness 3. Press impact 4. Competitive presence	1. Show audit and demographics 2. Postshow survey 3. Press analysis 4. Competitive audit
Increase Demand Generation	1. Lead quality and quantity 2. Reduced cost per lead 3. Sales opportunities	1. Lead analysis 2. Database tracking 3. Reduce sales cycle

© *White paper: Put Your Measurement Where Your Marketing Is: Turning ROI-Insight into Strategy and Results*
The George P. Johnson Company
Integrated Event Marketing
http://www.gpjco.com

tion, so they can no longer come back and say, "Hey the leads really aren't good because you didn't ask the right questions."

Let's take a major national trade show where if you are considered a player in your industry you must sponsor. From these events, your on-site team processes between 50 and infinity of leads via the lead retrieval system from badge swiping and a hard copy lead capture form. At the point of introduction. You don't know whether the attendee is someone who says that they are getting ready to purchase in zero to three months, or if they are even a decision maker. All you know is the person stopped by your booth, attended your breakout session, and the marketing department sent a contact to Sales.

As tacky as it sounds, badge-based systems still work very well in event measurement initiatives. Think of the attendee name badge as their credentials. You've spent all this money on your event program and understanding the patterns of your attendee can prove invaluable in planning, product positioning, and future trends. An electronic badge gives you a record of who actually attended each event and serves a dual purpose for security.

- Look at the data sorted by company name. Take a look at your event database and see how many people from the same company attended your event, stopped by your booth, or replied to your pre-event mailer.

■ **Hint:** By using the name badge effectively, you can do everything from scanning attendees' badges at each breakout session, to *politely* denying them access if it's a confidential program.

- You can also leverage this same data for ROE (return on experience). Your sales reps can follow up within a few days and have intimate data about the attendee they are contacting. They can ask: "How'd you like our cigar and martini reception?" "Did you find our panel discussion on the latest industry trends of value?" "How was your one-on-one conversation with the analyst and our partner?" With this personal approach you will be amazed at the positive reaction you get from people when you can speak to what they've experienced.

By using the attendee ranking system as outlined in the chapter on leads, you put your sales department one step ahead of their qualification process. Without it, here's what happens.

- The sales rep starts their calls and the first lead says, "Hmmm, not really, it's not something I'm interested in."

> The rep calls the next lead contact and hears the same thing. Seven phone calls later, each with the same response, the sales rep gives up, becomes frustrated, and trashes the rest of the contacts that were generated from the event. By qualifying and measuring, you create a track record that validates the leads you capture.

Typically, event measurement is done event-by-event. Ideally, measurement should be integrated into your complete event strategy, naturally yielding a slew of results. Ken Mortara explains what this means and shared the following:

> *"One of our clients is a major sponsor of a conference series that is held four times a year in New York, San Francisco, Phoenix, and Orlando.*
>
> - *For two years we did lead capture and reporting.*
> - *After the second year, we looked at all four shows and found that the New York and San Francisco area shows were producing tremendously better results than Orlando and Phoenix. The client didn't drop out completely, but they scaled down in those locations.*
> - *Next, they took the extra budget dollars and invested in a national trade show and monthly Webinars, extending the power of the event marketing strategy.*
>
> *"Without capturing the kinds of information that came out of the original conference series by measuring the value of the events, they would have continued on the path and never really maximized their event investment," says Ken. "It's one of the success stories that I really love to tell because it really is what this measurement program notion is all about. It is to find out what works and place your investment there. It doesn't mean to abandon everything else, but it means being prudent about where you place your budget dollars."*

The very first time you touch someone the lead qualification process begins, because *there* is the first impression. If it's the welcome/registration desk at an executive event and your VIP customers and press walk up, they will see the attention to detail. Besides the beautiful creative materials you've produced for the event, if your staff working the desk is sitting there eating a sandwich and drinking a Coke, that leaves a different impression than if the staff is standing, shaking their hand and smiling.

Like it or not, with events, the first impressions are lasting ones. Capturing the touch points and experience can provide you with invaluable planning and follow-up information. ethnoMETRICSsm Corp., is a company that specializes in conducting pricing and purchase experience market measurement and analysis utilizing lean six sigma methodology in the retail and exhibition industries. It compiles data with the traditional attendee card swipe information. However, they strategically place video cameras throughout the event to measure the effectiveness of trade show booths.

"Point of purchase, advertising, displays, and other marketing, spending buckets in the retail and trade show venues; this type of metrics has been designed to help companies display, price, and sell the maximum amount of product at the highest margin possible," says Martin Smith, President, ethnoMETRICS.org. "In turn, optimizing their spending dollars and maximizing the ROI, they provide an enticing purchase experience that will result in heightened sales and customer loyalty."

With events, the selling is more of qualifying and trying to understand how to get to the next steps in the deal. In measurement, the first impression begins the touch points. Let's make one thing clear as well, we all know why these events are held: to build relationships and accelerate the next step in the sales process! There is no need to be oblique about this objective. Your guests know that you aren't there for your health, so don't beat around the bush. Routinely put you and your prospects together into environments that promote business.

LEVERAGING AND MEASURING PROMOTIONAL ITEMS AND GIVEAWAYS

In the pharmaceutical world, giveaways are like penny candy. So much free product exchanges hands, at times it looks like a feeding frenzy. In the education market, teachers are the first to take advantage of free books, presentation tools, and any type of equipment. Executives, on the other hand, limit what they take and it's traditionally based on what they want, think is cool, or need.

In each scenario, money becomes the first variable, Look what it costs for the bag or package, the goodie item itself, shipping to the conference site, and distributing it on-site. ShowValue has an interesting system they use for monitoring and measuring this component of an event strategy in a trade show environment. The first time an attendee badge is scanned, a message comes up on the screen and a consistent script pops up: "Have you had a chance to check our XYZ product?" The second time the attendee comes to your booth the system puts up a message that says: "I see that you have received our 'product bag.'" The next custom message appears: "Have you had a chance to look over any of the products?" What you are delivering is the benign message to the person that you're not getting a second one. "We just ran an interesting report for a client," explains Ken Mortara, "At the end of a four-day trade show, we found they had about 3,000 people who came once, 375 came twice, 125 people came three times, and then 15 people that came four times, and no one came five or more times. So what they did was dramatically reduce the cost of their giveaway program and that translated in thousands of dollars."

At some point in your event cycle, there will be a commitment to event measurement. Lead capture forms are such a simple way, but the difficulty is having the information filled out. You need it filled-out to be able to measure your objectives. However, never forget the power of your gut instinct and contribute your comments to the measurement initiatives.

It's traditional to hold a briefing with your on-site team prior to the event opening. (See Chapter 8 on leads.) Typically, the briefing covers: logistics, messages, and promotional activity. Rarely, is measurement even mentioned or included. By simply announcing that you have a lead capture and measurement initiative in place, you've made incredible strides. What you want your on-site team to understand is your goal to improve the leads delivered.

You'll also want to reiterate that the leads be entered into the events database or Customer Relationship Management (CRM) application. If you have a paper system on-site, you will have to do manual data entry and hire a temp for a few days, and there's room for error. Alternatively, you can scan the lead capture forms and pick the data up that way. Keep an eye out for technology advancements in this area from handheld devices like those used on the TV shows *America's Home Videos* and *Who Wants to Be a Millionaire,* to BlackBerrys and PDAs, to your personal mobile phone. New ideas to capture and process attendee information are popping up all the time.

There's been a movement over the last several years that more and more companies only want electronic means of data capture. It's quick, efficient, and targeted. There are also some negatives. One is the cost. For example, putting out enough terminals at a conference where people can go after the session ends is the challenge. Do the math: 100 of your top customers have just come out of your breakfast presentation. They're running to their next session and you've got five computer stations set up outside the room in the foyer area in the hotel. The first five customers line up and within minutes the terminals are eight people deep. What do you think the odds are of you capturing their ROE at that time? A paper alternative in this scenario would actually work better. Paper lead capture forms are easy to use, cheap, and people know how to use them. They are very effective, but for a lot of companies they are viewed as a low-tech solution and that's not the image that they want to project. Think about what tools are appropriate and at what time.

By outsourcing event measurement you'll get the following:

- A third-party firm just does it better—it's their living.
- A third-party firm validates your results.
- A third-party firm uses the latest technology and methodologies.

Because developing a measurement plan is so laborious and frustrating, I've chosen to adopt the "Seven Step Process for Measurement Success," created by ShowValue. Here's why it works in relation to the EventBLT. "Seven Steps" starts out with the notion of setting the objectives: thinking about the impact to the sales process, why you are spending the money, why you're allocating the budget, why you're making the investment in a particular event, or any other opportunity that you have for event marketing. Then, the next step is to develop the measurement plan, in writing. Let everybody see it and sign off on it, it becomes real. Once the objectives are outlined and the plan is written, the next step is to create the survey instruments, which can be different depending on what the objectives are. In the plan they define what the instrument should be.

"If the event is a reaction sheet for a seminar, we typically do a paper evaluation form because it has the benefit of people being able to do it immediately," says Ken Mortara. "After the forms are created and the event has been executed, we recapture all of the data. First, tabulate the results so you will know what you are looking at. Next, analyze against the objective and try to look at the various effects of different conditions. One of the things we always advise is to have some segmentation kinds of questions. Is this about experience, age, or education, and is it pertinent to the event? The last component, and probably the most important in terms of the long-term effect, is to pull it into some sort of very professional executive-level report. For the most part, the reports I tend to see are very, very detailed, very analytical, and 20 pages long, and when you put it in front of someone they get the glazed-over look. We strongly advocate a one-page executive summary which people can read and will read, and then having all the supporting information followup."

Here is ShowValue's seven step process. It's not a religion, it's a process. I found that it works and when you take shortcuts it dramatically impacts your results. I would love to say that I follow this process every time I set out to do an event program. It's simply not the case. Most times it comes down to budget issues. Companies want the results, but they don't want to expend resources, time, training, or budget dollars in this area. The methodology is a very effective tool for making sure that you're capturing good, relevant information and that you're producing a report that carries some value. You'll also want to make certain that this information is easily imported into your event database or CRM solution, such as salesforce.com.

Seven Steps to Measurement Success:

1. **Define Measurable Objectives.** To be measurable, objectives must be quantifiable. Defining objectives such as the dollar volume of sales influenced, quantity and quality of sales leads, speaker ratings, range of positive-to-negative perceptions, and increased brand awareness. These form a solid basis for authoritatively demonstrating the effectiveness of your events program.

2. **Develop a Measurement Plan.** Methodology will differ, depending on the objectives being set and the type of event being measured. Mapping out a plan detailing the survey method(s), target audience, and associated time frames is critical to a successful measurement strategy.

3. **Create Survey Instruments.** Simply stated, you cannot analyze data you don't capture. Questions, and the selections you offer, must be clear, concise, appropriate for your targeted audience, and crafted to avoid errors and bias. And, they must support your stated objectives.

4. **Capture Data.** Data capture is a deceptively complex step which requires a thorough understanding of traffic flow dynamics, timing, and potential use of incentives to achieve optimum results.

5. **Tabulate Results.** Assembling the data, imputing results, calculating averages, and ensuring the accuracy of cross tabulations, are all critical elements leading to a clear understanding of whether objectives were successfully met.

6. **Perform Business Analysis.** Analysts with in-depth experience in events and business, scrutinize data to demonstrate event value and identify areas of success and areas for improvement.

7. **Produce Executive Report.** The final step in the process results in a document that is appropriate for all levels of management, including the executive office. A professionally prepared report proclaims the value of the information presented and leads the reader through a process of discovery.

ShowValue
http://www.showvalue.com

Chapter

10

THOUGHT LEADERSHIP

Our mantra:
Event Marketing is all about facilitating, easing, opening, accelerating, and shortening the sales cycle. That's it!

Is thought leadership attainable? I've heard the term described as everything from "intellectual property and capital" to, "Geez, that guy's an expert." Companies today market their thought leadership and it is based on expertise, knowledge, and a visionary mindset. The sales pitch does NOT fall into thought leadership. You will rarely hear a thought leader talk about products, services, and solutions. Thought leaders are "evangelists" for your company and thought leadership, whether you want to believe into it or not, is here to stay.

By taking a look at your event strategy, you have the foundation for a community where you can be identified as a thought leader. Your job is events, not the whole world. With each event there is a circle (your business environment). The circle represents: employees, customers, partners, press, and analysts. From this circle you can determine who will represent your company as the designated thought leaders. The "persons" selected will be at the forefront and will be able to live up to what they claim. This

Tip

What's a Thought Leader?

A thought leader is a recognized leader in one's field. What differentiates a thought leader from any other knowledgeable company is the *recognition* from the outside world that the company deeply understands its business, the needs of its customers, and the broader marketplace in which it operates.

Elise Bauer of The Pacifica Group
http://www.pacifica-group.com

is why consistent messaging is so important and their knowledge and charisma can fuel the brand equity. Yes, there are people behind the brand that live and breathe it.

Many people believe with events, you can buy your way into creating the perception that your company representatives are thought leaders. Events do NOT create thought leaders, they SHOWCASE thought leadership. The expertise, knowledge, and vision are what make the individual become the thought leader.

Each organization has their own identity with executives and subject matter experts. For events, it's up to you to leverage the individuals within your company to further your message. Just like sales, you'll need to engage a relationship with those in your company that will be touted to be the thought leaders. They need to trust you. You'll build and earn that trust through the successes you achieve with your overall event strategy. The tactical implementation will come "event by event," as reflected in that show's specific event plan.

Identifying who in your company can be used strategically at an event for speaking engagements, meetings, and networking will take some work on your end. In this stage, you still need Sales' input as to who in your organizational structure or among your third-parties should be included in the program. What's so impressive is that someone like Bill Gates from Microsoft would fit in multiple categories, based on everything from his vision in technology to his philanthropic initiatives.

THOUGHT LEADERS AT-A-GLANCE

In most companies you can segregate thought leaders into two sections. Some people fall under both categories, and there is actually a "Paid presenter" category as well.

1. *Internal:* Board of directors, evangelist, executive, founder, subject matter expert
2. *External:* Analyst, customer champion, editor/journalist reporter, speaker

- *Both:* Author, lobbyist, philanthropist
- *Paid presenter:* Celebrity

Look at possible candidates from within your company and also review the following list of thought leader types. Following the category descriptions is a "cheat sheet" for you to fill out and reference. (See Figure 10.1) Keep a copy in your daily calendar for those last-minute emergencies.

Internal—Thought Leaders

- *Board of Directors.* A group of individuals usually with diverse backgrounds elected to the board of your company. The president of the company reports to the board, but may also be chairman of the board. A board member's responsibility ranges from management policy issues, to company direction, to providing an independent perspective. Board members usually have great contact lists as well.

- *Evangelist.* A passionate and loyal messenger.
- *Executive.* Usually has a vice president title or above, and includes all the CXO levels—Chief Executive Officer, Chief Security Officer, Chief Financial Officer, etc. (Depending on the company, this person is also known as the honcho, bigwig, or money man.)

■ **Hint:** This is the first audience that will complain, and they'll either do it right to your face or through one of their assistants, or worse, their significant other. Either way, the lack of understanding of what's expected here will get you every time. *(Authors note: I'm talking down to the "I hate mushrooms in my food" to the "I want to meet with ten customers, two press, and one analyst and, if I come to your event, I want my time booked with no downtime until 1:00 AM!)*

- *Founder.* Typically, the individual who originated, invented, created, or established the company, product, or service.
- *Subject Matter Expert–internal.* Someone who is considered a specialist. This person is highly knowledgeable about a specific topic or product.

Tip

Spouse of an Executive

It is a good idea to brief spouses/significant others on company messages and to include them in communications. Some may not find the information interesting, but many will. It allows the spouse to understand how a partner is spending the majority of the day and presents the spouse with the chance to embrace and support the company's goals and values.

Incorporating a spouse into an event program can prove invaluable from initiating conversations, to networking on a partners' behalf.

Sarah Woodberry Trauner
President
Woodberry Events
http://www.woodberryevents.com

External—Thought Leaders

- *Analyst.* This person is a specialist who conducts independent research on the performance and prospects of companies, markets, or economies, and publishes reports on their findings. There are market research analysts and financial analysts. Many analysts have a team of people working on their efforts.
- *Customer Champion.* The biggest fans of your company, product, or service willing to speak on your behalf. These are people that are passionate about what your company does and will endorse you to the outside world. At an event, telling the story from your customer's perspective increases your success when creating your EventBLT.
- *Editor/Journalist/Reporter.* They are individuals who provide a totally independent perspective about your offering. Leveraging their expertise can be executed through their hosting or moderating an event or a panel discussion.
- *Speaker.* Hired to present a motivational speech or provide insight into a specific topic, a fee is usually required for their services. The National Speakers Association is comprised of more than 3,800 professional speakers.

Internal and External—Thought Leaders

- *Author.* The writer or creator of the intellectual property. A body of work that includes the written word or a creative piece.
- *Lobbyist.* A person who attempts to influence the legislative process.
- *Philanthropist.* A person who donates time or mega-money to help those in need.

Tip

Customer References and Event Marketing

For customer references, which is a budding professional service in high-tech marketing organizations, you must be tightly linked to events marketing. The events marketing staff puts on various events whether it's a major conference, a CIO Summit, or a product-focused panel to support a regional sales team.

A customer reference team is responsible for securing the customers for the events. While the events staff produces the various components of the event such as the content and the agenda, a customer reference team makes sure the customer speakers are briefed and can speak appropriately to the topic.

The goal is to take care of your customers when they are acting in a reference capacity. Make sure they are on message, are thoroughly briefed on any sensitive topics, and that they know their audience. They also must know every detail of their travel and logistics.

Since customers are generously giving your company their time when they speak at events, it's up to the customer reference organization to make sure their trip is as comfortable and easy as possible.

For example: "Our custom reference team relies heavily on the events marketing team and we know we can count on them to take good care of our customer references. They understand that we count on them to help maintain these customer relationships so we can go back to the customers for repeat speaking events. Our goal is to understand what our events marketing team is doing and what their plans are so that we can develop customer reference assets accordingly."

Start planning customer reference activities, such as videos and white papers, six months in advance of your largest events. It's critical that you plan in advance and that you have customers to support your key messages at the event, whether it's in a press release or a speaking slot.

Lara Shackelford
Director of Marketing
(Ten years at a large enterprise software provider)

Paid Presenter—Thought Leaders

- *Celebrity.* An individual who has achieved a great deal of fame and is widely recognized in the public eye. Status is achieved through sports, entertainment, political achievements, and now, "reality or media driven" recognition. Can be found through a speakers' bureau or an entertainment agency.
- *Mascot.* A character that represents your company or brand and is considered to bring good luck, such as Ronald McDonald or the Philly Phanatic. It's a stretch for most of my colleagues to put mascots in the thought-leader category. Most find it's a brand component. Others consider a mascot in many circles to be a "celebrity." In sports, they are required to do public appearances. Do you have a mascot that you can leverage?

SPEAKING ENGAGEMENTS

For thought leadership, events provide a forum for your company to talk about more than just the products and solutions, it is an opportunity to really talk about what's impacting your target market, the end users out there. Any time your company secures a speaking engagement at an event, it's an opportunity to discuss the issues and present your vision. Remember, this is not a sales pitch.

Basically, the individual that is positioned as the thought leader can impact your lead generation activities and brand recognition. If your thought leaders are dynamic at presenting the information, your company can reap great benefits. Any person that speaks on behalf of your company should go through media training where your thought leaders are taught everything from voice projection, to responding to audience questions, to body language.

Tip

Engaging and Managing Paid Presenters (speakers or celebrities)

- Start with a realistic budget.
- Write a scope of work, include:
  - Amount of time, how long they should speak or perform
  - What topics or messages you want covered or integrated
  - Add personal items like signing autographs
    - *Hint:* Even for a concert, the same rules apply.
- Select a reputable firm and read the celebrities' bios before making your initial selections.
  - View their videotape and biographies
  - Ask for references
  - Match the paid presenter to the message you want to convey
- Get internal approval and build enthusiasm for the selection.
- Negotiate directly with the speakers' bureau, agent, or manager.
  - Review the rider. This will advise you as to likes and dislikes. Read it carefully before you agree and make sure you deliver to specification.
  - Request additional time for public and private meetings.
    - Ask paid presenters to work the booth on the show floor or dine with VIP customers and executives.
  - Offer to exchange product or services for a lower fee.
  - Commit to purchasing their books or DVDs and offer it as a promotional item to your target audience.
    - Brand their items with a "compliments of" tag and an autograph.
  - Leverage the destination—if a desirable location
    - Offer to extend hotel room nights
- Brief them thoroughly on your three key messages and provide easy-to-understand reference material in advance.
    - *Hint:* Send a briefing package in advance with a company brochure. Articles are very helpful. Include an executive giveaway item.
  - Give them a chart and photos (if you've got them) of your key executives and customers.

- Be super nice and go out of your way, even if you are paying them a lot of money. You will get a far better engagement.
  - Keep in mind, they have full-time jobs whether in sports, entertainment, or politics. Your event is just another thing on their to-do list.
  - Send a thank you note after the event

FIGURE 10.1 *Thought Leader's Roles and Responsibilities*

Description	**Presenter** ***(includes: Contact Name, E-mail, Mobile Phone #)***	**Bio & Abstract**	**Event**	**Activity**	**Availability**
Analyst					
Author					
Board of Directors					
Celebrity					
Customer Champion					
Editor/Journalist/Reporter					
Evangelist					
Executive					
Founder					
Lobbyist					
Mascot					
Partner Champion					
Philanthropist					
Subject-Matter Expert					

- On-site you'll see an up tick to other activities you're doing, from increased attendance to your booth to scheduled meetings during the event.
- If there are members of the press or analysts in the audience, your company could be quoted in their articles or position papers.

Thought leaders in your company are evangelists. The key is to use them effectively in your live presence environment.

Your event strategy will be stronger if you have speaking engagements in the mix. When you decide on the marketing activities for each individual event, speaking engagements should be at the top of your list. A conference agenda and the quality of speakers or presenters is the first area in which an attendee looks to decide whether or not they should sign up for the event.

Speaking engagements are coveted and traditionally hard to get unless you buy your way in, or you are so hot that organizers are knocking your door down. Speaking engagements are also one of the major reasons why companies host their own events.

Tip

Speak

Identify trade shows and conferences that customers and industry influencers are attending and get on panels or lead workshops. Find out about local associations that host speaking events and submit yourself for giving a talk. Again, focus on providing useful information. No one wants to listen to you pitching your product. You are there to inform and educate, to provide a unique perspective.

Elise Bauer of The Pacifica Group
http://www.pacifica-group.com

There are usually three types of speaking engagements:

1. *Keynote Address:* The crème de la crème of speaking opportunities. It opens a conference and sets the tone for conference theme and message. It is held at what's referenced to as general session and all conference delegates are in attendance.
2. *Breakout Session:* Throughout the day educational tracks are run usually for smaller groups with a drill-down on the topics at hand.
3. *Panel Discussion:* Features a moderator and guest panelists who are subject-matter experts in their field.

Tip

Archive the Content and Presentations from a Proprietary Event

Just because an event is over, it's not really over. There are at least two to three months of followup that's usually done.

Keynote addresses and breakout sessions are rich with content that should be repurposed. This great resource can be used for your Positioning and Messaging Framework, as well as for sales tools

- Videotape or stream the sessions and post to your Web site during or post-event.
- Audiotape the various sessions and transcribe the presentations.

Check-out these resources:

Same Day Transcriptions—Web-based service that outputs audio files and written documentation. *http://www.samedaytranscriptions.com*

Conference Archives—provides technology solutions for distributing archives of conference educational sessions via the Internet. *http://www.conferencearchives.com*

A few years ago, I worked for a client that retained the services of Blanc & Otus, a PR firm with five offices worldwide that employs former journalists, to corporate communications executives, and to events managers. I found it interesting that their firm had an entire division dedicated to events. "With any good public relations work, the ultimate goal is to get our clients' targets (i.e., prospects) and not change their buying behavior, but get them to start buying our clients' products or services and/or thinking about them in new ways," says Greg Spector, Chief Executive Officer, Blanc & Otus. "Events can be a powerful way to influence and to affect that kind of change."

When you build your event strategy, the PR plan should work hand-in-hand. "The first link is down and dirty research and looking at your company's competitor," says Cece Lee, Account Director and Conference Strategist for Blanc & Otus. "Where are the competitors speaking and how are they positioning themselves in the marketplace? Sometimes you'll do a media analysis and it's different from what they're saying publicly. You can't go out there and just talk about topics that don't map back. If your media messages are different from your conference messages, your audience is going to see that. It will be a transparent disconnect! Included in the research phase is audience qualification, we look for events that match the target audience they want to reach. The final stage is how to leverage your presence at the event, from speaking opportunities to one-on-one coverage."

There are two ways speaking engagements can be included in the event strategy. Both ways showcase your thought leaders.

1. *Free.* You submit a session abstract and bio which are evaluated and hopefully accepted by the show organizer. Sometimes the same organizer will build an entire event around your industry, product, or service. If it's your own event, obviously it's free to you, but you may offer your partners "time–a speaking opportunity" to share their views.

2. *Pay to play.* You negotiate (for a fee) placement of your thought leader. A breakout session at a conference should be negotiated as part of your marketing sponsorship opportunities. The ultimate goal is to have your thought leaders speak at the conference's general session.

To secure a speaking engagement, the first step is to look at the strengths and weaknesses of the people who are representing your company as the thought leaders. A standard requirement in securing speaking engagements is to develop an abstract and a bio. Cece Lee from Blanc & Otus explained this process to me in detail. I've summarized her approach and added some tips of my own.

Here's an 11-step checklist of how to proceed in securing speaking engagements, followed by a speaker resumé checklist (Figure 10.2):

1. Look at the list of thought leaders you are seeking to present as a speaker to the conference manager. (See "Thought Leaders At-A-Glance" earlier in this chapter)
2. Develop a one-page biography, or bio, on each of your thought leaders. It's a marketing piece. Do NOT use bios that are normally on your Web site. Cece says, "It's not the bio the organizer wants to see. Your marketing piece should explain why the organizer should select your thought leader over your competitor's. A speaker's bio should include a detailed list of where they've spoken before, detailed articles in which they've been quoted and on what topics, if they've written books, and what is the perspective they bring to the conference at hand."

■ **Hint:** If you are hosting your own events, I strongly recommend conducting the abstracts and bio exercise because this documentation will keep your agenda content organized and provide you with key points for your Positioning and Messaging Framework, which will be used to create your visual materials

3. Develop an abstract that addresses the issues of the conferences and the topic that best matches what you can deliver. An abstract for an event is a short and compelling summary of the presentation you'd like considered for inclusion in the agenda.
4. Fill out the paperwork (on time and submit as requested). Abstracts are usually due six to eight months prior to the actual date of the event.
5. Call conference organizers in advance to get a sense of how they're looking. A good question to ask is: "Can you provide me with some insight as to what your audience really wants to hear, based on last year's survey results?"
6. Be proactive–don't rest on your laurels and don't fall into the trap of thinking your job is done. Follow up with the organizers to see if the info you submitted is a fit. If not, discuss in detail so you can pitch additional ideas. Remember to check for last-minute cancellations and be ready to go.

■ **Hint:** If a submission deadline has passed, chat with organizers about what's missing and be ready to pitch a new idea or story on the spot.

7. Panel discussions are a great way to get noticed. Consider including a competitor. It doesn't mean you have to have your main competitor there, but you do want to have a contrary opinion on that panel, someone who is able to present a different perspective. Adding a partner, customer, or editor gives the panel abstract more punch.

■ **Hint:** Promote the panelists with their bios and session details in your event marketing activities.

8. Engage your thought leader(s) early on to make sure you schedule the time on their calendars. Schedule well in advance, not days before, and double-check because this will nail you every time.

■ **Hint:** Make sure people show up. Confirm and reconfirm. Find out what their arriving and departing dates are, as well as their mode of transportation. Then, the day before, call to say, "Looking forward to seeing you tomorrow at date, time, place, and room name. Leave your mobile phone number for any last-minute changes (which will happen).

Make it worthwhile. Time is valuable. Work with Sales and your PR team to arrange for customer-, prospect-, editorial-, and analyst-related meetings.

Have an emergency back-up plan, just in case someone flakes and doesn't show up. What would you do?

9. Prepare the thought leader(s) in advance with key messages you want them to get across during the speaking engagement.
   - Develop and review the presentation. Typically, this includes PowerPoint slides and/or multimedia support.
   - Create a briefing kit. By setting the correct expectations you'll eliminate confusion. The information in this kit should include logistics and key messages.
   - Distribute everything in advance.
10. Enhance the live speaking engagement.

■ **Hint:** Do an in-chair drop featuring a postcard with a new product announcement with call-to-action, special offer, and branded promotional item.

11. Be seen. Attend even if you don't sponsor. Sending your thought leaders as a conference registrant has great advantages.

■ **Hint:** While the registration fee and travel and expenses (T&E) could be as high as $4,000, all the right people (your target audience) will be there and "it pays to be seen." In some cases, it could be just as important as speaking.

FIGURE 10.2 *Speaker Resume Checklist*

Materials	Checklist
Speaker biography that includes responsibilities at current company. What is his/her most important success at the company (e.g., spearheaded $1.2 million in cost savings by implementing supply chain efficiencies)?	
Speaker's full contact information, including assistants	
List of the speaker's previous speaking engagements from the past two years in the following format: conference name (month year), level of opportunity, and presentation title or title of the panel.	
Areas of expertise	
Past presentations (if available)	
300 dpi electronic head shot in .tif or .jpeg format	
List of most relevant news coverage in the past 6 months featuring the speaker in the following format: publication (date published), title of article, by author	
List of professional affiliations and board memberships	
List of personal or professional awards received. When did you receive them?	
Conference referrals, including phone number and e-mail address (if available)	
Conference evaluations. List score received (e.g., 4.5 out of 5) and from which conference.	
Testimonials from moderators or conference organizers	

Provided by: Blanc & Otus, Conference Strategies (CLS)

Tip

Gain Speaking Success

Today's speaker is challenged, perhaps as never before. He or she has to be even more convincing and work harder at holding an audience used to communicating in bullet points rather than flowing rhetoric. So, how do you grab and keep your audience's attention?

Here are eleven pointers that can help lead to a more interesting and lively presentation.

Public Speaking Success

1. Beware of electronic dependency.
2. Be prepared for possible electronic malfunctions.
3. Don't leave your personality behind.
4. Use guideposts.
5. Face up to the situation.
6. Vary your rhythm and speed.
7. Project yourself.
8. Add color and intensity.
9. Try word painting.
10. Practice makes perfect.
11. Have fun!

Beware of Electronic Dependency

The electronic and computer age has made us lazy, giving many a false sense of security. We have grown to rely on sophisticated sound systems, lulled into thinking that a good microphone will amplify and enhance our words. However, it is not unusual for audiovisual equipment and microphones to malfunction, or for digital presentations to fail because an appropriate adapter or other integral part is missing. Perhaps you discover a corrupted PowerPoint file on your computer at the last minute, or your Web browser malfunctions for a live presentation.

(continued)

Are You Prepared for Possible Electronic Malfunctions?

Practice your presentation as if you had no microphone or visual to rely on. Ask yourself whether your voice is projecting sufficiently. Can you motivate your audience with your verbal delivery? Be prepared for any situation, and you will have a better overall delivery, and greater confidence to handle any eventuality.

Don't Leave Your Personality at the Door

Your friends and colleagues usually prize you for your unique qualities. However, often when a speaker is in front of the podium, suddenly he or she becomes someone else . . . someone far more stiff, formal, and constrained. It's like walking into a room and leaving your personality behind. Don't be afraid to be you, to let your emotions in and color your presentation. People who are connected to their emotions make far more compelling speakers.

Use Guideposts

In the course of my public speaking seminars someone will invariably ask about using a script or cue cards. Many people are under the misconception that it is wrong to read from a prepared text. Nonsense! A text serves as your road map.

What polished speakers know is that the real trick is delivering your presentation so that the audience thinks it is spontaneous, even though you may be reading from a text. If you are reasonably confident, boil the main points down to 5 × 7 cards with major headlines. Whichever way you prefer, make sure that the type is large enough for you to read your notes or your script, and that you are comfortable with handling the pages or cards.

Face Up to the Situation

It's fine to read from a script or cue cards. However, the trick is to let the audience know you're talking to them. When following a script, be sure to study it well in advance so that you can scan ahead and look up at your audience. Don't bury your face by looking down; and, for women, be sure that your hair does not cover your face. Let your face and your eyes speak, conveying emotion and variety with both your expression and your voice.

Vary Your Rhythm and Speed

In our fast-paced, digital world, the "new" communications style forces us to deliver increasingly compact messages. As a result, we have become so used to speaking fast that we often trip over our tongues, swallowing or gulping the words down. In live presentations, the listener needs time to digest information. Just like the song, "Fascinatin' Rhythm," altering the pace and speed at which you speak can add interest and variety. For instance, slow down to emphasize a phrase or sentence. Don't be afraid to pause before and/or after an important point. A good pause gives the listener an opportunity to digest what you have to communicate, and underscores the importance of the point.

Project Yourself

When speaking before a smaller group, say 50 or fewer people, a microphone can actually be an obstacle to intimacy between speaker and listener. Learn to project your voice so that you can be heard without a mike. Good breath support is the key to being heard. While proper breath control takes time to learn, you can get off to a good start by breathing deeply and being sure to use, not hold, your breath while you speak. Deep breathing also helps to calm jittery nerves and stagefright butterflies.

Color and Intensity

Add interest by "coloring" your voice. Experiment with beginning and ending your phrases on a higher or lower pitch. Add expression by "trying on" different emotions as you practice your presentation. And, verbally "lean into" those words you want to emphasize.

(continued)

Word Painting

Learn to infuse your words with meaning. Think of using words the way a painter would use color, texture, and form to communicate. What are the primary words you want to emphasize, what are the background words and phrases?

Practice Makes Perfect

No matter how good your speech, practice makes perfect. Practice delivering your presentation until you are comfortable with it. Audiences are smart—they can tell when you haven't done your homework. Become aware of what you like and dislike in other speakers, and try to incorporate some of the positive attributes into your presentation.

Let the Sun Shine Through

Also, having fun and imparting a sense of enthusiasm will energize and interest your audience. Let your personality shine through your presentation. By being yourself, you will add credibility and believability. And, remember, just as there is no substitute for the experience and impact of live theatre, there is no substitute for old-fashioned public speaking . . . even in the 21st century.

Linda Kundell
Public Speaking Coach
http://www.publicspeaking4u.com

PRESS AND ANALYST RELATIONS

Again, with events and as it relates to thought leadership, the key is leveraging the body of work developed and output from the PR and analyst relations side. Usually, this is managed by a PR firm or internally could be handled by a marketing or PR manager. I have found that the most success I've had in events is when the PR engine runs parallel with and integrates into the event strategy. What PR does for events is that it maps to the larger message that the company is seeking to achieve and accomplish.

Press/media and analysts provide you with a channel to communicate and validate your key messages. A lot of time, money, and resources are spent cultivating relationships with these two audiences. The efforts are ongoing and unlike advertising where you can just pump out a lot of media placements on a set schedule, you cannot just turn your PR and analyst relations initiatives on and off. In some cases, these two groups are the cornerstone and become the outlet for your thought leadership positioning.

In certain industries, analyst relations is continuing to grow very rapidly because of their influential objective role in the marketplace. Analysts, for example, will even help you construct your messages. This is not for free. Your company would retain (for a fee) an analyst firm. Research reports, white papers, and one-on-one briefings would all be included in the contract fee. Many times these same firms hold their own events. When an analyst firm becomes the event organizer, you have a built-in target audience: their qualified clients. Remember, if you've been invited to sponsor, so have your competitors.

Press and analysts provide an independent view of your offering and their articles or reports "influence" the action of your target audience. The sales tools/collateral you've already produced (see Chapter 7) should be leveraged and used as support resources.

There are some basic guidelines that hold true much across all events and it's important to match the thought leader to the constituent.

- Press: General, business or trade
- Analyst: Financial or market

Tip

Cultivate the Press

Don't leave it solely to your PR agency. If you are the CEO or the VP of marketing of your company, you should have a list of 20 writers and editors who regularly report on your market. You should be calling them, meeting with them, and calling them some more. Journalists are very busy people, often working on ridiculous deadlines. When you call you need to give them something that they can use to make their life better—a lead, a story, some insight, a quote, customers they can talk to for quotes. Warning: Journalists have a sometimes well-deserved reputation for being incredibly curt, arrogant, and annoying. You may find this true or not. In any case, you need to treat them with respect. You need them more than they need you.

Elise Bauer of The Pacifica Group
http://www.pacifica-group.com

Press

Usually restricted to senior-level managers and above that your company has identified as authorized spokespersons. This means they can be quoted in the press. Events held for and by press require extra handling.

- If the press has been invited to your event, set up a press room for them to submit their stories.
- Arrange for a VIP meet and greet whereby one-on-one meetings are held. The messages become sound bites. Identify long-lead press and target accordingly.

Financial Analyst

Usually restricted to senior management, specifically the CEO or CFO who can speak to financial issues and regulations.

Events held for and by financial analysts range from quarterly conference telephone calls that may be supported simultaneously with an online application (WebEx, NetMeeting, etc.), to a two-day conference in an upscale resort location. You also need to be invited to sponsor.

Market Analyst

Multiple levels within a company can speak effectively about the company product managers to developers, and sometimes even the sales force. Events held for and by market analysts range from horizontal to vertical industry themes (i.e., healthcare security). Market analysts deliver the presentation (content) to the audience. Your goal here is to get your messages embedded in their presentation.

During an analyst presentation, representatives from your company should attend the session and "hang out" afterward to answer questions.

Tip

Analyst Meetings at Events: Prepare . . .

- Qualify the appropriate analysts.
- Book time on analysts calendar in advance.
- Notify your marketing team and thought leaders immediately.
- Prep all parties, including customers, the analyst, and thought leader, and brief them on the analyst's prior research

Tip

Analyst Relations

Market analysts are decision drivers and by having a laser focus to this audience you help sales.

- Customers seek analyst feedback when contemplating the buy.
- Press quote analysts for news stories and company profiles.
- Mentions in analyst research reports validate your position.
- Analyst firms hold conferences and analysts moderate panels.

Market analyst input is highly valuable when leveraged correctly.

- Provide insights on the competition.
- Recommend partnerships.
- Sales leads result from analyst meetings. Analysts do consulting work and solve very specific problems.
- Ongoing perception that you are a player.
- A good test market for new messages. It gives candid feedback on what resonates and what does not.

In addition to branded apparelwear, give your representative a branded portfolio to hold in their hand and show them how to hold it: logo face out!

THE VALUE OF AN ANALYST EVENT

Participating or partnering with an analyst firm can prove invaluable to your event strategy. You can sponsor or exhibit at a conference the analyst firm hosts, or engage the organization to speak (for a fee) at your company's proprietary events. For example, Gartner, the leading provider of research and analysis on the global IT industry, recognizes the core of their business is the senior technology buyer. Gartner events are designed to provide value to that constituency, by addressing their issues and by focusing on the specific technology areas in which *they,* senior IT, are focused on. The event environment has been designed with insight and education as its heart (based on Gartner's rigorous, independent research), and offers delegates varied opportunities to network and exchange information with leading technology providers and their peers. While it's the classic conference model, its laser focus on fact-based insight and custom solutions for the end-user provides a targeted event that technology companies seek to sponsor. The target audience is prequalified.

"It is important to understand that buyers and decision-makers have a myriad of industry events they can attend. But, if they *choose to attend an analyst event,* it's because they trust and rely on the insight of that analyst firm," says Alister Christopher, Senior Vice President, Worldwide Events for Gartner. "It behooves technology solution-providers to position themselves at those events relative to what industry analysts are saying about them, and to be part of the dialogue, rather than outside of it. We have many, many delegates who only attend Gartner events, and who tell us that they use our conferences to catch up with existing partners and evaluate future partners. So if a company (especially small-to-mid-size) is not present at one of our industry events, chances are slim that our delegates will seek them out through other channels or respond to pull marketing efforts."

"Having a strategy for connecting with key analysts at an event is often overlooked, but is just as important as having a marketing strategy for delegates," continues Alistair.

- Make contact well in advance of the event with important analysts.
- Spend time briefing them on what's new, products or services that will be unveiled at the event, etc.
- Never "jump" analysts at an event to introduce your product leads. This leads to frustration, as the analyst generally

likes to do premeeting research and come to the first meeting as prepared as you are.

- Be respectful of analysts' time and confine meeting requests to the hours outside of the core agenda. Remember, the analysts' first priority on-site is delivering presentations, having one-on-one meetings with delegates, and spending time on the show floor.

If you've been under the impression that the role of a PR firm or an internal public relations department was press and analyst coverage, you're right. What I've found over the years is the changing nature of PR and the role of "media-analyst" relationship which now includes participation in events. Don't get caught in the cycle of an event is happening, and three days before you're trying to figure out what to do in terms of PR. Marry the two together at the planning stage. If the event is something that happens at the last minute, then you'll have a foundation from which to pull information.

When you write your event strategy, consideration of press and analyst events should be top of mind. Companies that sponsor or host press and analyst events find the momentum helps them in *facilitating, easing, opening, accelerating, and shortening the sales cycle.* When you don't have a lot of news, events are a way to keep the momentum of a program going. Speaking engagements build a solid vertical strategy and provide a forum for high-profile recognition within an industry or market segment, or multiple industries or market segments.

Traditionally, a PR firm will assign an account team to every client and one person is designated as the lead. As an event marketer, it's important to befriend PR and integrate their initiatives into each event. *(Author's note: If you are an internal PR manager, the same principles apply.)*

- The account team maintains a contact database of the press and analysts your company targets. Prior to each event a review should be done on the exact people who are either preregistered or believe they should attend.
- The account team will schedule the briefings, do the inviting, and draft the messaging. From a logistics standpoint you may need to arrange meeting space, food and beverage, and support materials. Remember to brand the meeting space with notepads, pens, table tent cards, etc.
- Measuring the success of your PR and analyst programs is NOT originally based on the number of leads. In the short-term it's often measured on ROO (return on opportunity). It's not based on sheer numbers, it's the quality of the members in the audience and the coverage received, whether next day or six months from the event.

One of the benefits of using a PR firm like Blanc & Otus is that a lot of their work is repurposed for multiple clients. You have the benefit of leveraging other company's research and findings. At B&O, they have a proprietary database called the Conference Intelligence Resource (CIR). Every staff member in their agency has access to it. As a client of their firm, so do you, by tapping into their expertise. From a preplanning to postevent planning, it's an excellent resource. I find investing my event marketing budget in services like this actually puts money back into my budget. Blanc & Otus's CIR tracks everything from historical data about the conference to activities on behalf of their clients. I let them do the work since they've already got the established relationships.

Again, the messages you communicate should be consistent and should all support your over-arching initiatives.

When it comes to events and the PR process, here's what I find useful when it comes to announcing a deal or product.

What's the story? PR team interviews the customer, product management staff, as well as the sales lead to gather data for the press release, FAQs, etc. Press release is cycled between sales, marketing, and legal in all related organizations.

Time announcements. Clarification during the sales cycle to announce the deal at the time of closing, or product upon release or availability.

- Time the press release and announcement to the event schedule. It's a great hook for your events and so many companies forget to do timely announcements.
- Event team collaborates with customer or partner's marketing team on timeline and go-to-market strategy.

Develop a press release/briefing. Schedule meetings and telephone calls with reporters and market analysts.

- *Pre-brief 1:* High-level customer point of contact for technical lead brief market analysts
- *Pre-brief 2:* Executive-level briefing in advance of the news announcement crossing the wire

Press release hits the wire.

- On-site support materials match timing
- Web site communications updated
- Reuse and repurpose what's been written about you for future events

I would love to say there's a formula with events for press and analyst relations. When working on your event program, here are some things to keep in mind:

Tip

Press and Analyst Relations Make a Difference

1. Schedule meetings in *advance and extend the discussion.* Editorial and lead analysts are usually accessible at their own events. Be prepared with invitations to a private VIP dinner and possibly lure them with an exclusive meeting with a customer.
   - Review how you can leverage your existing relationships on behalf of your company.
   - Assess the topics being covered and match the press and analysts, deciding which individuals are important to you.
2. Treat press and analysts as VIPs. Cultivate the relationship. Treat this audience as you would treat your top customers.
   - Get a list of who's who at the event and brief your team. Don't be a stalker, but do stay on the look-out for these key people. *(Author's note: I know all customers should be treated the same. Okay, fine. But recognize that it doesn't happen that way.)*
3. Avoid panic. Putting customers in front of press and analysts panics everyone because you never know what someone's going to say.
   - Prep work is critical here. At events, set up prebriefing areas to go over key points prior to the meeting.

- Take advantage of the media list the conference organizer generates and match it to your own. Monitor the updates regularly up until the start of the actual event. Use all the tools available to you (e.g., virtual press room, media kit).
- Press kits. The online press room is HOT and has become the fastest way to deliver information. The formal press kit is NOT. The media does NOT want to carry a book around with them. From a print perspective, a one-page overview with a call-to-action, such as directing them to access more information via an exclusive URL, can be equally compelling. The press kit should not be replaced, just rethought. Think about the items you include in the kit carefully. Jour-

nalists are a touchy-feely bunch, so think about including a CD or a complimentary sample of your product.

- Regularly monitor the press room. Do you have enough media kits or do you need to replenish? During the event pick up other's materials and keep it as reference materials.
- Gift-giving: Yea or nay? Be careful here. It's okay to give a gift, but it needs to be useful or innovative and it must hammer home the message.
- Update your public and internal Web sites to reflect the same messages you're communicating at the event.
- Make sure your press release is featured on your home page.

Press and analysts are often categorized in the same crowd and attend the same conferences or events, but they do have different needs. It's all about what you are trying to accomplish with them at the event.

Let's say you're hosting a lunch seminar. You're previewing your hot new product for an elite group of prospects, customers, press, and analysts, and only high-level executives from your company are included. The luncheon is at the top-rated restaurant in the city where your corporate headquarters is located.

- Strategic seating. Seat the right people together to get your message out. The eight to ten people seated at your table are the messengers.
- No shows—You will have holes at each table since some do not show up (keep fillers on the side).
- Arrange a table host. Look to place a mix of folks and always have someone from your company as the host of that table.
- Assure that both press and analysts are the right advocates for these ideas.

Tip

Innovative PR Event

"Eight-Minute PR" is a concept Blanc & Otus adopted from the speed dating idea. The purpose is multi-fold. The evening event begins with cocktails and guests immediately get down to what's called the "round-robins." The rules of engagement are covered and then they're off. Every eight minutes a bell rings, there's a brief break, and then it's off to the next meeting. It's fun, fast, and produces results.

The events bring together a group of companies and journalists. The companies get eight minutes with each journalist to present who they are, what they do, what makes them different, but without the aid of PowerPoint or support tools. It's just talking and conversation and in this process we work with our clients to be able to communicate effectively and voice these ideas within the time frame.

The journalists enjoy it because they don't have to sit through long meetings to decide whether or not there is a good story here. This can be the beginning of a relationship; the beginning of a story idea that's all it needs to be, and to the clients' benefit because they get quick exposure to many journalists in an evening.

Greg Spector, President, and Cece Lee, Account Director and Conference Strategist
Blanc & Otus
http://www.blancandotus.com

Foresight and integration is what makes for a strong PR and analyst relations program. The last-minute stuff just guarantees a screw-up, but know that last-minute stuff will always pop-up. It's important to be solutions-oriented. Think on your feet. Proact, not react. Take the right amount of time and spend the money it takes to do it right, or don't do it at all, because if you don't do it well it's going to work against you. It's pretty basic thinking, but sometimes the oldest clichés ring true. By recognizing the needs of this audience and understanding that you are creating "events within events," you will create results.

PUBLISHING

The publishing community and broadcast media provide a great resource for branding, lead generation, and thought leadership for events. Technically, both the publication and broadcast media could be classified under "press," however, both provide a whole other level to the event mix. These media have loyal and passionate readers, viewers, and listeners. If partnered correctly, you'll have an outlet that will deliver the target audience you want to reach. Your press and analyst relations efforts are further realized with this environment. Interestingly though, there is still the matter of objectivity.

Up until the explosion of the Internet, print advertising was all about the page. It was basically the only thing a magazine publisher had to worry about. Today, the publishing community operates on multiple platforms often referred to as the "four pillars" in order to provide value to their readers and advertisers.

The four pillars are an integral part of a medium's strategy and are known as:

1. *Print*
2. *Online*
3. *Research*
4. *Events*

In order to compete for advertising dollars this mix gives an added boost to your event strategy since they deliver both your target audience (customers) and editorial. This is one of my favorite ways of delivering and leveraging events.

Consumer and trade magazines serve a particular market; read their media kits for complete details. Their media kits are loaded with audience profile data and purchasing trends. The publishing industry spends a fortune on market research. Publisher's media kits alone and their back-end research (they don't even share), can be great tools in your marketing efforts.

With magazines, there's an affinity between the editorial team and the readers. "The publishing community's primary job is to make the connection between the reader and the vendor (advertiser) who supplies the products and services. The editors are a conduit to the reader by providing them with new or timely information," says Mark Durrick, publisher of Eye Care Business, a trade publication.

The magazine's ad sales reps sell you a variety of marketing vehicles that provide you with ways to reach your target audience. The key to an event with a magazine is that the content is not a sales pitch. It is trend or vision related. It's objective and controversial. It's prevalidated before delivery and has shelf life. People spend the time reading. They'll even rip or print something out if they find it of particular interest. They have already warmed up to a particular idea or notion. With a face-to-face event or a Web cast the printed page from that magazine regarding your product or service comes to life.

One of the benefits in partnering with a magazine publication is that the events you'll create or sponsor with them are objective, scalable, and turnkey. The program structure features innovative content, compelling presentations, and current research. The events are editorially driven so both sponsors and attendee find value. Types of events that partner well with a trade magazine are seminars, peer-to-peer forums, summits, and Webinars. For consumer programs, you'll often find a publication like *Vanity Fair* sponsoring or hosting a large gala event but perhaps partnering with a charity or a liquor company.

Content is one of the hardest pieces to deliver at an event. I like publications because they have editors who deliver the message for you. These editors provide you with a voice and they can often bring out the best in what your company offers. Deciding to leverage a magazine's infrastructure at your event may be a

Tip

Leveraging Marketing Dollars

Print, broadcast, and billboard advertising is often forgotten about during an event. It's important to link together your marketing efforts. Using your advertising dollars and merchandising credits gives you greater leverage within your event strategy.

challenge. If you partner with a particular publication, it will allow you to achieve your initiatives based on these universal themes: *innovation* and *optimizing the business.*

Leveraging your product to find the pressure point:

- Grow the customer base
- Build new markets
- Create new sales opportunities
- Reduce costs
- Secure the business environment

Product feeds the pressure point:

- Creates the need for interactive resources that promote the mindset
- Opens the door for a forum dedicated to helping the target audience
- Demands cutting edge information be shared

From a marketing perspective, negotiating a deal with a magazine to co-brand an event program has other value-added benefits. Find your account rep and have your rep find out who else in your company they are working with. Research, sales lead generation, and advertising dollars can all come out of different budgets. The goal is to get all the constituencies together in a meeting and have a goal in mind, whether to sell product or increase brand recognition.

Tip

"Techniques for Effective Public Speaking"

Ten Tips for AudioVisual Presentations

1. Find out in advance what type of electronic equipment is available, and be certain that it is compatible with your visual aids.
2. Do dry runs in advance: test microphone levels and rehearse with the equipment and any personnel running the equipment.
3. Try to get into the room and have it set up as early as possible; check the lighting and find out who will control it.
4. Test all electronic equipment in advance to be certain it is working properly.
5. Keep slides and PowerPoint presentations as simple and visually interesting as possible.
6. Intersperse your presentation with blank slides to give the audience a pause and focus attention on you.
7. If using videotape, be certain there is enough leader at the beginning and end of your tape segments. Be certain that videotape is cued and rewound before presentation.
8. For safety, carry an extra set of your presentation with you. Backup your PowerPoint presentation onto a flash drive or CD, and carry it separately from your computer and presentation.
9. Have your presentation readily accessible on your computer's desktop.
10. Be certain your script has cues appropriately marked.

Linda Kundell
Kundell Communications
e-mail publicspeaking4u@aol.com or Speechdoctor@nyc.rr.com
http://www.publicspeaking4u.com

What's a Thought Leader?

A thought leader is a recognized leader in one's field. What differentiates a thought leader from any other knowledgeable company, is the *recognition* from the outside world that the company deeply understands its business, the needs of its customers, and the broader marketplace in which it operates.

Trust is built on reputation and reputation is generally NOT built on advertising. It is built on what others say about you. Become a thought leader in your field and it won't matter as much how big you are. Companies will look to you for insight and vision. Journalists will quote you, analysts will call you, Web sites will link to you.

How does one become a thought leader?

Before one takes the first actionable step, a fundamental shift in mindset is needed. Thought leadership requires a spirit of *generosity.* Generosity of one's time, intelligence, and knowledge. It requires a trust that by being open with what you know, and by sharing your time and knowledge, the world will reward your efforts. With that in mind, here are steps that will help you on your way to being a thought leader:

1. **Cultivate the press.** Don't leave it solely to your PR agency. If you are the CEO or the VP of marketing of your company, you should have a list of 20 writers and editors who regularly report on your market. You should be calling them, meeting with them, and calling them some more. Journalists are very busy people, often working on ridiculous deadlines. When you call you need to give them something that they can use to make their life better—a lead, a story, some insight, a quote, customers they can talk to for quotes. Warning: Journalists have a sometimes well-deserved reputation for being incredibly curt, arrogant, and annoying. You may find this true or not. In any case, you need to treat them with respect. You need them more than they need you.
2. **Write.** White papers, case studies. Prepare lists of useful resources. Show that you understand and care about the problems your customers are trying to solve. Assemble a valuable knowledge base of

materials that demonstrate, not only your expertise, but also your commitment to solving your customers' problems. Write industry specific pieces that have useful information for potential customers, rather than sales pitches for your products.

3. **Spread the word.** Get what you've written into the hands of anyone who might care. Submit articles to editors of newsletters, trade magazines. Post them on your Web site. Make them free and easily accessible. Put your name on them and give them to anyone who will listen.

4. **Speak.** Identify trade shows and conferences that customers and industry influencers are attending and get on panels or lead workshops. Find out about local associations that host speaking events and submit yourself for giving a talk. Again, focus on providing useful information. No one wants to listen to you pitching your product. You are there to inform and educate, to provide a unique perspective.

5. **Use your Web site.** Your site should be a source of useful information for customers, potential customers, and influencers. It is surprising that so many companies still view the Web as a place to park their corporate brochures versus a dynamic, highly interconnected exchange of knowledge. The Web is a *marketplace* of ideas, not a kiosk. Your site increases in value the more people know about it and link to it. The more reference-able your Web site is, the more it will be referenced.

6. **Unlock your white papers!** Don't make people register to learn more about you. You want as many people to know about you as possible. If you want to do lead generation, use direct response ads rather than holding the information on your Web site hostage. Be generous with your expertise. Or the market will favor someone else who is.

7. **Make thought leadership a strategic imperative for your company.** Ideas and insight do not require dominant market share or millions in capital expenditures. Your company does not need to

(continued)

be a leader in sales to be considered a thought leader (though of course, it doesn't hurt). In high tech especially, the rules of the game change so quickly that insight becomes currency. But, becoming a thought leader does require work and commitment. It demands the often difficult task of looking at your company from the perspective of the world outside. Most companies fail miserably at this. Generating an ongoing effort towards thought leadership is the best way to ensure that it actually happens.

Elise Bauer of The Pacifica Group
http://www.pacifica-group.com

Chapter

11

STRATEGIC PHILANTHROPY

Our mantra:

Event Marketing is all about facilitating, easing, opening, accelerating, and shortening the sales cycle. That's it!

Every day companies get requests for some sort of charity donation. Usually, the request flows to community affairs, HR, or the marketing department. At some point, it falls into the realm of events. This is called strategic philanthropy: the power that adding a charity component brings to your sales initiatives and business objectives while also doing a really good thing!

One component people miss all the time is the emotional hook. You need to hit them in their heart. It's about giving and giving back and still earning a profit. It's about the moment at the end of the day when you know you've made a difference in someone else's world. In business, events with this angle reap wonderful rewards and set you apart from your competitors. The key in this area is that it all makes sense. Does your positioning and messaging directly tie-in to the charity component you want to introduce and support? Consider this case study.

"It's a very funny thing about charities, not everybody relates to just one charity. I just had dinner with Colin Powell and we were talking about America's Promise (the program's focus is on teen volunteer opportunities) and some of his new initiatives for America's youth. I do believe that children are a great uniter," says Ray Lane, General Partner, Kleiner Perkins Caufield & Byers. "We were in Japan for the Special Olympics Winter Games. At a very special dinner honoring the board of directors, the city of Nagano presented taiko drummers for entertainment. The amazing thing was that they were all intellectually disabled and to my untrained ear sounded as professional as I've ever heard. Afterwards we spent a lot of time talking and dining with the performers, allowing us to put a face on each individual. Not only appreciating their art, but doing it in an inclusive manner."

People feel good when they are a part of something, whether it's helping children, people with cancer, or something else they can relate to. With corporate events, the key is finding the right philanthropic initiative so it that makes sense to your brand and message.

- *The scene.* In the 1990s, the technology industry worked together in developing the age progression technology used by the National Center for Missing and Exploited Children, or NCMEC. Each year during Comdex in Las Vegas a small graphics software firm hosts a Chili for Children Cook-Off benefiting the NCMEC.
- *Be seen.* The graphics firm created an entire sponsorship program where other software manufacturers and their competitors would buy-in for a fee (anywhere from $7,500–$50,000). The premise was for the 50 software manufacturers to submit a homemade chili recipe and serve it on-site to their distribution channel of 15,000 resellers in the con-

course of the Thomas & Mack Center. Beans, beans, they're good for your heart, and needless to say, it was a blast! Following the cook-off was a dance concert.

- *Overheard.* While the 50 head chefs were scooping chili, representatives from the respective sponsor companies were raising money via raffle items. At the height of the *Beanie Babies* craze, one color printer company purchased over 1,500 of these stuffed toys at the "mishpukah" price.
- *Branding.* Each toy was branded with a small button featuring the company logo. A *Warhol-inspired* company logo in four-color temporary tattoos were specifically made for the event—very inexpensive. An in-house artist created this design and the concepts were repurposed to decorate their chili concession-style kiosk.
- *Lead generation.* Resellers were lined 10 deep filling out contact info cards and on their cell phones or running to pay phones, calling home to find out what they should get. The Beanie's sold for over $10 a piece and all the proceeds went to the NCMEC. Over 5,000 people stopped by and the sales reps did all the followup, postevent.
  - The info cards contained the added incentive "enter to win the prized Princess Beanie," which was very hard to get.
  - Reps were positioned on the aisles as greeters/ "Beanie sellers," and each person received a tattoo stamped on his or her hand, similar to "in and out" privileges in a nightclub.
- *Thought leadership.* The PR and Event team pitched to the CEO the goal of showing how color printing makes a difference in the world. During the concert portion of the event, the announcement was made that the color printer company would replace the NCMEC black and white printers with color printers. So now when a photo of a

child was released to the media you could see hair, skin, eye color and distinguishing features such as freckles.

POSTEVENT

At the time, the NCMEC received photos of missing kids by fax or overnight mail, delaying the release to the media. So the color printer company took their donation to the next level and teamed with their hardware partner, Compaq, their software partner, Adobe, and their distribution channel, Kinko's, to provide parents and guardians a way to provide photographs immediately by walking into any Kinko's and arranging for photo distribution instantaneously to the media. Thus, a new initiative was executed.

The program launched with events in multiple cities in the United States and fell with the company's third quarter. Here's how the events were executed. This should provide you with some creative ideas to help you enhance a similar program.

- Speakers ranged from politicians to policeman to customers to celebrities.
- The guest list was VIP by invitation only. Over 500 customers, prospects, partners, press, analysts, politicians, and celebrities joined the gathering.
- Red carpet arrivals featured the company's logo and a photo gallery display of NCMEC missing kid stories as guests made their way to the registration table.
- Full-color name badges were given to each person.
- During the cocktail hour reception all food and beverages were served in black and white.

- During the 20-minute presentation regarding the ongoing efforts, the company announced that their donation was made on behalf of their customers.
- To showcase the recognition, the donation included a custom-designed print called a *Symbol of Hope.*
- Prints were output to various printers from the company's product line.
- Each print was framed and presented to customers at the events. The donation to the NCMEC was made in honor of the color printer's customers.
- After the presentation, a two-hour reception continued however, now serving full-color food and beverages; even the linen colors were changed out.

Think about the example and how technology and partnering made a difference in the world. Imagine a photo in black and white on TV of a missing kid today. In just a few short years after that, e-mailing photos over the Internet now takes a matter of minutes. This time is valuable and precious in such tragic cases.

Can you think of how your company can make a difference in the world? Look closely at what you do and create your event network to brainstorm ideas. To kick-start your thought process, one of the best ways to understand "strategic philanthropy" is to see a program in action.

Opts Ideas, based in New York and San Francisco, recently created and won four national awards and one international award for an event for the financial institution Washington Mutual. The goal was to introduce their brand and company to the New York market. Washington Mutual had acquired Dime Savings Bank and had a lot of stiff competition with established players like Chase, JP Morgan, and Citibank, and they wanted to communicate to New Yorkers who they were in a way that made them feel like they were not the "out-of-towners."

Business partners Michael Christman and Lisa Holland explain their unique program in detail. It's one of my favorite stories and I often reread their case study for inspiration (so I've included that, too).

Opts Ideas explains:

Spotlight on Teachers

We took a look at who Washington Mutual is, what their core values are, and created a series of events and programs that would introduce the brand to New Yorkers. One of the values is that Washington Mutual is actively involved in the community, and in particular with education, focusing on teacher development, recruiting, and retention. We created a program called Spotlight on Teachers that would be splashy, visible, news worthy, but also resonate with the core values and the community-based interest of Washington Mutual. After brainstorming ideas and working through various themes, we thought—"What if we bought every single seat on Broadway and then gave the tickets to teachers?" What was great about that was that no one had ever done it before. Broadway is clearly something that only exists in New York, and whether you are from out of town or in town, it has a deep and meaningful attachment to New York. By giving all the tickets to teachers, we also communicated Washington Mutual's commitment to education to the hearts and minds of New Yorkers.

The program took a number of months of development with a number of key stakeholders to get off the ground. It required hours of deep outreach with school boards, teacher unions, theater organizations, and civic and business leaders in Times Square. We had 100 percent support for the event program from Washington Mutual (sometimes referred to as WaMu). It was probably one of the largest regional marketing events that they had done. We closed a section of Times Square and had 28,000 teachers gathered for a pre show rally featuring a performance by Joel Grey and The Broadway Kids. The preshow event concluded with Deanna Oppenheimer, WaMu President, speaking from the stage and receiving a thunderous round of applause from 28,000 very happy teachers. The whole event was capped off by ticker tape falling from the sky (in WaMu colors, of course) then the teachers all went to see the shows. It was an incredibly moving experience for everybody and by being an integral part of the event the Washington Mutual team got to experience firsthand the value and emotion.

(Author's note: It's moving . . . compare that feeling to just seeing a video or photos of the event and a PowerPoint slide that shows how many people attended. Emotion is the relationship grabber.)

Programs like are a lot of fun and have a great pay-off. It's also a lot of work. I asked Lisa to explain what she actually did to make it happen.

"With the Opts Ideas outreach program it was all about one-on-one meetings. So we would find out who was the head of the New Jersey Teachers' Union, and who was the head of the Theater Development Fund, a nonprofit organization located on Broadway that was to make theater more available to educators. We had figure out who has a stake in Broadway, how to reach the teachers, and how to get the businesses in Times Square on board.

Just to get it off the ground, we worked with the heads of teachers' unions, heads of principals' unions, school boards, the president of the theater development fund, the head of the Schubert Theater, the head of the Times Square Business Improvement District. We created a little coalition of a broad range of people who would be involved in this program and had some stake in its succeeding. Our goals were to get them on board and integrated in a way that added value to the program.

Here's an example: we worked with the Times Square Business Improvement District that represent all of the merchants in the Times Square area. Now, they might have had an issue with this event because we were asking to close sections of the street to traffic on a Saturday for a long period of time, which potentially could mean a loss of revenue for them. We wanted to have them on board, and there had been a lot of uproar about events in Times Square, especially after the NFL had done their big kick-off event with Jon Bon Jovi, so it was important that we had everyone feeling good and positive about the program and how it could benefit them as well. We worked with the merchants and New

(continued)

York and Co., essentially the Visitor Convention Bureau, to offer the teachers attending this event special discount coupons to shops, restaurants, and are hotels—valid only that weekend and only to the teachers. The teachers had an added incentive to stay, shop, and experience that whole area, and the merchants had increased traffic, so everybody won in the exchange. The teachers felt like they got something special and the merchants and businesses in the area felt they got added value with additional marketing and increased revenue.

For the branding components, Opts Ideas designed a wide variety of materials. It included everything from posters to 3D point-of-sales tools. For lead generation, Opts designed a nomination form. The only way a teacher was able to attend this event was that they would be nominated by an individual who would drop off this form at a Washington Mutual branch. For thought leadership, Washington Mutual's president spoke, as well as NY dignitaries and education leaders.

For the next phase of the event, once we had our teachers that had been nominated and selected to win the tickets, we sent notification mailings to them with an appealing and an eye-catching twelve-page full-color magazine-style booklet entitled, "Broadway Bound," that had all the information they needed. It offered the discounts and it told the teachers how they could call and use a unique ID number to select the show they wanted tickets to, and how to use their experience on Broadway back in their classroom. We wanted to make sure that while we acknowledging the teachers and giving them something fun to experience, that this could also be something that they could take back to their classroom (again getting some more brand extension from the teachers talking to their students about the day they had at the show). We provided links to how they could get curriculum guides for each of the Broadway shows. The next piece they received was a final confirmation with their custom-printed tickets. Besides the typical Broadway ticket info: date, time, show, we had the special logo we designed and used throughout the event in conjunction with the Washington Mutual brand.

On the day of the event, we closed a section of 45th Street between (Broadway and 8th Ave) for about eight hours. We installed the stage, Jumbotron screens, hospitality areas, and then we had a preshow event with Mr. Broadway, Joel Grey performing. Also speaking to our elite group of teachers, was Deputy Mayor, Dennis Walcott, the president of Actors' Equity all alongside the President of Washington Mutual. We capped it off with a ticker tape parade and sent all 28,000 teachers marching through the streets of Times Square to see their shows. Events like this exude energy and power. You could feel it in the streets.

Our ROO included broadcast press coverage all over the New York metro evening news. The event received fantastic press coverage in the New York Metropolitan Area:

- The New York Times 11/7/02 Sunday edition ran a photo and caption. Many additional regional papers, including *Newsday,* picked up the story from the AP wire.
- Major broadcast coverage from local news stations: Fox 5 news and Eyewitness News ABC 7.
- From Mayor Michael Bloomberg's address read at the Times Square event: *"On behalf of the city of New York, I recognize those associated with Washington Mutual Bank for your efforts in making this afternoon possible and for rewarding the hard work of our teachers with a fun-filled afternoon at the theater. Spotlight on Teachers is an outstanding program and our teachers are most deserving of this wonderful recognition."*

A number of surveys were done afterwards and they indicated that postevent WaMu had moved up in brand awareness to second place, behind JP Morgan Chase.

There are many components that go into producing a great event. If you are looking for an emotional hook, strategic philanthropy should be included as an integral part of your event plan.

Michael Christman, President, Partner
Lisa Holland, Vice President, Partner
Opts Ideas, Inc.
http://www.optsideas.com

Chapter

12

MEETING TECHNOLOGY

Our mantra:
Event Marketing is all about facilitating, easing, opening, accelerating, and shortening the sales cycle. That's it!

Event management is a process. Today, technology rules our world and enhances our lives. In business, the beauty of technology is that it allows you to be more efficient and productive, provided the software and hardware works. Data you input is saved and archived for immediate and future use. In the event management arena, technology has become a life saver.

These new, easy-to-use, online meeting and event management systems are designed to ease the pains of event managers and meeting planners. But, the latest generation of systems offer visibility and intelligence on meetings spend to corporations, without the burden of additional reporting from the event managers. *Meetings spend* is a buzzword describing how all meetings and events roll-up for accounting purposes, as opposed to event-by-event. These tools provide you with the ability to put money back into your budget and contribute to your company's bottom line.

Online software helps you in managing customer events, trade shows, internal meetings, conferences, seminars, Webinars, hospitality programs, internal meetings, and more.

Executives, administrative assistants, field marketing professionals, and basically any job title can take advantage of the features built into these software applications. These products are delivered online via the Internet. The software application functions in real-time and can be a hosted or nonhosted model. I prefer the hosted model (the software is monitored and managed by a third- party organization).

As an event marketer, one of my biggest complaints all these years has been the lack of standardization in the industry. Every time you do something you are basically recreating it time and time again, and it has traditionally been a manual process. With a standardized platform for event management, approval and attendee registration information becomes instantly available.

- Event management is a planning solution. Features include: event framework, sourcing hotels, air, and other suppliers, as well as managing a budget.
- Attendee management is a registration or housing solution. An event-specific Web site is created to retain details of your event such as: agenda, registration, housing, travel, communications, name badges, process meeting fee transaction, surveys, and reports.

Over time, all information, from registration numbers and agenda details, to budget parameters, approved and declined events, measurement of traffic, leads, surveys, comments, and business generated, is filtered, compressed, and available to team members around the world on a program everybody has, understands, and can access. "With technology, planning and managing an event becomes a whole lot easier," says John Pino, founder and executive chairman of StarCite, who has been honored numerous

Tip

Know The Law

Besides the cost savings, a standard event technology platform provides an accurate reporting mechanism that gives companies the back-up documentation to address the requirements outlined in the Sarbanes-Oxley Act (SOX) that was passed by the U.S. Congress in 2002 whereby both CEOs and CFOs must sign-off on the accuracy of their company's filings with the U.S. Securities and Exchange Commission.

times as one of the most influential executives (thought leaders) in the meeting and event planning industry. "StarCite's technology, for example, features a series of modules: plan, budget, buy, attend, and measure. Within buy is our marketplace of over 77,000 suppliers and a wizard-like feature called RapidRFP™. These components are configurable so the company can actually track data they need. Preferred suppliers can also be loaded up front. We've also designed our software to be customized to fit a corporation's policies, preferred vendors, procedures, workflow, divisions, products, and any cost centers that they may have," Pino continues, "We look at the specifications that corporations need to run meetings and events in alignment with the way they go to market, how they motivate and educate people. Corporations look at this as a business issue. There is a business purpose behind it. The overall benefit to companies is to try to help them drive some best practices and policies throughout their organization to gain visibility, savings, and control."

You can look at ROI (return on investment) in a number of ways and that's important for events. There are direct-cost savings, indirect-cost savings, time savings, and efficiencies. "Let's take attendee management and cost-effectiveness in ROI," says John Pino. "If you are outsourcing attendee management to a service company you're going to pay somewhere between $25 and $50 per attendee. With 24/7 accessibility 'in-house' your cost is going to be somewhere between five and ten dollars. Not only is the cost less, but because of the technology and 24/7 accessibility, there is actually the improvement of service to the attendee," continues Pino. "Other savings include dramatic decreases in the number of errors you'll find in the overall attendee data, the ability to run hotel savings reports as well as the basic reduction in manual labor. In terms of quantifying direct and indirect savings, the system and the process allow this to happen naturally, because of the process and efficiency of the standardization and data capture. Corporations are getting significant returns (minimum 10 percent) and in some cases where there is no event department within a corporation you can get returns as much as 25 to 30 percent. It varies based on the sophistication and the size of the company."

When your company decides to implement an online meeting and event technology solution, it is important to have other players involved in the process. The team should include key stakeholders like procurement and IT. "Some event managers and marketers do NOT want procurement involved in this area," says John. "But corporations spend a lot of money on meetings and events and it needs to be managed like other spend categories."

As an event marketer, what I've found is that the more I engage procurement in the process, the more I can get my job done and their involvement actually puts money back into my budget. So I've had a different approach. I have worked for companies where I've met with the CFO or controller and I request a marketing project accountant, just like a major motion picture has. The controller or CFO is usually very receptive and will assign someone to pay special attention to events and it really helps you get what you want (negotiations). "The perception is that procurement is ineffective because they only buy commodities and they don't understand marketing," says John Pino. "But by changing the perspective that they are buying projects–procurement can be your friend. It's worth the effort. All they really want to do is to make sure that every dollar spent is spent effectively and with a good process."

In most companies there are a lot of simultaneous initiatives, so you have to have some urgency as to why this one is better than another one. Having buy-in from internal constituents is key.

As an event marketer it is important to stay ahead of the trends. I am very encouraged and excited about the possibilities for events. With technological tools at your fingertips, you provide a whole other level to the marketing mix.

Tip

Implementing a Meeting Technology Solution

- Do some homework. Take a step back and sort through what's really going on with meetings and events within your company.
- Find out the number of events being planned, who's planning them, what your standards are, etc.
- Try to show where you will be able to save money and by how much.
- What would implementing this solution mean to your company's bottom line?
- How will you get an approval for this type of initiative to change the process? When you look at the numbers you have both arguments: efficiency and cost-savings.

John Pino
Founder and Executive Chairman
StarCite, Inc.
http://www.starcite.com

StarCite, Inc., is the provider of On Demand Global Meeting Solutions

Chapter

13

PUTTING IT ALL TOGETHER—THE EVENT PLAN WITH LOGISTICS YOU NEED TO KNOW

Our mantra:
Event Marketing is all about facilitating, easing, opening, accelerating, and shortening the sales cycle. That's it!

Events require a lot of attention to detail. The littlest thing can become your biggest nightmare. It is important to understand that something will go wrong. It does and it always will. It's your state-of-mind that carries you through an event program. Being calm and solutions-oriented is a critical component to the success of the logistics implementation.

The route of entry for many event managers is the logistics component, and it is still considered a required skill even for an event marketer position. Jobs in events require attention to detail, as well as the baseline of understanding the logistics component. In larger corporations, a trend is to bring in professionals from other departments to events, such as sales and/or operations. "I spent ten years in sales and sales support before I was asked to head up a specific end-user customer event many years ago," says Stuart Gold, former Vice President, Global Forums and Sponsorships, for BEA Systems. "It's about the customer, partner, press, and analyst relationship. At the end of the day our job is to impact the bottom line."

You know you have to get it done right. Leverage all facets, look at the entire picture. The content is the most critical. Creative follows content and logistics. Unfortunately, nobody remembers when it's done right, but if there's something wrong you'll hear about it in long-winded detail. Move on. Something will go wrong. It always does. You'll live. Remind yourself and your colleagues it's still about the content. The logistics don't mean anything without strong content and positioning. Logistics are part of the ingredients.

You must be thorough and you must think through the "what ifs." Never say, "shoulda, coulda, woulda." You've got to just *do*.

BUDGET

The budget takes a lot of organizational skills, finesse, and patience and "mishpukah pricing." In Yiddish "mishpukah" means "family," and strong relationships with your external vendors (your event network) will yield even healthier results. For every individual event you produce and every event strategy you build, you will need to have a budget. You'll dread the day when you are over budget! You'll get very creative in leveraging your marketing dollars. The key word is "leveraging." It's imperative to look at the scope of your event plan and as previously mentioned, "gang" sales collateral, promotional items, PR folders, multimedia efforts, and more.

▪ **Hint:** Procurement, purchasing, legal, and accounting are your friends. They'll negotiate side-by-side with you and for you. Engage them as part of your event network.

Managing an event budget is similar to managing your personal finances. You want to spend it, but you want to "own" something for it. Ask yourself: "What's the value you derive from this purchase?" A line-item budget is essential to gaining the most from your event strategy.

Make sure you manage your budget. There's nothing much more to say on this topic. It's not your money. Figure 13.1 is a line-item budget. Budgets are usually kept in Excel, but note that online meeting and technology solutions (Chapter 12) automate this process for you. You may use some or all of the parts as you execute each event. Customize the line items to your needs. This budget is also a good starting point for submitting requests for additional program funding.

EXHIBITING

When there is an exhibit component to your event, it's advisable to have a general service contractor involved from the beginning. There are numerous details that need to be coordinated: labor, rigging, shipping, materials, and handling are just a few of the things that are required for trade shows and events.

One of the largest exhibit contractors is Freeman. I think of them as my general service contractor, just like I would if I was renovating my home. Dealing with multiple subcontractors is a full-time job. If you have a general contractor, like Freeman, who works with over 300,000 exhibitors a year and manages over 3,600 tradeshows, events, and small meetings, you now have a single point of contact. From a logistics standpoint they make your job easier by providing services that range from general way-finding information and entrance treatments, to handling of materials.

Once you are at an event, it's important to keep the attendee involved and motivated by your program. The number one request at an event is "face-time." When you sponsor or exhibit at an event, the amount of time you get to meet with actual attendees contributes to the success for your event.

FIGURE 13.1 *Budget Template*

Company Name: ______________________________

Event Name: ______________________________

Location: ______________________________

Date: ______________________________

Program Budget: ______________________________

Anticipated Attendees: ______________________________

BUDGET (revision #): ______________________________

Description	**Vendor**	**Item Cost**	**Quantity**	**Apprx. Cost**	**Actual Cost**
Air Transportation					
Roundtrip Coach Class					
Roundtrip Business Class					
VIP Air					
Agency Air Ticketing Fee					
Agency Project Management Hours					
Air Information Transfer Fee					
Total Airfare					
Hotel Accommodations					
Location:					
# of Rooms On Hold (# nights)					
# ROH Early Arrivals (# nights)					
# Junior Suites (#nights)					
# One-Bedroom Suites (# nights)					
# Duplex Suite (# nights)					
1 Presidential Suite (# nights)					
# Staff Rooms (# nights)					
# Additional Staff Room (# nights)					
Hotel or Resort Levy					
Estimated Resort Fee for Children (if applicable)					

FIGURE 13.1 *Budget Template (Continued)*

Description	Vendor	Item Cost	Quantity	Apprx. Cost	Actual Cost
Mandatory Gratuities for ROH and Jr. Suite					
Mandatory Gratuities for 1-Bedroom Suites					
Mandatory Gratuities for Duplex Suite					
Mandatory Gratuities for Penthouse Suite					
Complimentary Rooms (estimate)					
Commissions (estimate)					
Miscellaneous Gratuities					
Fitness Club					
Total Hotel Accommodations					
Ground Transfers					
Arrival Transfers					
Airport Porterage					
Golf Bag Transfers					
Departure Transfers					
VIP Transportation					
Total Ground Transfers					
Food & Beverage					
Day One:					
Reception					
Breakfast					
AM Break					
Lunch					
PM Break					
Dinner					
Crew Meals					
Sub Total					
Day Two:					

(continued)

FIGURE 13.1 *Budget Template (Continued)*

Description	**Vendor**	**Item Cost**	**Quantity**	**Apprx. Cost**	**Actual Cost**
Reception					
Breakfast					
AM Break					
Lunch					
PM Break					
Dinner					
Crew Meals					
Sub Total					
Day Three:					
Reception					
Breakfast					
AM Break					
Lunch					
PM Break					
Dinner					
Crew Meals					
Sub Total					
Day Four:					
Reception					
Breakfast					
AM Break					
Lunch					
PM Break					
Dinner					
Crew Meals					
Sub Total					
Total					
Production/AV/Staging					
Electrical/Engineering					
Scripts/Creative Concepts					

FIGURE 13.1 *Budget Template (Continued)*

Description	Vendor	Item Cost	Quantity	Apprx. Cost	Actual Cost
Multimedia Video					
Lighting and Rigging					
Audio					
Video					
Scenic/Staging					
Graphics					
Freight					
Miscellaneous					
Lifts					
Local Labor					
Preproduction					
Evening Entertainment					
Special Entertainment/Bands					
General Session					
Break Out Rooms					
Private Meetings					
Workshops					
Graphics Management					
Video Production					
Phones					
Internet Access					
Electrical					
Communications/Radios					
Photographer/Videographer					
Per Diem/Travel Expenses					
Production Company Fee/Project					
Management					
Project Management					
Production Staff					
Production Staff Overtime					
Estimated Costs					

(continued)

FIGURE 13.1 *Budget Template (Continued)*

Description	Vendor	Item Cost	Quantity	Apprx. Cost	Actual Cost
Total Production					
Exhibits and Structure					
Booth Design					
Booth Space					
Sponsorship Fee					
Property Build					
Signage/Banners					
Event Services (misc.: banner hanging, etc.)					
Lead Retrieval					
Electrical					
Shipping/Freight/Dryage/Materials					
Handling					
On-Site Labor					
Pre-Event Labor					
Travel Expenses					
Project Management					
Total					
Equipment					
Phones					
Internet Access					
Electrical					
Communications/Radios					
Security					
Office Equipment Rental					
Computer/Hardware Rental					
Printer/Fax Rental					
Shipping/Freight					
Event Management					
Pre-Event Labor					

FIGURE 13.1 *Budget Template (Continued)*

Description	Vendor	Item Cost	Quantity	Apprx. Cost	Actual Cost
On-Site Labor					
Administration					
Travel Expenses					
Project Management					
Total					
Marketing Deliverables					
Name Badges					
Invitations					
Signage					
Event Agenda					
Banners					
Online Marketing					
Direct Marketing/Direct Mail					
Advertising					
Press Relations Initiatives					
Mailing/Postage					
Staff Shirts					
Executive Gifts					
Prize Drawing					
Creative Materials Tool Kit Items					
Promotional Items and Giveaways					
Sales Tools/Collateral					
Recognition Awards					
Event Web Site Development					
Web Registration					
On-Site Registration and Equipment					
Credit Card Transaction Fee					
Program Management					

Tip

Increase Face-Time

People love food! Keep it flowing! Especially when you are wandering a floor all day. When you are in meetings all day, when you put the food out, people are naturally drawn to it. Spread it out and don't forget it drives attendees to visit you or your exhibitors and sponsors.

Jeff McCaw
Vice President of Sales Exposition Services
Freeman
http://www.freemanco.com

"At Freeman, we manage an event every year where the show organizer does not want attendees to leave the exhibit floor," says Jeff McCaw, Vice President of Sales Expositions Services for the company. "So in essence they created a contained environment with registration and name badges, small theaters for presentations, food and beverage, hospitality receptions, and education sessions occur within the venue space. Education plays a huge role in any event program and keeping it part of the exhibit program adds another element for face-to-face time," continues Jeff. "This strategy keeps the event managers happy, versus the meeting planners having to cram in 300 concurrent sessions in a four-day period. Scheduling 'limited exhibit only hours' and 'session only hours' is a great way to eliminate session time competing with floor time. Another big trend for face-time is that people are always wanting private one-on-one little meetings and want to have a home somewhere on-site to do business. At a trade show for example; a "shared meeting space package" will be made available to sponsors and/or attendees. A concierge will manage the meeting room and you can sign up to use the space in hourly increments. It's a very affordable way to take advantage of the value added marketing benefits a show offers."

When you sign-up to be an exhibitor you will receive a kit that provides you with what you need for your exhibit. A sample of the most common logistics that need to be planned and paid for prior to your on-site arrival is shown as Figure 13.2. This information has been pulled from a typical exhibitor kit. Often, this information is available online. I was an early requestor/early adopter of online event kits and the benefits are quite valuable. Time savings and automatic confirmation are two reasons why online kits are the future. While there are obvious conveniences to online exhibitor kits, I still request a hard copy of the kit. It's a comfort level, not a requirement.

I also use the exhibitor kit-type information when I am producing a proprietary event like an executive dinner at a five-star hotel that includes a presentation or a golf outing. The line items serve as a reminder of the details that need to be covered. Not every event requires the same things, but there's a ton of overlap.

BOOTH/SPACE DESIGN

Okay, you've got the contractor in place. What's the space look like? How is the space designed? The next component is called booth design or space design and it is produced by an exhibit house that builds trade show exhibits and displays. Some companies allow you to rent the booth property. The key in booth and space design is to match the look and feel to your message. The configuration itself is the conduit for interaction.

Remember to use your booth property when you host a meeting. A 10 × 10 pop-up booth, for example, can serve as the backdrop to a registration area and a tabletop display could be used as a way for you to showcase product outside a break out room.

Figure 13.3 presents samples of various booth configurations, each providing you an opportunity to communicate your message.

FIGURE 13.2 *Event/Exhibitor Checklist Form*

General Information	Show Schedule	Due Date	Completion Date
	Important Dates and Deadlines		
	First Time Exhibitors Fact Sheet		
	Vendor Director		
	General Information		
Registration and Housing	Online Registration		
	Hotel Accommodations		
	Hotel List and Map		
Rules and Regulations	Use of Exhibits: Aisles		
	Use of Exhibits: Giveaways		
	Exhibit Construction: Smoke Detectors		
	Exhibit Construction: Engineering Certificate		
	Exhibit Height Restriction: Hanging Signs		
	Security		
	Exhibitor-Appointed Contractors		
	Policy on Halogens		
	Parking/Directions		
	Notification of Event to Authorities		
	Alcoholic Beverages Authorization		
	Acknowledgement of Rules and Regulations		
Shipping and Material Handling	Shipping Info		
	Target Freight Move-In		
	Freight Handling Advance Receipt		
	Storage Rates		
Labor	Exhibitor Appointed Contractor (EAC) Labor		
	Booth/Venue Labor		
	Outbound shipping		
	Rigging and Forklift		

FIGURE 13.2 *Event/Exhibitor Checklist Form (Continued)*

General Information	Show Schedule	Due Date	Completion Date
Decorator Services	Order Form Checklist		
	Order Form Recap		
	Credit Card Authorization		
	Furniture and Accessories		
	Carpet and Padding		
	Standard ID Sign Order		
	Booth/Venue Layout		
	Booth/Venue Cleaning and Porter Services		
Utilities	Electrical Service Part 1		
	Electrical Service Part 2		
	Electrical Service Part 3		
	Electrical Forklift Rental Order		
	Stagehand Labor Order Form		
	Lighting Truss/Motorized Hoist		
	Electrical Totals Estimate		
	Electrical Service Diagram		
	Labor to Run Communications Cables		
	Internet Service Contract		
	Network Security Declaration		
	Wireless Internet		
	Water		
Marketing Services	Lead Capture		
	Deadlines		
	Contact Information		
	Opportunities		

- *Brand recognition:* Signage, sales tools/collateral, promotional items and giveaways
- *Lead generation:* Retrieval systems
- *Thought leadership:* Theater presentation with multimedia, demo, or experts on hand to discuss with target audience

FIGURE 13.3 *Booth/Space Design*

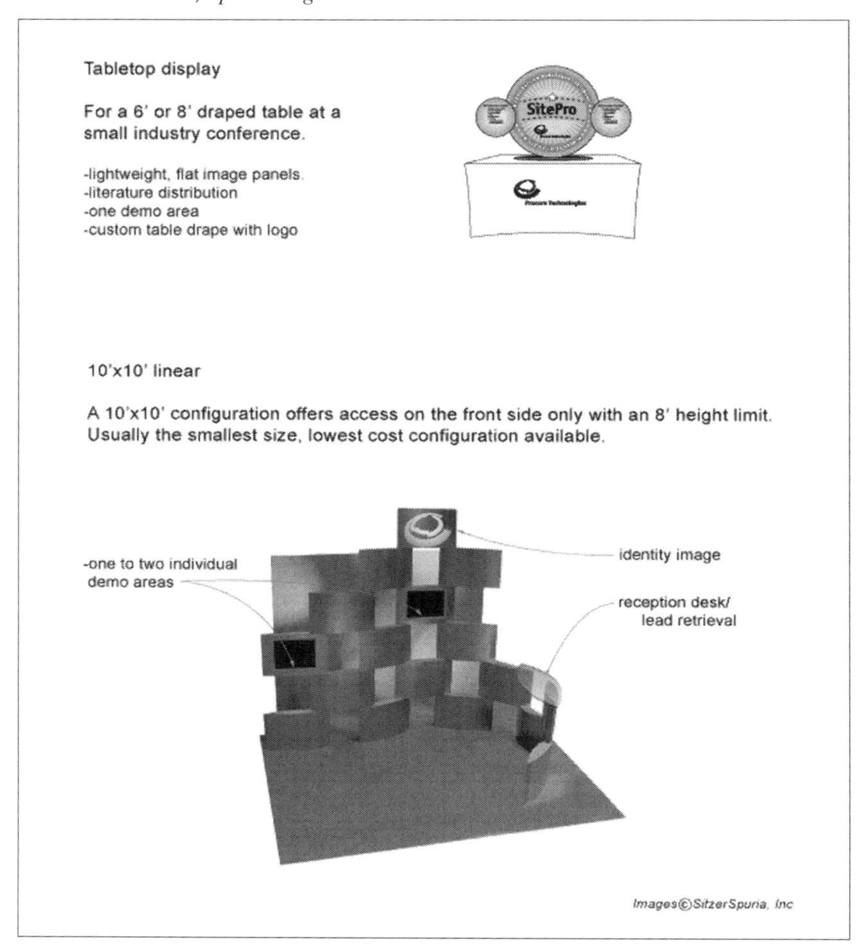

(continued)

FIGURE 13.3 *Booth/Space Design (Continued)*

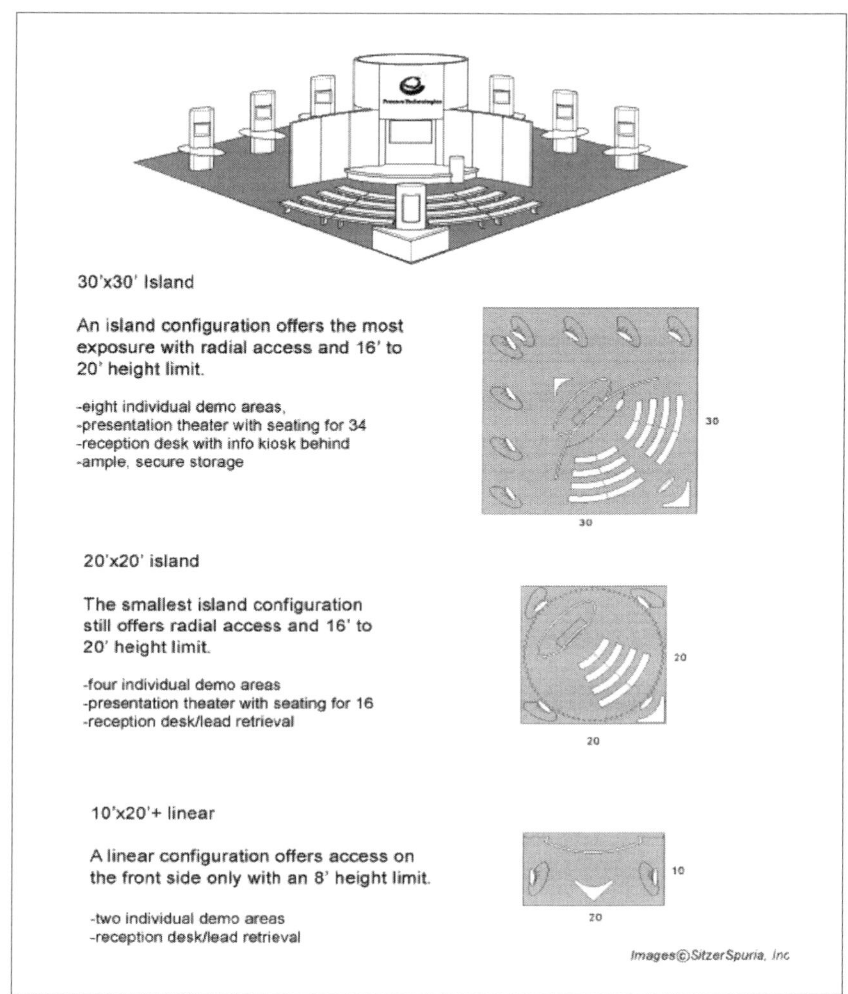

INTERNAL COMMUNICATIONS

For every event you produce, it is your responsibility to provide internal communications materials regarding the content and logistics components. "In any size program, people will come to you with a variety of questions," says Kim Millen, Marketing Resultant at Marketing in Motion, Inc." "Everything, from what is our key message, to what should I wear, to can I bring my customer or my wife."

The frequently asked questions become overwhelming after about a minute, so I create what I call the event master kit. Included in the documentation are details regarding attending the event, dress/attire, hotel accommodations, meals, and more. Think of it like FAQs but in a different format. The logistics component of the event marketing plan takes about 30 minutes to put together. However, the content component that reflects the EventBLT is ongoing and it takes many hours to actually fill in the template.

Start with an event plan to communicate the message to your internal audience. Figure 13.4 is a blank template for you to use. Most of its topics have been covered in previous chapters. I would be remiss in writing *The Event Marketing Handbook* without including the "ya gotta' know stuff" category. With logistics it's knowing and having access to the information quickly. Hopefully, you will find the logistic section of *The Event Marketing Handbook* a valuable resource when you go to write your own event marketing plan.

What I found from the logistics side is that your colleagues, salespeople, thought leaders, PR, and ad teams, etc., need to know the same details for every event.

At the onset of your planning, begin by creating an event master kit. You should update the information in the kit as you work on the project. I like to post the kit to a common site and send e-mails to the key constituents throughout the cycle so they can make the necessary arrangements to attend.

What I've put together are the logistics and planning details with suggested ways on how you think about or communicate the information. This is meant for you to use as a guide. You'll need to examine your program and decide what best represents what you're doing and your company.

FIGURE 13.4 *Event Marketing Plan Template*

Name of Your Company ___________________________

Name of Event: ___________________________

Web Site URL ___________________________

Day and Date of Event ___________________________

Location of Event ___________________________

Address ___________________________

City, State, Zip ___________________________

Overview

Insert a 50-word summary about the event

The conference features:

Education

Include a list of the high-profile content

Networking

Showcase the hospitality-style functions

Launch Plan

Event Goal:

Objective:

Strategy:

Positioning and Messaging Focus

Refer to Chapter 2 and insert your position framework template here.

Audience Profile

Refer to Chapter 3 for information on identifying your target audience.

Approximate number of attendees:

Example: Demographic Profile—Custom Home Builders High-Priced Contractors Building: $1,000,000+ homes

(continued)

FIGURE 13.4 *Event Marketing Plan–Event Master Kit Template (Continued)*

Sponsor List

Include a current list of companies that will be showcased at the event. Determine if the sponsors are a potential partner.

- Use the conference Web site for this info. (For a proprietary event, you should already know this info.)
- Highlight all competitors.

Conference Agenda

Include the time and the description of what is scheduled.

Use the preconference mailer or the Web site to fill in this info.

Example: DAY, MONTH/DATE

7:00 AM–2:30 PM
9:00 AM–3:00 PM
8:00 AM–5:00 PM
3:00 AM–5:00 PM
6:00 PM–8:00 PM

Show Participants

In order to achieve our show objectives, the following people have a specific role during the conference.

Name	Title	Show Role	Clothing Size
	CEO	Press/Media Relations	
	President	Exhibit Staff Speaker/Podium Presenter (2 minutes)	
	Account Manager	Exhibit Staff	
	Regional Sales Executive	Exhibit Staff	
	Regional Sales Executive	Backup/Exhibit Staff	
	Event Marketer Consultant	Event Management/Set-Up	

Event Marketing—EventBLT

☐ Sponsorship Package includes:

- Include full list of negotiated benefits.

FIGURE 13.4 *Event Marketing Plan–Event Master Kit Template (Continued)*

☐ Brand Recognition
- Creative materials
- Promotional items
- Sales collateral

☐ Lead Generation Program
- Business development opportunities/Meetings schedule
- Marketing and hospitality initiatives ideas

☐ Thought Leadership
- Speaking engagements
- Press and analyst plan
- Press list and analyst list

Logistics

☐ Attending the Event/Name Badges/Credentials
☐ Audio/Video Requirements
☐ Booth/Event Scheduling and Etiquette
☐ Climate
☐ Destination Management Services
☐ Dress/Attire
☐ Help Me/Emergency
☐ Ground Transportation
☐ Hotel Information
☐ Holidays
☐ Know Your Stuff
☐ Laptops
☐ Meals/Alcohol
☐ Medical Emergencies
☐ Packing
☐ Personal Expenses
☐ Photo Opportunity
☐ Room Set-Up
☐ Shipping/Materials Handling
☐ Time Zone
☐ Tipping/Gratuity Guidelines
☐ Travel

The next section, "Logistics and Planning At-a-Glance," features the generic or most common actions that one needs to know on the topics being covered. These are also the questions that get asked over and over. Again, the info in an event master kit includes attending the event, dress/attire, hotel accommodations, meals, and more. Think of it as FAQs. By creating and distributing an event master kit you keep everyone on the same page. With this information you will be able to create your own kit.

LOGISTICS AND PLANNING AT-A-GLANCE

Attending the Event/Name Badges/Credentials (Trade Shows and Conferences)

You, or members of your team, are responsible for preregistering all company personnel and invited guests to the event. Registration is typically done online and in advance of the event. In some cases, name badges and credentials are sent in advance to the attendees. Here are some typical instructions to include in the kit.

- Go to the event registration area in the venue to pick up your name badge and conference materials.
- The registration area is open throughout the event at the following times (list the hours).
- As a participant in the event you will receive the necessary credentials to attend all respective events.
- It is crucial that you wear the respective credentials during your participation. Name badges are a great identifier, while you may feel like a "dweeb," it establishes your identity.

FIGURE 13.5 *Credentials Chart*

	Name	Title	E-mail	Mobile Phone Number	Shirt Size	Arrival and Departure Info
Executives						
Speakers						
Sales						
Marketing						
PR						
Technical Support						
Staff						
Customers/ Prospects						
Partners						
Significant Other						
Other						

While at this conference think of yourself as the point person on the team. It will be up to you to introduce yourself and the company to every person you come in contact with. In addition, you will need to keep track of everyone and contact them after the conference. The tool shown as Figure 13.5 may be useful in tracking attendees.

Audio/Video Requirements

Any time there is a presentation or any use of media, you'll have requests for some sort of AV support tools. Here's a basic list of what's usually requested.

- LCD projector
- 35mm slide projector
- Overhead projector

- Video projector
- DVD player
- Screen
- Audio Taping
- Video Taping
- Flip Chart and Markers
- Rear Screen Projection

Booth/Event Scheduling and Etiquette

Use the exhibit house's sketches and share the booth or stage design with your internal teams so they have a visual picture of what to expect once they are on-site.

These six principles apply when you are working assigned booth duty:

1. Do not eat or drink in front of people and do not leave cups, wrappers, etc., on the information counters.
2. NO chewing gum—provide breath mints instead.
3. Carpeting is top-of-the-line with nonfatigue padding underneath.
4. If you see garbage or trash, pick it up and keep your space looking clean.
5. Keep mobile phones on vibrate if you have that feature, and never, ever, pick up a call while speaking with an attendee at the event. Mobile phones with ringer-only features should be kept on the lowest volume possible. Remember phone chargers.
6. Your very smiley happy face :) :) :) is mandatory. This is a show and you still need to make it fun!!!

It's also a very good idea to create a booth schedule, like Figure 13.6, to keep all booth personnel and events organized.

FIGURE 13.6 *Sample Booth and Event Schedule*

Time	Theater	Demo Center or Session #1	Demo Center or Session #2	Info Desk	One-on-One Meetings
7:30 AM *Set-up*				Allison Tony	
8:00 AM *Team Meeting*	ALL	ALL	ALL	ALL	ALL
8:30 AM *Expo Opens*	Spenser Sam	Simone Austin	Michael Robert Christina	Matt H. Steven Travis	Matt S. Madison
9:00 AM					
9:30 AM					
10:00 AM *Staff break*	Spenser	Simone	Robert Christina	Steven Travis	Matt S.
10:30 AM *Staff break*	Sam	Austin	Michael	Matt H.	Madison
11:00 AM	Spenser Sam	Simone Austin	Michael Robert Christina	Matt H. Steven Travis	Matt S. Madison
11:30 AM	ALL	ALL Kirra	ALL Kyle	ALL	ALL
1:00 PM *Staff lunch*	Spenser	Simone	Robert Christina	Steven Travis	Jenna Jamie Jake
1:30 PM *staff lunch*	Sam	Austin	Michael	Matt H.	
2:00 PM– 4:00 PM	Spenser Sam	Simone Austin	Michael Robert Christina	Matt H. Steven Travis	Aubrey Lara Jennie
4:01 PM *Expo Closes*					
6:00 PM *VIP Dinners*					Barbara Lee Peggy Frank
7:00 PM *Welcome Reception*	ALL	ALL	ALL	ALL	ALL

* TBD executives to rotate in booth

Climate

Below is a sample of what you should state regarding general weather conditions. You'll obviously need to revise this based on where you are in the world.

> *"At this time of year, 'the city' experiences temperatures in the 60s to 80s. Be prepared with spring-like clothing. Daytime temperature averages 74°F. At night, the average is 50 to 65°F. Use these averages as guidelines when planning your travel wardrobe. Please note, it may become quite windy or you may see a touch of rain. Please be prepared for this weather."*

Destination Management Services

When planning an event, you may find that you need to hire a destination management company (DMC). The official definition of a DMC according to the Association of Destination Management Executives is: "A professional services company possessing extensive local knowledge, expertise and resources, specializing in the design and implementation of events, activities, tours, transportation, and program logistics."

"One of the most important values of a DMC is they can find special places well off the beaten path," says Karen Gordon, president of Activity Planners based in Las Vegas. "An excellent DMC knows their city inside and out, including its hidden treasures. They can point you towards restaurants, galleries, and private clubs (where they have memberships) that are too new, unique, or private to be found in any guidebook." The biggest advantage of using a DMC is the level of expertise you can depend on!

DMC's can also partner with meeting professionals to:

- Obtain an experienced back-up team that handles meeting details on site.
- Develop customized events that fits their budgets and meets their deadlines.
- Choose the best transportation routes in crowded cities.
- Find interesting local personalities to serve as speakers.
- Secure a group's access to private screenings at important museum shows.
- Create extraordinary events on a moment's notice.

Dress/Attire

Image is everything and at an event your company can shine! Your ratio of "event wear" to team member depends on the number of days the event will be held.

Consider giving people two each of the items you select. This becomes part of their wardrobe and serves as brand messengers postevent.

It is important to pay attention to women's needs. Dress women like women and not like men. For some reason when it comes to company logo clothing for women, we lose our sensibilities on how to present ourselves.

Sizes:

- Men: range from small–6X
- Women: range from XS–2X (some styles will go as large as 5X)

Please make certain your teams are properly groomed for the event. Nose and ear hairs should be clipped, shoes should be shined, teeth whitened and brightened, and hair styled. If you put this line in your event plan it is sure to be remembered without you having to tell someone.

Executive-Style Attire and Speakers/Presenters:

Men: When selecting your attire for the event please keep in mind the following guidelines:

- *Wardrobe:* Dark suit (grey, blue, or black); dress shirt (white, pale blue; subtle patterns); tie wear (subtle patterns). In a more relaxed conference, no tie is needed.
- *Accessories:* Dress leather-soled shoes (black); dress leather belt (black); dress socks (black is always safe); eyewear (please wear contacts, if possible, as stage lights will reflect and cause glare and shadows).

Tips:

- Suit style and fit:
  - The sleeves should taper, gradually ending just over the wrist so the shirt cuff extends about a half inch beyond the jacket sleeve.
  - The length of the pants in the front should touch the front of the shoe and angle towards the back of the shoe to fall just above the heel.
- Color and Patterns:
  - Keep in mind that when you are on stage, it is important that your audience is not distracted by what you're wearing. You want them to stay focused on the content of your presentation.
- Grooming:
  - Have your hair cut or styled at least two days prior to presentation. This will give you a less rigid and more relaxed, comfortable appearance.
  - Manicure and groom your fingernails and hands.

Women: When selecting your attire for the event please keep in mind the following guidelines:

- Wardrobe: Dark suits (grey, blue, or black preferred); colorful shirt or sweater; business dress
- Accessories: Dress leather-soled shoes; jewelry should be understated but showcase your personality. Handbag should be a smaller size so it fits under a podium or table.

Tips:

- If you choose to wear an open-toe shoe, please see that your feet are properly groomed.
- Color your hair or go in for a cut at least two weeks prior to your presentation. This will give you a less rigid and more relaxed, comfortable appearance.
- Manicure and groom your fingernails and hands.

Business Casual/Resort Style Attire

Men: When selecting your attire for the event please keep in mind the following guidelines:

- Daytime Wardrobe:
    - Shirt (option A)—Short-sleeve shirt with company logo; cotton or rayon/polyester blend in your size. It's a contemporary and clean look. Wear the shirt on the outside. Do NOT tuck in the shirt.
    - Shirt (option B)—Long-sleeve, three-button, knit polo sweater with company logo; style is made from 100 percent fine gauge rings spuncombed cotton.
    - Pants—Complement colors according to the shirt and base slack choices on the following: khaki, black, olive green, tan, navy.
    - Shoes—Brown or black loafers
    - Socks—The temperature and location will dictate whether socks or no socks. For example, no socks in

Hawaii, but in all other cases, black socks are usually a safe choice.
  - Belt—Black or brown
- Evening Wardrobe:
  - Shirt—Long-sleeve V-neck sweaters with company logo. This versatile V-neck style looks great either tucked in or worn out, and should be made from the softest 100 percent ringspun combed cotton. Think evening out with friends.
  - Pants—Complement the sweater with black or tan slacks. Black jeans are also acceptable.
  - Shoes—Wear black shoes that are polished and be very careful with sandals. Your feet, and especially toenails should be well presented.
  - Belt—Black or brown

Women: When selecting your attire for the event please keep in mind the following guidelines:

- Daytime or Evening Wardrobe:
  - Shirt (option A)—Twin sweater set with logo on both cardigan and sleeveless or short sleeve shell, made in 100 percent soft combed cotton with the feel of cashmere.
  - Shirt (option B)—Twin sweater set with cardigan and long sleeve crew or V-neck sweater underneath, made in 100 percent soft combed cotton with the feel of cashmere.
  - Shirt (option C)—Blouse is fashionably feminine button front shirt, V-neck style with color ¾"-length sleeves made from fine pima cotton pinpoint oxford fabric that is wrinkle resistant. Wear in or out.

- Pants—Complement colors according to the shirt and base slack choices on the following: khaki, black, olive green, tan, navy.
- Skirts—Clean lines are always acceptable. If you go for the peasant look, make sure you are in-style with current trends. Don't look like a potato sack.
- Jeans—A darker denim will carry you through evening. NO HOLES.
- Shoes/Sandals—Wear a comfortable pair; high-heels will kill your feet. Wear a dress pair of sandals and NOT flip-flops.
- Socks—The temperature and location will dictate whether socks or no socks. For example, no socks in Hawaii, but in all other cases, black socks are usually a safe choice.
- Belt—if needed

For the Golf Course:

Men and Women

- Shirt—A quality 100 percent short-sleeve polo shirt featuring logo on front.
- Slacks—Khaki or tan
- Jacket—A windbreaker or sweater
- Golf Shoes—Make sure they are clean.
- Baseball Cap/Sun Visor—Logo on front
- Suntan or sunscreen lotion

For the Gym:

Men and Women

- Shirt—A quality 100 percent cotton tee shirt featuring logo on front and back.
- Shorts—No extremely short cut-offs.
- Sweat Pants—No holes in the crotch or knees.
- Sneakers—Check for the scent and make sure they are clean.
- Etiquette—Watch your spitting and coughing.

For the Pool or Beach:

Men and Women: Remember that you are with business colleagues and you will be talked about.

- Bathing Suit—Bring one and make sure it's relatively new. Suits wear out quickly.
- Cover Up—A wrap or shorts are appropriate.
- Sandals—Flip-flops are fine here.
- Baseball Cap—With logo on front or back of cap.
- Beach Towel—With logo and leave on chairs or sand while you go do something else.
- Tote Bag—With logo on both sides if possible, and large enough to carry magazines, books, file folders.
- Suntan or sunscreen lotion

Help Me/Emergency

Is your team in a panic because they lost the paperwork, forgot something, or are confused? It is important to provide "HELP ME" information in your event kit. Designate a specific person and provide the appropriate contact info, including a mobile phone number.

Ground Transportation

- Bus–Check to see if the conference is providing transportation around town. A shuttle schedule should be posted in the hotels that are part of the conference.
- Cab–Local services are usually outside the venue. 4:00 PM is usually a shift change, so you may want to arrange alternate transportation if you have important meetings.
- Limo–A service that is at your beck and call without having to pay 24-hour fees is ideal.
- Subway/Train–This is based on city or area availability.

Hotel Information

Where To Stay:

- Always look to book hotel rooms at the host hotel for the event. It may cost a little bit more, but it's worth it for the extra networking time you'll get with the bulk of the attendees, who are usually those with the strongest influence.
- Wherever you stay use the full name of the hotel (e.g., don't just say "Westin," instead, say "Westin Times Square").

Discounted rates: Secure accommodations immediately to take advantage of the conference's discounted rate.

- Large company–Ask for your corporate rate.

- If you are a small company and are participating as a partner with a large company, you are probably entitled to use their transient rate as well. As a member of AAA you can take advantage of their rate.

Room Deposit/Cancellation Fees:

- Be aware that certain conferences and/or hotels may require a stay of a specific number of room nights.
- Get creative. You can use the same hotel room, but switch out guest names over the required time period.
- When you book a block of hotel rooms, be aware of cancellation charges and room deposit fees that will show up on the credit card you used to hold the reservations.

Name of Hotel ______________________________

Address ______________________________

City, State, Zip, Country ______________________________

Phone Number ______________________________

Fax Number ______________________________

Toll-free Central Reservation Number ______________________________

URL Address ______________________________

Check-In/Arrival Date ______________________________

Check-Out/Departure Date ______________________________

Confirmation Number(s) ______________________________

Holidays

Here's a guideline for widely recognized and acknowledged U.S. holidays. However, always check a calendar before scheduling any event. For international holidays, remember to reference the host countries' calendar as well as those from where the delegates are invited. One year, a major analyst firm held their largest conference over the Jewish holidays. There was a great deal of apologizing to do. Always check dates and make sure you are aware of any potential conflicts.

January–June	**July–December**
New Year's Day—January 1st	Independence Day (U.S.)—July 4th
Martin Luther King Day	Labor Day
Chinese New Year	Rosh Hashanah
Valentine's Day—February 14th	Yom Kippur
Presidents' Day	Ramadan
Ash Wednesday	Columbus Day
St. Patrick's Day—March 17th	Halloween—October 31st
Palm Sunday	Election Day
Purim	Veteran's Day
Good Friday	Thanksgiving
Passover	Christmas Eve—December 24th
Easter Sunday	Christmas Day—December 25th
Mother's Day	Hanukkah
Memorial Day	Kwanzaa
Flag Day—June 14th	New Year's Eve
Father's Day	

Know Your Stuff

Remind your teams that they have been specially chosen to represent the company at an event. Attendees will ask them all sorts of questions. Reinforce that they need to be prepared and re-familiarize themselves with the positioning and messaging documentation. Make sure you advise your team and executives to bring business cards. A minimum 50 cards to every event.

Laptops

In some companies an internal team member will provide their own laptop to run demos at the event or meeting. Other companies designate equipment just for events. Because of storage and security issues, try to keep all unnecessary equipment off the show floor or that of a hosted event.

Meals/Alcohol

There are a variety of scenarios that play out at every event in regards to feeding the attendee base. Whether you sponsor or attend, you should be aware of what the conference provides.

- All meals are provided to attendees throughout the duration.
- All breaks are open all day long featuring coffee, soft drinks, water, snacks.
- Meals are only provided to conference attendees; sponsors are on their own (this is tacky, but it's done).
- No meals are provided and all attendees are on their own for the duration.
- Breaks only feature water stations.

Tip

Food

Enhance food presentations at hosted meal functions with logo items Ideas include:

Tastes Great

Know Your Audience

- Custom design your own menu with the head chef.
- Understand likes, dislikes, and dietary restrictions.

Brand It

Dessert Items

- Speak with the chef and select custom cookies or plate writing.
- Remember to use your branded chocolates at each place setting.
- Purchase a custom-designed cake in the shape and color scheme of your product.

Sculptures

- Your company or product logo is carved in ice or chocolate. Ask the catering manager in the venue for assistance to arranging for this item.

- All attendees are on their own each evening. This is an excellent opportunity to entertain prospects and customers in local restaurants.

Medical Emergencies

Be aware that there may be a medical emergency. Find out the venue's policy and include it in your plan. In my experience, there have been two situations when medical attention has been required at an event: the death of a speaker in the middle of a presentation, and an allergic reaction to nuts that were ground up into a tray of brownies.

Tip

Beverages

When providing beer and wine only, don't be limited to just two selections of wine. A variety costs the same amount of money and is much more interesting.

Beer

- Beer is domestic and imported, but if you're doing a Mexican theme, you may want to change out the selections and feature a wide range of Mexican beers.

Champagne/Sparkling Cider

- When welcoming attendees into a room, a server with a tray of champagnes glasses and water is such a nice touch. Of course, these are also great for a toast.

Cocktails

- Martini's, Manhattans, and tequila shots; a full bar is always appreciated.
- Make sure if you are hosting that there is NO tip jar left on the bar. Make it clear to the venue that you will provide the gratuity. (It's very tacky in a business reception otherwise.)

Be Responsible and Accountable

- People will get buzzed or drunk. Never let anyone drink and drive. Err on safety. Escort people to their rooms in a hotel if necessary. Have a policy and plan in place.

Packing

The following tips have been provided by Amy Hyatt of WorldTravel BTI:

- If you hate dealing with luggage at the airport, consider sending your clothes via overnight delivery to the hotel.

Just list your name and "hold for arrival on the date you plan to arrive," and your clothes will be waiting upon your arrival. It's always recommended to phone the hotel ahead of time. International destinations may take longer to arrive, so research and send in advance. You can arrange for items to be sent back home in the same manner.

- To maximize the space in your suitcase, roll your clothes! Rolling clothes tightly will take the air from them, allowing more room.
- Pack heaviest items (such as shoes) on the bottom. The lighter clothes at the top will allow more give when closing your suitcase.
- Fill up all empty space. Fill shoes with socks, hose, and accessories.
- Call the hotel ahead to check amenities. If they provide a hair dryer, ironing board, and shampoo, you may be able to leave these items at home for a great deal of additional space.
- Consider travel-size amenities to save space. Shampoos, deodorants, toothpaste, toothbrushes, soaps, etc., all come in compact sizes to save a considerable amount of space.
- Stick with one or two color schemes in your travel wardrobe. This will eliminate the need for multiple shoes and bags.
- Consider the dry-cleaning service at the hotel. If staying multiple days, it may be worth dry cleaning so you can rewear outfits again.
- Have you wanted to buy something, but didn't feel you had enough room in your suitcase? You can have the hotel box up your purchases and send either overnight to you, or just put your address (hidden, of course) on the box and treat it as normally checked luggage at the airport. Your wonderful new items will arrive in baggage claim.

Personal Expenses

Be clear about how personal expenses for an event are covered. In some cases, staff members' costs may go to what's called a master account. The charges usually go to a master account if they are a key player in the execution of an event. Your internal teams should keep track of their expenses throughout the duration of the event. To be reimbursed, they should submit their expense report according to your company's policy. You should request that all expense reports be submitted within two weeks of a particular event.

Photo Opportunity

Photos and video provide a graphic archive of your event. There are two options: either hire a professional photographer to take pictures, or purchase your own digital camera and do it yourself. I like to make a photo album after the event for all to enjoy. Always make duplicate pictures to hand out as mementoes.

Room Set-Up

Depending on the type of event there are a variety of room set-up options available to you. The handy guide offered here (Figure 13.7) describes some set-up options and illustrates the various configurations. "While the exact figures listed may be a little tight, the idea is for meeting planners to experiment with the formula and write down what works best for their meetings," says Jonathan Vatner, Senior Associate Editor of *Meetings and Conventions* magazine and writer of the article "Cheat Sheets, Planner-Approved Formulas for Figuring Room Setups, F&B and More," November 2003, in which I found most of this information.

FIGURE 13.7 *Room Set-Up Guide*

Style	Description with Configuration Illustration
Auditorium/Theatre/Amphitheater *Conversion info:* *Space Needed:* • 9–13 square feet per person • more than 33" between rows • 4' – 6' for aisle space • Twice the screen height between the from row and the stage, 4' or more behind the last row	Set up in rows without tables. There's a stage in the room that serves as the focal point for presentations. Side sections are set herringbone or curved for better sight lines. The room features a podium and platform riser. Usually used for general and keynote sessions. 
Boardroom/Conference Style	Small groups that require a lot of interaction. Substitute a rectangular table with an oval. 
Chevron Schoolroom style with the two sides on an angle. Optimizes viewing. Think of the shape of an arrow.	See classroom or schoolroom for description. 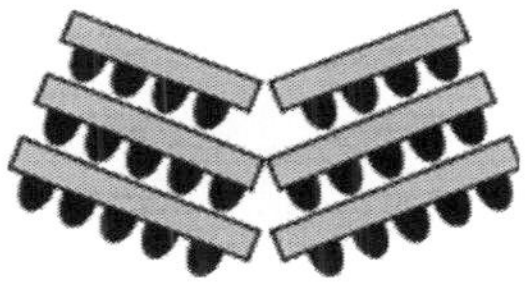
Classroom or Schoolroom *Conversion info:* *Space Needed:* • Allow from 14.5 to 24-square feet per person and 3' – 5' between tables. • For tight set-ups put three attendees at each 8' × 18" table • If space is available, put two attendees at each 6' × 30"	Rows of table with chairs. Attendees have room to take notes and spread out materials. Size of table is typically 18" or 30" wide and 6' or 8' long. Allow two feet of space if possible. If attendees are bringing laptops make sure you have enough power sources and Internet/wireless service if needed. 

(continued)

FIGURE 13.7 *Room Set-Up Guide (Continued)*

Style	Description with Configuration Illustration
Crescent Rounds/Dinner Theater	Round banquet tables with chairs around ½ to ¾ of the table facing the focal point of the room. This is common for breakout sessions or events featuring motivational speakers or entertainment. 
Rounds *Space Needed:* • 60" round: 80–120 square feet per table; each seats 6–9 • 66" round: 90–135 square feet per table; each seats 7–10 • 72" round: 100-150 square feet per table; each seats 8–11 • Dance floor space: 2–3 square feet per person	Used for meal functions and can seat 6, 8, 10, or 12 comfortably. Also good for roundtable discussions and birds-of-a-feather sessions. 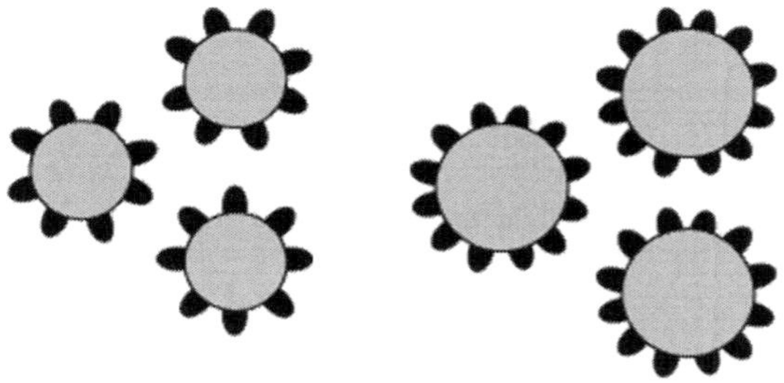
Reception 7- to 15-square feet per person provide enough seating for 2 –30% of attendees	*YOUR TURN—Draw the configurations based on the charts and description provided.* • Cocktail rounds: use 3 chairs per person • Bar height rounds-no chairs are needed.

FIGURE 13.7 *Room Set-Up Guide (Continued)*

Style	Description with Configuration Illustration
U-Shape/Hollow Square *Space Needed:* • 37.5 to 45-square feet per attendee • 2' to 3' between seats • Keep extra chairs on the perimeter for last-minute additions to the meeting.	*U-Shape:* A hollow square or rectangle with one side removed. *Hollow:* Square or rectangle shape all sides touch.

Shipping/Materials Handling

Materials handling is the unloading of your exhibitry, as well as promotional items and sales collateral. Here are the shipping options. Reconfirm shipping addresses and mark all boxes with the related contents on a separate inventory sheet.

Advanced shipment to show site

- For trade shows primarily, exhibit property is sent 30 days prior to show date and stored at a warehouse.
- Most inexpensive option, but requires the most advanced planning.
- Reduces possibility of lost shipments.

Direct shipment to show site

- For trade shows, meetings, and events, all materials are sent directly to the location.
- Overnight carriers are used, like FedEx, UPS, and DHL.
- Return tracking numbers for all packages.

Walk it in

- Best for last-minute items like sales tools/collateral.

Time Zone

Most countries observe daylight savings time (spring forward, fall back). The date varies, but around the world it typically starts in March or April and ends in September, October, or November.

For example, When it is 3:00 PM in Los Angeles (Pacific time), it's 5:00 PM in Chicago (Central time), and 6:00 PM in New York City (Eastern time). You'll adjust quicker if you change your watch as you are flying across the country.

Tipping/Gratuity Guidelines

Make it clear to your on-site team what's covered as far as tipping and gratuities.

- Gratuity and/or Service Charge: Automatically added to your bill (usually when you've pre-arranged payment or established a master account).
- Tip: Voluntary amount given at an individual's discretion. (At an event it is NOT uncommon for the attendees to tip the parking valet, even though your event is picking up the tab.)

Deciding how much to tip and to whom is up to your discretion. It depends on your budget and the work and service these folks do for you. At the end of each event, you'll most likely tip in cash, usually in increments of $20s, $50s, and $100s. Figure 13.8 is a useful tip sheet that will help you with the process, whether it's at your hotel postconference session (after the event is over) or as you do it yourself.

Travel Tips

- Always attach a luggage tag, but keep your address hidden. This will keep strangers from knowing your address and that you are leaving town. Turn your information around in the tag, and try to avoid using the airline's paper tags, if possible. Any luggage store will sell leather tags for $3-$5 and it's worth the investment. Another popular option is to insert your business card into the tag, thus protecting your home address.
- Many laptops look the same. Tape your business card or personal information upside down on the face of the laptop. This will easily identify your computer through security and keep your personal information confidential.
- Make copies of all credit cards, passport, and other identification (front and back) before leaving home. If something is lost or stolen, you can phone home and quickly have your information. Credit cards should immediately be cancelled and the U.S. Consulate should be contacted immediately if your passport is lost or stolen.
- Keep a currency conversion chart. Convert $1, $5, $10, $20, and $50 bills into local currency. Write on a small piece of paper. Keep in your wallet for easy calculations of true spending.
- Upon hotel check-in, take a matchbook or business card so you always have the hotel address and phone number with you during the trip. This will help if you get lost, or if the taxi driver is not familiar with the hotel location.

Courtesy of Amy Hyatt of World Travel/BTI

WHERE ARE YOU?

This quick reference chart (Figure 13.8) is a handy item for preplanning. It is also important to advise your internal attendees where they are going. Both a U.S. and international version is provided for quick reference.

FIGURE 13.8 *Who's Who in Service Personnel*

Position	Name of Person	Cash	Add to Master Account
AV Technicians			
Banquet Captain			
Bell Captain/Staff			
Chef/Kitchen Staff/Servers			
Concierge			
Conference/Conventions Services Staff			
Doormen			
Front Desk/Reservationists			
Ground Transportation Team (car service, limos, shuttles)			
Housekeeping			
Housemen/Day & Night Crews (who rework meeting space and floor set-ups)			
Parking Valet			
Porters/Baggage Handlers (planes, trains)			
Security			
Shipping/Receiving Department			

FIGURE 13.9 *Preplanning Quick Reference Chart*

- Time zones are based on 12:00 PM (noon) eastern standard time and also reflect a 24-hour time period (military time). Any city with an asterisk (*) indicates that it is the following morning.
- Temperature is indicated in Fahrenheit. Conversion info to Celsius temperature.

F	C
32°	0°
40°	5°
50°	10°
60°	15°
70°	20°
75°	25°
85°	30°

U.S. City	Airport Code	Temperature (Jan/July)	Time	Telephone Area Code
Atlanta, Georgia (GA)	ATL	58/88	12:00 PM	404 or 678 or 707
Boston, Massachusetts (MA)	BOS	25/81	12:00 PM	617 or 857
Chicago, Illinois (IL)	ORD	31/84	11:00 AM	312 or 773
Cleveland, Ohio (OH)	CLE	31/82		216
Dallas, Texas (TX)	DFW	54/95		214 or 469 or 972
Denver, Colorado (CO)	DEN	43/88		303 or 720
Honolulu, Hawaii (HI)	HNL	80/88	8:00 AM	808
Houston, Texas (TX)	IAH	61/91		281 or 713 or 832
Las Vegas, Nevada (NV)	LAS	57/104	9:00 AM	702
Los Angeles, California (CA)	LAX	66/85	9:00 AM	213 or 310 or 323 or 714
Miami, Florida (FL)	MIA	75/89	12:00 PM	305 or 786
New York, New York (NY)	JFK LGA	37/85	12:00 PM	212 or 347 or 646 or 718 or 917
San Diego, California	SAN	45/75	9:00 AM	619 or 760 or 858
San Francisco, California (CA)	SFO	55/71	9:00 AM	415
Seattle, Washington (WA)	SEA	45/75	9:00 AM	206
St. Louis, Missouri (MO)	STL	37/88	11:00 AM	314
Washington, DC (District of Columbia)	IAD	42/88	12:00 PM	202

(continued)

FIGURE 13.9 *Preplanning Quick Reference Chart (Continued)*

International City	Airport Code	Temperature (Jan/July)	Time	Country/City Telephone Code
Amsterdam, Netherlands	AMS	50/85	18 00	31/20
Athens, Greece	ATH	56/ 88	19 00	30/01
Auckland, New Zealand	AKL	3/56	5 00*	64/01
Bangkok, Thailand	BKK	89/89	0 00	66/2
Beijing, China	PEK	34/87	1 00	86/10
Buenos Aires, Argentina	EZE	86/59	14 00	54/1
Cairo, Egypt	CAI	65/96	19 00	30
Calcutta, India	CCU	79/90	22 00	91/33
Geneva, Switzerland	GVA	51/91	18 00	4/22
Havana, Cuba	HAV	78/88	12 00	53/7
Ho Chi Minh, Vietnam	SGN	88/88	0	84/8
Hong Kong, China	HKG	74/92	1 00*	852
Istanbul, Turkey	IST	47/82	19 00	90/212 or 216
Johannesburg, South Africa	JNB	86/70	19 00	27/11
London, England United Kingdom	LHR	44/71	17 00	44/171 or 181
Madrid, Spain	MAD	47/87	18 00	34 / 1
Melbourne, Australia	MEL	79/55	3 00*	61/03
Mexico City, Mexico	MEX	70/73	11 00	52/5
Montreal, Canada	YUL	21/79	12 00	1/514
Moscow, Russia	MOW	21/76	20 00	7/095
Munich, Germany	MUC	34/73	18 00	49/89
Paris, France	CDG	42/76	18 00	33/1
San Juan, Puerto Rico	SJU	83/88	13 00	787
Rio De Janeiro, Brazil	GIG	84/77	14 00	55/21
Rome, Italy	FCO	55/83	18 00	39/06
Seoul, South Korea	ICN	33/82	2 00*	82/2
Singapore, Singapore	SIN	85/87	1 00*	65
Sydney, Australia	SYD	79/62	3 00*	61/02
Tel Aviv, Israel	TLV	62/87	19 00	972/3
Tokyo, Japan	NRT	49/83	2 00*	81/3
Toronto, Canada	YYZ	29/77	12 00	1/416 or 905
Vienna, Austria	VIE	50/89	18 00	43/1

Resources

As an event marketer, you can never have enough resources. In this section you'll find everything from the obscure to the traditional, or from the fun to the serious. Create and maintain your own list.

INDUSTRY ASSOCIATIONS

Many organizations exist in the industry. Also check these associations for specific conferences they organize. Most associations focus on education and networking for their members. Joining an association is up to you. Some find value and others do not. Here's a short list that will get you started.

SmithBucklin
The world's largest association management company, providing tailored services to more than 185 trade associations, professional societies, technology user groups, and government institutes/agencies.
http://www.smithbucklin.com

American Management Association
The largest membership-based management, development, and executive training organization.
http://www.amanet.org

American Society of Association Executives
Serves members who manage leading trade, professional, and philanthropic associations, representing over 10,000 associations and 25,000 members.
http://www.asaenet.org

Asian Association of Convention and Visitor Bureau (AACVB)
Represents China, Hong Kong, Indonesia, Japan, Korea, Macau, Malaysia, the Philippines, Singapore, and Thailand.
http://www.aacvb.org

Association of Corporate Travel Executives (ACTE)
Spans all sectors of business travel, from corporate buyers to agencies to suppliers.
http://www.acte.org

Convention Industry Council (CIC)
Represents more than 100,000 individuals, as well as 15,000 firms and properties involved in the meetings, conventions, and exhibitions industries.
http://www.conventionindustry.org

Direct Marketing Association
Telephone, mail, and internet marketing association for users and suppliers in the direct, database, and interactive marketing fields, offering seminars and resources, and lobbying for . . .
http://www.the-dma.org

Hospitality Sales and Marketing Association International (HSMAI)
http://www.affordablemeetings.com

International Association of Convention and Visitor Bureaus (IACVB)
Serving convention and visitor bureaus (CVBs), with more than 1,200 members in over 550 destination management organizations in 30+ countries.
http://www.iacvb.org

International Association of Exhibition Management
Focuses on individuals with business interests in the exhibition industry and includes 3,500 members. (Formerly the National Association of Exposition Managers)
http://www.iaem.org

International Special Events Society (ISES)
Spans caterers, meeting planners, decorators, event planners, audiovisual technicians, party and convention coordinators, educators, journalists, hotel sales managers, and others; nearly 4,000 members active in 38 chapters throughout the world.
http://www.ises.com

Meeting Professionals International (MPI)
The largest association for the meeting profession; 18,000 members in 60 countries; a heavy focus on education and career pathways.
http://www.mpiweb.org

Professional Convention Management Association (PSMA)
An international nonprofit organization of meeting professionals and supplier partners.
http://www.pcma.org

Promotional Products Association Internationals
A not-for-profit association dedicated to professionals of the $17.3 billion promotional products industry.
http://www.ppa.org

Society of Incentive and Travel Executives (SITE)
Spans airlines, cruise lines, corporate users, destination management companies, ground transportation companies, hotels and resorts, incentive houses, official tourist organizations, trade publications, travel agencies, and supporting organizations such as restaurants and visitors attractions. Nearly 1,800 members in 82 countries, with 28 local and regional chapters.
http://www.site-intl.org

Trade Show Exhibitors Association (TSEA)
Specifically for event managers who use exhibits to promote and sell their products, as well as to those who supply them with products and services; 2,100 members and 4,500 customers.
http://www.tsea.org

INDUSTRY ASSOCIATION CERTIFICATIONS

For meetings and events, you can get certified through various associations or continuing education programs. Many courses are offered online. It is up to you whether you want to pursue this in your career.

CSEP–Certified Special Events Planner
Certified by: ISES

CMP–Certified Meeting Professional
Certified by: CIC

CMM–Certification in Meeting Management
Certified by: MPI

CAE–Certified Association Executive
Certified by: American Society of Association Executives

CEM–Certified in Exhibit Management
Certified by: International Association for Exhibition Management

CTSM–Certified Trade Show Marketer
Certified by: Northern Illinois University Outreach Program

SPEAKER INFORMATION

Speakers' bureaus are known as lecture agencies that provide professionally paid presenters a fee for a speech during a designated time during an event. They represent all types of experts (media personalities, politicians, entertainers, professional and amateur athletes, educators, humorists, motivators, authors, adventurers, futurists, and more.)

Topics include:

- Arts
- Children
- Education
- Entertainment
- Environment
- Ethnic and Gender Issues
- Family
- Health, Fitness, Well Being
- Humanitarian Issues
- Humor
- Inspirational
- Lifestyle
- Literature
- Motivation
- Politics—National and International
- Religion
- Science
- Spiritual
- Sports
- Technology

National Speakers Association (NSA)
3,500 members
http://www.nsaspeaker.org

Washington Speakers Bureau (WSB)
http://www.washingtonspeakers.com

American Program Bureau
http://www.apbspeakers.com

Greater Talent Network
http://www.gtnspeakers.com

Leading Authorities
http://www.leadingauthorities.com

Keppler Speakers
http://www.kepplerspeakers.com

JOB SITES

- Meetingjobs.com
- craigslist.com
- Monster.com
- CareerBuilder.com

PUBLICATIONS—MAGAZINES, NEWSPAPERS

There are a variety of magazines and newspapers that specifically target the meeting and event industry. Additional publications provided in this section include advertising, brand, incentive, and business publications.

Meetings and Events

***Corporate Event Magazine* (quarterly)**
Case studies of business-to-business event marketing.
http://www.exhibitoronline.com

***Event Marketer* (Seven times a year)**
Serves the information needs of brand-side event marketers and agency executives across the spectrum of face-to-face media; including mobile marketing, mall marketing, street events, trade shows, corporate events, proprietary events, sponsorships, business-to-business events, and press events.
http://www.eventmarketermag.com

Special Events Magazine
http://www.specialevents.com

***Meetings and Conventions* (monthly)**
Offers in-depth features, informative columns, destination insights, news analysis, original research for meeting and event planners in cor-

porations, associations, incentive houses, and independent planning companies excel at their jobs and effectively manage their careers.
http://www.meetingsandconventions.com

Successful Meetings **(monthly)**
Targeted to meeting planners across all industries, articles on thought-provoking and timely issues, to innovative ways to motivate a staff;
http://www.successmtgs.com

Meeting News **(18 times a year)**
Offers news and product/destination information with "how-to" features and perspectives for executives, managers, and meeting and convention planners who are involved in planning in corporate businesses and services, associations, and travel agencies.
http://www.meetingnews.com

Corporate Meetings and Incentives
Association Meetings
http://www.meetingsnet.com

Corporate & Incentive Travel **(monthly)**
Targeted to meeting and incentive travel planners, featuring issue-oriented features, examinations of professional concerns, thoroughly researched destination reports, and columns by industry experts.
http://www.corporate-inc-travel.com

Event Solutions **(monthly)**
Targeted to event, meeting, and incentive industry professionals who are responsible for choosing destinations and locations, selecting outside planners, producers and suppliers, and setting budgets and spending limits on these events.
http://www.event-solutions.com

BizBash
Ideas and resources for special events and meetings.
http://www.bizbash.com

***Business Travel News* (29 issues per year)**
For corporate travel managers.
http://www.btnonline.com

***T&E Magazine* (monthly)**
Focuses on travel and entertainment expense management by offering policy advice, legal insights, and trend analysis.
http://www.temagazine.com

***Convene* (10 times a year)**
Members of the Professional Convention Management Association automatically receive the magazine.
http://www.pcma.org/resources/convene

Advertising and Entertainment

***Adweek, Brandweek,* and *Mediaweek* (weekly)**
Key sources of information for advertising, media, and marketing executives, and influencers at advertising agencies, major brands, and media buying agencies.
http://www.adweek.com
http://www.brandweek.com
http://www.mediaweek.com

***Advertising Age* (weekly)**
Comprehensive weekly news on all aspects of the U.S. advertising business.
http://www.adage.com

***Creativity* (monthly)**
Focuses on creative work and the talent that produced it, features on advertising, production, postproductions, design, and photography.
http://www.adcritic.com

***Entertainment Marketing Letter* (bi-monthly)**
Discusses trends in entertainment-based sponsorship, online promotions, direct response sales, product placement, interactivity, and product sampling.
http://www.epmcom.com

Promotional Items and Incentives

***Incentive Magazine* (monthly)**
Devoted to motivation and performance improvement through the use of incentive programs and consumer promotions; also prints an annual *Buyers' Guide* with *Potentials.*
http://www.incentivemag.com

***Potentials* (monthly)**
Features ideas and products that motivate; focuses on tactics that get results; covers new products, case studies, and trends that will help you put together a successful motivation program; also prints an annual *Buyers' Guide.*
http://www.potentialsmag.com

***Presentations* (monthly)**
For individuals and organizations that create and deliver presentations; tracks trends and provides info on presentation hardware and software.
http://www.presentations.com

Business and Sales

Sales and Marketing Management Magazine (monthly)
Published for executives who manage the sales and marketing functions in their companies.
http://www.salesandmarketing.com

CRMguru.com
An online community focused on Customer Relationship Management (CRM).
http://www.crmguru.com

Business Week, Forbes, Fortune, Wall Street Journal, USA Today

Trade Show Magazines

Exhibitor Magazine
A resource for corporate exhibit/event managers and marketing executives; offers range of educational and informational tools for trade show and event industry professionals in the United States and abroad.
http://www.exhibitoronline.com

Trade Show Week **(weekly)**
Targeted to trade show executives offering news, analysis, and trends. Features include "The Annual Survey of Labor Rates" and "Corporate Exhibitor Survey."
http://www.tradeshowweek.com

Trade Show Week Data Book **(annually)**
A comprehensive directory of trade shows and consumer expos featuring nearly 5,000 shows.
http://www.tradeshowweek.com

BOOKS

How to Advertise, Kenneth Roman and Jane Maas (New York: Thomas Dunne Books, 2003)

Strategic Brand Communication Campaigns, Don E. Schultz and Beth E. Barnes (New York: McGraw-Hill, 1999)

Trade Show and Event Marketing, Ruth P. Stevens (Cincinnati: South-Western Educational Pub, 2005)

Death by Meeting, Patrick Lencioni (San Francisco: Jossey-Bass, 2004)

The Sports Event Management and Marketing Playbook, Frank Supovitz and Joe Goldblatt (New York: John Wiley & Sons, 2004)

Guerilla Marketing, Jay Conrad Levinson (Boston: Houghton Mifflin, 1998)

The Complete Guide to Advertising, Torin Douglas (Secaucus, NJ: Chartwell Books, 1984)

The Soft Edge: A Natural History and Future of the Information Revolution, Paul Levinson (New York & London: Routledge, 1997)

Digital McLuhan: A Guide to the Information Millennium, Paul Levinson (New York & London: Routledge, 1999)

Cellphone: The Story of the World's Most Mobile Medium, and How It Has Transformed Everything! Paul Levinson (New York & London: Palgrave/ Macmillan, 2004)

INDUSTRY EVENTS, TRADE SHOWS, AND CONFERENCES

Exhibitor Show
http://www.exhibitoronline.com

TS2
http://www.ntpshow.com

The Next Big Idea Conference
http://www.adweek.com

Promo Marketing Conference & Expo
http://www.promoexpo.com

The Incentive Show
http://www.theincentiveshow.com

The Motivation Show
http://www.motivationshow.com

RESEARCH

Center for Exhibition Industry Research (CEIR)
Promotes the image, value, and growth of exhibitions.
http://www.ceir.org

IEG
Provider of independent sponsorship research, analysis, tools, and training.
http://www.sponsorship.com

Case Study Forum
Writers of ROI case studies.
http://www.CaseStudyForum.com

WHITE PAPERS

"MPI/GPJ Events Trends Report"
Provides understanding of how events are currently being used within the United States.
http://www.gpjco.com

"Integrated Event Marketing (IEM)"
Overview on the practice of IEM in which trade shows, proprietary events, sponsorships, and channel events converge to form a single integrated event portfolio.
http://www.gpjcom.com

"Event Measurement"
Outlines seven ways to measure events, as well as industry practices for designing a measurement program.
http://www.gpjco.com

"Rise of Proprietary Events"
Outlines how to use events more strategically to gain new customers.
http://www.gpjco.com

"Emerging Procurement and Cost Issues"
Focuses on cost management strategies.
http://www.gpjco.com

"Building Brand Communities"
Discusses how customer communities are transforming the way companies build their brands and business.
http://www.gpjco.com

"Experience Design"
An independent overview of the emerging practice of experience design.
http://www.gpjcom.com

"The Marketing Profitability Path: Mapping Your Journey"
A four-part series article that provides an approach for managing the integrated sales and marketing funnel to maximize profitability. Written by Jim Lenskold and Hugh Macfarlane (author of *The Leaky Funnel*), originally published by MarketingProfs.com.
http://www.customerpathing.com

"Pharmaceutical Thought Leaders: Brand Strategies and Product Positioning"
Learn how "pharmas" and biotech companies approach budgeting decisions, build and maintain strong relationships, measure performance, and use thought leaders to impact brand strategy and drive product growth.
http://www.cuttingedgeinfo.com

RANDOM RESOURCES

Venue Enablers

AgendaOnline
Business-to-business corporate event planning resource, providing sites and services that event planners need to plan and produce special events.
http://www.agendaonline.com

Zagat Survey
Locate the top restaurants by cuisine in various U.S. cities.
http://www.zagat.com

Conference Centers
Dedicated complex with state-of-the art AV equipment and wireless/Internet connection, adjacent sleeping rooms, amphitheaters to concon-current breakout session rooms.
http://www.iacc.org

Party Centers
Plan someone's personal birthday party, anniversary, or wedding. (If this is not your forte, direct them to friends you have in the business, or to these two Web sites):

Bridal Goddess
http://www.bridalgoddess.com

Shindigz by Stumps
large party superstore
http://www.shindigz.com

Marketing Resources

Corbin Ball
A comprehensive site about meeting planning and events technology.
http://www.corbinball.com

CMO Council
Dedicated to high-level knowledge exchange, thought leadership, and personal relationship building among senior marketing and brand decision makers in the technology and communications industries.
http://www.cmocouncil.org

eMarketer
Data, research, and analysis on e-business, online marketing, and emerging technologies.
http://www.emarketer.com

MarketingProfs.com
Marketing know-how from professors and professionals.
http://www.marketingprofs.com

iMedia Connection
Connecting the marketing community.
http://www.imediaconnection.com

Allison Saget
Event Marketing Consultant.
http://www.eventblt.com

Index

S

T